Exploring China's Religious Sites

This book employs cutting-edge digital and spatial methodologies to tackle the critical issue of religious site scarcity across China for five major religions: Protestantism, Catholicism, Buddhism, Daoism, and Islam, spanning the period from 1911 to 2004.

Drawing from Chinese government datasets and Geographic Information Systems (GIS), this comprehensive work presents official information concerning religious sites and pinpoints specific cities facing shortages in such sites. The book also offers an in-depth analysis of religious sites, delving into their statistical, historical, comparative, and religious contexts and evolving significance within China, shedding light on the unique challenges and opportunities each religion faces.

This groundbreaking book uncovers spatial patterns and relationships, providing new insights into the distribution of religious sites and the evolution of Chinese religious practices since 1911. It will be an invaluable resource for students and scholars of modern China, religious studies, and digital and spatial humanities.

Zhaohui Hong is a Professor of the Graduate School of Religion and Religious Education at Fordham University, USA. His research interests include religious economics, economic history, digital humanities, and Chinese religions.

Routledge Contemporary China Series

255 **Ancestor Worship in the Diaspora Chinese and China Universes**
The Making of a Collaborative Cultural Basis
Khun Eng Kuah

256 **Rethinking the Occupy Movement in Hong Kong**
Origins, Processes, and Consequences
Shen Yang

257 **Perspectives on Plagiarism in China**
History, Genres, and Education
Yongyan Li

258 **City Branding in Chinese Megacity Regions**
Against the Background of Ecological Modernization
Haiyan Lu

259 **Modernization in Eastern Tibet**
Leviathan the Forager
Su Hu

260 **Inside The Expressive Culture of Chinese Women's Mosques**
'This Turmoil of the Soul'
Maria Jaschok

261 **Exploring China's Religious Sites**
Digital and Spatial Insights
Zhaohui Hong

For more information about this series, please visit: www.routledge.com/Routledge-Contemporary-China-Series/book-series/SE0768

Exploring China's Religious Sites
Digital and Spatial Insights

Zhaohui Hong

LONDON AND NEW YORK

First published 2025
by Routledge
4 Park Square, Milton Park, Abingdon, Oxon OX14 4RN

and by Routledge
605 Third Avenue, New York, NY 10158

Routledge is an imprint of the Taylor & Francis Group, an informa business

© 2025 Zhaohui Hong

The right of Zhaohui Hong to be identified as author of this work has been asserted in accordance with sections 77 and 78 of the Copyright, Designs and Patents Act 1988.

All rights reserved. No part of this book may be reprinted or reproduced or utilised in any form or by any electronic, mechanical, or other means, now known or hereafter invented, including photocopying and recording, or in any information storage or retrieval system, without permission in writing from the publishers.

Trademark notice: Product or corporate names may be trademarks or registered trademarks, and are used only for identification and explanation without intent to infringe.

British Library Cataloguing-in-Publication Data
A catalogue record for this book is available from the British Library

ISBN: 978-1-032-79961-2 (hbk)
ISBN: 978-1-032-80104-9 (pbk)
ISBN: 978-1-003-49545-1 (ebk)

DOI: 10.4324/9781003495451

Typeset in Times New Roman
by KnowledgeWorks Global Ltd.

To Qian and Emma, my beloved daughters.

Contents

List of Tables	ix
List of Figures	xiv
List of Maps	xv
Preface	xvii

1	Introduction	1
2	The Shortage of Protestant Churches in Hangzhou City	9
3	Case Studies in Hangzhou, Zhengzhou, Hefei, and Fuzhou Cities	22
4	Taipei and Provincial Capital Cities on China's Southeast Coast	31
5	Growth of Officially Registered Protestant Churches since 1949	43
6	The Nationwide Shortage of Chinese Protestant Churches	57
7	Multi-Methods Research Design	69
8	The Evolution of Buddhist Temples	83
9	Quantitative Analysis of Daoist Abbeys	100
10	A Spatial Exploration of the Catholic Market	112
11	Quantitative Studies on Islamic Mosques	131

12 Spatial Analysis of Mosques: Case Studies in Xinjiang
   and Ningxia   148

13 Religious Sites of Five Religions during the Cultural Revolution   167

   Index   *185*

List of Tables

2.1	Comparative Protestant Churches and Participants in China and the US.	11
2.2	Church Availability and Accessibility: Chicago vs. Hangzhou.	17
3.1	Distribution of Protestants and Percentage of Protestants in the Total Population in Four Provinces, 2004.	24
3.2	Comparison of Protestants and Protestant Churches between the United States, China, and Four Chinese Provinces, 2004.	25
3.3	Comparison of Church Availability in the Four Cities (2.5 km Radius).	26
3.4	The Estimated Driving Time for the Four Cities (12.5 Minutes).	27
3.5	The Estimated Driving Time for the Four Cities (25 Minutes).	28
3.6	Comparison of the Three Criteria for Assessing Protestant Church Shortages among the Four Provincial Capital Cities.	29
4.1	Protestant Population in Mainland China, Taiwan, and the Six Capital Cities (2010–2015).	33
4.2	The Number of Protestant Churches in Mainland China, Taiwan, and the Six Capital Cities.	34
4.3	Protestant Density Rankings.	34
4.4	Church Accessibility Statistics.	36
4.5	Protestant Church Accessibility in the Six Cities by the NAM (30 Minutes).	38
4.6	Protestant Church Availability and Accessibility in the Six Cities by the LAM (10 Minutes and 3 km).	40
4.7	The Combined Rankings of Protestant Church Accessibility in the Six Cities.	40
5.1	The Density of Protestants per Church in Hangzhou.	47
5.2	Density of Protestants per Church in Harbin.	47
5.3	Density of Protestants per Church in Chengdu.	48
5.4	Comparison of the Growth Rates of Protestant Churches in the 31 Provincial Capital Cities of the Three Regions, 1949 and 2004.	49
5.5	Comparison of the Growth Rates of Protestant Members in the 31 Provincial Capital Cities of the Three Regions, 1949 and 2004.	50

5.6	Density of Protestants per Church in the 31 Provincial Capital Cities of the Three Regions, 1949 and 2004.	50
5.7	Regional Province Comparison of the Church Growth Rates.	51
5.8	Regional Province Comparison of the Protestant Growth Rates.	51
5.9	Density of Protestants in Regional Provinces, 1949 and 2004.	52
5.10	The Growth Rate of Churches and Protestants in the 31 Provincial Capital Cities.	52
5.11	Comparison between Protestant Church and Other Chinese Religious Sites.	53
5.12	Comparison on the Growth Rates between Protestantism and Population.	54
6.1	Protestant Congregations in Eastern China, 2004.	58
6.2	Protestant Population Density in Eastern China, 2004.	59
6.3	Comparative Church Availability in Eastern China, 2004.	60
6.4	Rankings of Church Shortages in Provincial Capital Cities in Eastern China, 2004.	60
6.5	Protestant Congregations in Central China, 2004.	61
6.6	The Density of Protestants in Central China, 2004.	61
6.7	Comparative Church Availability in Central China, 2004.	62
6.8	Rankings of Church Shortage in Provincial Capital Cities in Central China, 2004.	62
6.9	Protestant Congregations in Western China, 2004.	63
6.10	The Density of Protestants in Western China, 2004.	64
6.11	Comparative Church Availability in Western China, 2004.	64
6.12	Rankings of Church Shortage in Provincial Capital Cities of Western China, 2004.	65
6.13	Correlations between Church Shortage and GDP Per Capita in Three Regions.	65
6.14	The Nationwide Density of Protestants in Provincial Capital Cities, 2004.	66
6.15	National Comparisons on Church Shortage, 2004.	67
7.1	Church Accessibility in Eastern China by the 2SFCA.	75
7.2	Church Accessibility in Eastern China by the NAM (30 Minutes).	75
7.3	Church Accessibility in Central China by the 2SFCA.	77
7.4	Church Accessibility in Central China by the NAM (30 Minutes).	77
7.5	Church Accessibility in Western China by the 2SFCA.	78
7.6	Church Accessibility in Western China by the NAM (30 Minutes).	79
7.7	Provincial Capital Cities with the Shortage of Protestant Church in China.	80
8.1	Evolution of the Number of Buddhist Temples in the Four Cities Surrounding the Four Famous Mountains (1911–2004).	85
8.2	Growth Rates of Buddhist Temples in the Four Cities from 1978 to 2004.	86
8.3	Number of Buddhist Temples in Eastern, Central, and Western China (1911–2004).	88

8.4	Growth Rate of Buddhist Temples in Eastern, Central, and Western China (1911–2004).	89
8.5	Number of Buddhist Temples in China (1911–2004).	91
8.6	Comparative Growth Rates of Buddhist Temples across the Four Mountain Areas, Three Regions, and the Entire Nation (1978–2004).	91
8.7	Comparative Growth Rates of Five Religious Sites in China (1911–2004).	92
8.8	Comparative Growth Rate of Religious Sites of Five Religions in China (1978–2004).	93
8.9	Comparative Growth Rates between Buddhist Temples and Other Socioeconomic Factors (1966–2004).	94
8.10	Correlation Coefficient between Buddhist Temples and Other Religious Sites and Socioeconomic Factors.	96
9.1	Changing Number of Daoist Abbeys in the Three Cities (1992 and 2004).	102
9.2	The Growth Rates of the Daoist Abbeys in the Three Cities from 1992 to 2004.	103
9.3	The Average Annual Growth Rates in the Three Cities (1992–2004).	103
9.4	Number of Daoist Abbeys in Eastern, Central, and Western China (1911–2004).	104
9.5	Growth Rates of Daoist Abbeys in Eastern, Central, and Western China (1911–2004).	104
9.6	The Average Annual Growth Rate of Daoist Abbeys in the Three Regions of China (1911–2004).	105
9.7	Daoist Abbey Counts in China (1911–2004).	106
9.8	Comparative Growth Rates of Daoist Abbeys among the Three Cities, Three Regions, and the Entire Nation from 1978 to 2004.	107
9.9	Comparative Growth Rates of Religious Sites for the Five Major Religions in China (1911–2004).	107
9.10	Comparative Growth Rate of Religious Sites for the Five Major Religions in China (1978–2004).	108
9.11	Average Annual Growth Rates of Religious Sites for the Five Religions.	108
9.12	Comparative Average Annual Growth Rates between the Religious Sites of Five Main Religions and Other Socioeconomic Factors.	109
9.13	The Coefficient between Daoist Abbeys and Other Religious Sites and Socioeconomic Factors.	110
10.1	Catholic Population in China and Its Nine Cities, 2000–2010.	115
10.2	The Number of Catholic Churches in the United States, China, and the Nine Cities (2004).	116
10.3	The Density of Catholics in China and Its Nine Cities, 2004.	117
10.4	Catholic Church Accessibility in China by the 2SFCA.	123

xii List of Tables

10.5	Catholic Church Accessibility in the Nine Cities by the NAM (30 Minutes).	127
10.6	Combined Rankings of Catholic Church Shortage in the Nine Cities.	128
11.1	Percentage of Xinjiang Mosques in China (1911–2004).	133
11.2	Evolution of Islamic Mosque Numbers in the Four Xinjiang Cities (1911–2004).	133
11.3	The Growth Rates of the Islamic Mosques in Four Cities (1949–2004).	134
11.4	The Average Annual Growth Rate of Islamic Mosques in the Four Cities (1911–2004).	135
11.5	The Changing Islamic Mosques in Xinjiang (1911–2004).	136
11.6	Number of Islamic Mosques in Eastern, Central, and Western China (1911–2004).	138
11.7	The Growth Rates of Islamic Mosques in Eastern, Central, and Western China (1911–2004).	138
11.8	The Average Annual Growth Rate of Islamic Mosques in the Three Regions of China (1911–2004).	139
11.9	Number of Islamic Mosques in China (1911–2004).	140
11.10	Comparative Growth Rates of Islamic Mosques between the Four Cities of Xinjiang, the Three Regions and the Whole Nation (1978–2004).	140
11.11	Comparative Growth Rates of Religious Sites across Five Religions in China (1911–2004).	141
11.12	The Comparative Growth Rates of Religious Sites for the Five Religions in China (1978–2004).	142
11.13	The Average Annual Growth Rates of the Religious Sites of Five Main Religions.	143
11.14	The Comparative Growth Rates between the Islamic Mosques and Other Social Economic Factors (1966–2004).	143
11.15	The Coefficient between the Islamic Mosques and Other Religious Sites and Socio-Economic Factors.	144
12.1	Muslims in Xinjiang, China (2004).	153
12.2	The Density of Muslims in Xinjiang, 2004.	154
12.3	Number of Muslims in Ningxia, China (2004).	154
12.4	The Density of Muslims in Ningxia, 2004.	155
12.5	The Density of the Muslims in China and the United States, 2004.	155
12.6	The Density of the Muslims in the Eight Areas, 2004.	156
12.7	Comparative Mosque Availability in China, 2004 (LAM).	159
12.8	Mosque Accessibility in China by the 2SFCA.	162
12.9	Mosque Accessibility in the Eight Cities by the NAM (30 Minutes)	164
12.10	Average Rankings of the Mosque Supply in the Eight Areas by the LAM, NAM, and 2SFCA.	164
12.11	Combined Rankings of Mosque Supply in the Eight Cities.	165
13.1	Number of Religious Sites for the Five Main Religions (1966–1971).	168
13.2	Number of Religious Sites for the Five Main Religions (1972–1976).	169

13.3	Growth Rate of the Religious Sites for the Five Main Religions (1966–1976).	169
13.4	Comparison of Growth Rates of Religious Sites from 1949 to 2004.	171
13.5	Annual Average Growth Rate for the Four Periods from 1949 to 2004.	171
13.6	Growth Rate of Religious Sites for the Five Major Religions during the Two Cultural Revolution Periods (1966–1970 vs. 1971–1976).	173
13.7	Leading Provinces in the Construction of New Daoist Abbeys (1966–1976).	174
13.8	Leading Provinces in the Construction of New Buddhist Temples (1966–1976).	174
13.9	Leading Provinces in the Construction of New Catholic Churches (1966–1976).	174
13.10	Leading Provinces in the Construction of New Protestant Churches (1966–1976).	175
13.11	New Mosques in the Five Leading Provinces (1966–1976).	175
13.12	Locations of New Religious Sites: Rural and Urban, 1966–1976.	175
13.13	Comparison between Population and Growth of Religious Sites, 1966–1976.	176
13.14	Comparison between the Growth Rates of GDP Per Capita and the Religious Sites, 1966–1976.	177

List of Figures

2.1	Evolution of New Protestant Church Construction in Zhejiang (1855–2004).	12
5.1	Comparison of the National Growth Rates between Protestant Members and Church Numbers.	53
8.1	Evolution of Buddhist Temples in the Four Cities Surrounding the Four Famous Mountains (1911–2004).	85
8.2	Trends in the Growth Rates of Buddhist Temples in Zhoushan, Xinzhou, Chizhou, and Leshan Cities (1911–2004).	87
8.3	Evolution of Buddhist Temples in Eastern, Central, and Western China (1911–2004).	89
8.4	Varied Growth Rates of Buddhist Temples in Eastern, Central, and Western China (1911–2004).	90
8.5	Patterns of Buddhist Temple Development in China (1911–2004).	93
8.6	Comparative Growth of Buddhist Temples and GDP Per Capita (1966–2004).	95
8.7	Comparative Growth of Buddhist Temples and Urbanization (1949–2004).	96
9.1	Differential Growth Rates of Daoist Abbeys in Eastern, Central, and Western China (1911–2004).	105
9.2	The Patterns of Average Annual Growth of Daoist Abbeys in the Three Regions of China (1911–2004).	106
10.1	The Density of Catholics in China and the United States, 2004.	118
11.1	Evolution of Islamic Mosque Numbers in the Four Xinjiang Cities (1911–2004).	135
11.2	Growth Rates of Islamic Mosques in the Four Xinjiang Cities.	136
11.3	The Different Growth Rates of Islamic Mosques in Eastern, Central, and Western China (1911–2004).	139
13.1	Comparison of the Religious Sites for the Five Main Religions (1966–1976).	170
13.2	Comparative Growth Patterns of Religious Sites for the Five Major Religions (1949–2004).	172
13.3	Comparative Trends in Population Changes and Growth of Religious Sites (Islamic, Catholic, and Protestant), 1966–1976.	177
13.4	Comparative Trends in GDP Per Capita and Growth of Religious Sites, 1966–1976.	178

List of Maps

2.1	Protestant Churches in Chicago: A Spatial Overview.	13
2.2	Nine Hangzhou Protestant Churches.	14
2.3	Church Availability in Chicago (1 km) (2,383,800 residents or 96.55%).	15
2.4	Church Availability in Hangzhou (1 km) (270,026 residents or 12.8%).	16
2.5	Church Availability in Hangzhou (10 km) (2,044,030 residents or 96.87%).	17
2.6	Driving Times around the Churches in Hangzhou.	18
2.7	Hangzhou Christian Church with Street Map.	19
3.1	Driving Time around the Protestant Churches in Fuzhou.	27
4.1	The Protestant Church Accessibility Scores in Taipei and Guangzhou by the 2SFCA.	35
4.2	The Protestant Church Availability and Accessibility by the NAM.	37
4.3	The Protestant Church's Availability and Accessibility in the Six Cities by the NAM.	39
7.1	The Sample by the Two-Step Floating Catchment Area (2SFCA).	71
7.2	Sample by the Network Analysis Method (NAM).	73
10.1	Location of the Nine Cities in the Three Regions of China.	115
10.2	The Best Areas of the Catholic Church Accessibility Scores by the 2SFCA (Wenzhou).	119
10.3	The Second Best Areas of the Catholic Church Accessibility Scores by the 2SFCA (Shijiazhuang).	120
10.4	The Third Best Areas of the Catholic Church Accessibility Scores by the 2SFCA (Xi'an).	121
10.5	The Worst Areas of the Catholic Church Accessibility Scores by the 2SFCA (Guiyang).	122
10.6	The Best Areas of the Catholic Church Availability and Accessibility by the NAM (Fuzhou).	124
10.7	The Second Best Areas of the Catholic Church Availability and Accessibility by the NAM (Wuhan).	125
10.8	The Worst Areas of the Catholic Church Availability and Accessibility by the NAM (Chongqing).	126
12.1	The Selected Eight Cities and Prefectures in Xinjiang (top) and Ningxia (bottom).	151
12.2	Spatial Maps of Mosque Availability in Urumqi (LAM).	157

12.3　Spatial Maps of Mosque Availability in the Four Areas in Yinchuan (LAM). 158
12.4　Spatial Maps of Mosque Accessibility in Yining, Xinjiang, by the 2SFCA. 161
12.5　Spatial Driving Maps in Wuzhong, Ningxia by the NAM. 163

Preface

In 2009, I assumed the position of co-director at the Center on Religion and Chinese Society (now the Center on Religion and the Global East) at Purdue University, igniting a profound interest in Chinese religious studies. Drawing from my background in history, particularly economic history, I embarked on an invigorating yet challenging journey to integrate history, economics, and religious studies. My goal was to leverage my existing expertise while embracing new dimensions of knowledge.

Religion has always intrigued me, and it shares intricate academic connections with history and economics. Religion relies on history as its backdrop and stage to manifest its divinity and spirituality, while metaphysical religion also depends on the economic foundation to sustain both spiritual and material prosperity. Thus, in 2009, inspired by experts and scholars, I decided to employ cutting-edge digital and spatial technologies to conduct interdisciplinary research on modern Chinese religious economics and religious markets. This approach allowed me to apply historical research methods to observe the evolution of Chinese religious sites longitudinally. I also employed classical economic theories of supply and demand to analyze the supply side—mechanisms governing religious site operations in the religious market. Furthermore, this topic lent itself well to comparative research, enabling both longitudinal comparisons of the same religious sites across different historical periods and lateral comparisons among the five major Chinese religions (Protestantism, Catholicism, Buddhism, Daoism, and Islam), including Christian churches, Buddhist temples, Daoist abbeys, and Islamic mosques. Comparing religious site characteristics across diverse regions and countries enriched the multidimensional perspective of religious site studies, adding depth, vitality, and richness to the research. Importantly, applying novel digital and spatial technologies to address the shortage of modern Chinese religious sites added further significance to the research.

As the Principal Investigator (PI), along with co-PIs Fenggang Yang of Purdue University and Shuming Bao from the University of Michigan, we submitted a grant proposal to the Henry Luce Foundation in 2010. The result was a successful grant of $300,000 under the theme "Establishing Spatial Information Network for the Study of Christianity in China (No. 4301-41573)." Due to our outstanding progress, the Luce Foundation awarded an additional $400,000 in 2013 to expand the study from Christianity to other major religions in China, under the theme "The Spatial Study of Chinese Religion and Society" (No. 4301-59088). This expansion also allowed us to intertwine religious studies with socioeconomic development, resulting in a comprehensive project that spanned seven years.

Building upon this foundation, I, along with my undergraduate and graduate students at Purdue University Northwest campus, dedicated nearly a decade to digitizing and spatializing various data. My students, well-versed in STEM disciplines, excelled in statistics, Geographic Information Systems (GIS), and mathematics, providing valuable support and contributions to my research. I also extended invitations to them for co-authorship, resulting in over ten published papers.

In 2023, recognizing my research achievements in religious digital and spatial studies, the journal *Religions*, based in Switzerland, invited me to serve as a guest editor for a special issue on digital and spatial studies of religions (Hong, 2022). Following rigorous double-blind peer reviews, the special issue successfully published ten refereed articles, primarily focusing on Chinese religious themes. Additionally, I was invited to compile and edit this special issue into a book (Hong, 2023). This experience of being a guest editor motivated me to comprehensively revise, expand, reconfigure, and compile my previous papers into this current book.

I want to sincerely thank my students, Le Zeng, Jiamin Yan, Jianfeng Jin, Lu Cao, and Yunbiao Zhang, for their invaluable technical and statistical support. I'm also deeply thankful to Professor Fenggang Yang of Purdue University and Professor Xiangping Li of East China Normal University for their guidance and enlightenment in the field of religious studies. Dr. Shuming Bao from the University of Michigan provided significant assistance and inspiration in data statistics, generation, and spatial processing. I have also learned a great deal and benefited immensely from the insights of numerous scholars in the field of religious studies, including Peter Bol, Jiang Wu, and Huaiyu Chen. I am grateful to Mr. Nolan Zhang and Mr. Jiyuan Zhang for their assistance with maps and statistics. Finally, I extend my sincere appreciation to Helena Kolenda and Lin Li of the Henry Luce Foundation, whose funding and encouragement have been the key to the success of this project.

Of course, I bear sole responsibility for any shortcomings in this book.

March 10, 2024, New York

References

Hong, Z., ed. 2022. "Special Issue on Digital and Spatial Studies of Religions," *Religions (Guest Edition)*.

Hong, Z., ed. 2023. *Digital and Spatial Studies of Religions*. Basel, Switzerland: Multidisciplinary Digital Publishing Institute (MDPI).

1 Introduction

As an integral part of digital humanities and spatial humanities, the digital and spatial studies of religious sites have emerged as a burgeoning area of interest among scholars (Meng, 2011; Hong, 2023: ix–x). However, a fundamental question that arises when applying these non-traditional research methods to the humanities and religious studies is whether these new methods are effective. Can these innovative approaches address longstanding issues? Do they offer unique perspectives and solutions that traditional methods cannot? If they do, then digital and spatial scientific methods hold allure and vitality; if not, they might merely serve as showcases for new tools, discouraging more humanities scholars from learning and applying these new methods.

Digital and spatial research, with orientations rooted in both natural and social sciences, must demonstrate the capacity to uncover, interpret, and solve new problems if they aim to collaborate and intersect with the humanities, yielding a synergy where "1+1 is greater than 2." This capability should convince humanities scholars that digital and spatial humanities can provide tangible evidence to address issues in fields such as literature, history, philosophy, and religious studies. Furthermore, digital and spatial tools are merely advanced means in academic research; their utility is fully realized when they establish academic connections with specific disciplines; otherwise, they lose their significance as tools.

Meanwhile, interdisciplinary collaboration has become a prevailing trend and mainstream practice in academia, but the humanities, to a certain extent, remain committed to the solitary pursuit of single disciplines and single scholars who believe that true scholarship necessitates depth in a single discipline rather than breadth in multiple disciplines. It was argued that genuine scholars are those who engage in individual independent research and do not require or find effective teamwork collaboration necessary. However, research in digital and spatial humanities inherently possesses interdisciplinary, multidisciplinary, and cross-disciplinary characteristics. Because of its interdisciplinary nature, especially its involvement across humanities, social sciences, and natural sciences, it often requires collaborative efforts involving more than one individual scholar. Regardless of how knowledgeable an individual may be, it is generally challenging for one person to excel in both the humanities and STEM fields.

DOI: 10.4324/9781003495451-1

Thus, this book seeks to address the questions of whether digital and spatial humanities are effective and whether humanities scholars need to engage in interdisciplinary and multidisciplinary research. The primary research focus of this book revolves around the scarcity issues of religious sites related to modern Chinese Protestantism, Catholicism, Buddhism, Daoism, and Islam, within their respective sites and locations. This research area falls under the purview of religious economics (Stark and Finke, 2000: 218–250; Bankston, 2003: 155–171; Finke and Stark, 2003: 96–109; Finke and Stark, 2005: 1–25), which is an interdisciplinary intersection of religious studies and economics. Simultaneously, the issue of religious site scarcity is a significant challenge within the field of religious market studies (Stark and Iannaccone, 1994: 230–252; Sherkat and Wilson, 1995: 993–1026; Jelen, 2002: 93–112; Yang, 2006: 93–122). This shortage of religious sites specifically focuses on the supply side of the religious market equation, concerning the institutions responsible for providing religious venues. Just as business economics can be distinguished by its supply and demand factors, religious economics follows a similar pattern (Finke and Stark, 2003: 100). Yang also contends that "religious economics is determined by the interaction of three major elements: demand, supply, and management" (Yang, 2010: 3).

Here, the demand in the religious market is primarily determined by the number of believers, while the supply is mainly represented by the quantity of religious sites, such as churches, temples, abbeys, and mosques. So, the general definition of the shortage of religious sites is when the number of religious sites cannot meet the demands of religious believers, resulting in a situation where demand exceeds supply. Currently, most scholars studying church scarcity focus on two main aspects. First, there is empirical observation and theoretical generalization, but it lacks quantitative research and a spatial perspective. For example, Yang suggests that overcrowding in Chinese churches and temples has become a common phenomenon today (Yang, 2010: 23) and that China's religious market is severely underdeveloped (Yang, 2006: 114). However, he doesn't provide precise data on the extent of "overcrowding" or the degree of "underdevelopment." Yang's observations are also supported by other scholars (Sherkat and Ellison, 1999: 363–394). Second, research has focused on the visible and invisible factors influencing the Chinese religious market, such as government intervention and regulations (Yang, 2006: 93–122) and atheistic consciousness (Hamberg and Pettersson, 2003: 91–114; Yang, 2010: 3–33), but there is minimal quantitative research and spatial studies on the visible factor of churches. Additionally, many scholars tend to investigate the demand issues in the religious market rather than the supply side (Yang, 2010: 3–33), although Yang (2018) and his team have explored the atlas of religion in China through social and geographical contexts.

This book aims to use digital and spatial humanities methods to concentrate on the scarcity of religious sites in modern China between 1911 and 2004. Historically, the issue of religious site scarcity has mainly been addressed using conventional statistical methods, which means determining the ratio of the number of religious practitioners to the number of religious sites to observe how many believers each religious site can accommodate on average. However, this traditional and simplistic statistical method fails to calculate the time and distance believers need to travel from their residences to the nearest religious site to participate in religious activities. Only through such spatial research can we more accurately, comprehensively, and innovatively determine whether local religious sites are in surplus or shortage.

For example, even if there are 1000 believers using ten churches in a given area, with an apparent average of 100 believers per church, it may not seem crowded or scarce at first glance. But if these 100 believers need to spend 5 hours' round trip, covering a distance of 300 miles, to reach the nearest religious site, then this area should be identified as suffering from a shortage of religious sites. Conversely, if there are only two religious sites in the area, shared by 1000 believers, with an apparent average of 500 people per site, it may appear more crowded and scarce than the former scenario. Still, if these 1000 believers only need to spend one hour and cover 100 miles by average for their round trip, the latter situation is less problematic than the former.

Therefore, to determine the distance and time it takes for believers to travel from home to the nearest religious site, traditional statistical methods are no longer sufficient. We need to leverage scientific tools like geographic information systems (GIS) to measure distance and time, transforming flat statistical data into visual and map-based representations. This is where the true utility of digital and spatial approaches comes in. They not only complement traditional methods but also have the potential to replace them, allowing us to discover, explain, and solve problems that traditional methods struggle with. Digital and spatial humanities thus gain vitality and sustainability. They are not only feasible but also deliverable, measurable, and sustainable.

Regarding the standard questions surrounding the shortage of religious sites in China, this book employs three primary principles. First of all, it assesses the density of congregations in a specific area, primarily by comparing the number of believers to the number of religious sites, calculating the average number of worshippers per site. The more worshippers per site, the more severe the scarcity of sites. In addition, it evaluates the accessibility of religious sites, primarily through GIS, measuring the distance residents in a specific area need to travel to reach the nearest religious site. The farther the distance, the more severe the scarcity of churches. Furthermore, the book examines the availability of religious sites, mainly by mapping spatial streets and determining the average driving time for residents to reach the nearest religious site. The longer the travel time, the more severe the scarcity of churches. Additionally, to supplement spatial data, the book combines various empirical research methods, including on-site investigations, interviews, and participatory observations.

The highlight, feature, and contribution of this book lie in its application of digital and spatial methods, showcasing the unique advantages of these new approaches in addressing religious site issues. The relationship between digitization and spatialization follows a logical sequence. It begins with the collection, identification, analysis, comparison, and differentiation of the number of religious sites and the number of worshippers in different locations and periods for the five major

4 *Introduction*

religions in China since 1911. This data is then uploaded to appropriate internet platforms, scientifically categorized and generated into a digital online database. Once we have this digitized religious site data, spatial methods and GPS as valuable tools are employed to process the digitized data spatially. This includes visualizing the geographical coordinates of religious sites and calculating the time and distance needed for believers to reach the nearest religious site from their residences. Finally, by comparing different regions, religions, and time periods, and considering specific local factors, a standardized scarcity criterion consistent with common sense is proposed. This helps identify the locations and names of cities facing scarcity, allowing scholars to make reasonable and scientifically sound recommendations regarding where new religious sites should be established to meet the religious service needs of congregations.

The significance of this spatial research lies in its ability to scientifically choose appropriate locations for constructing new religious sites, ensuring that these sites are neither too remote to discourage attendance nor overcrowded due to a high concentration of residents. This helps achieve a balance in the supply and demand of religious markets in specific regions, promoting social harmony and facilitating economic development and employment opportunities around religious sites. Just as we carefully select locations for establishing new bank branches, gas stations, or medical clinics to prevent hasty decisions and blind construction, the help of GIS is required to scientifically pinpoint the service locations urgently needed by the public.

This book not only employs digital and spatial methods to study the shortage of religious sites but also integrates traditional historical research methods and cross-sectional comparative research methods. The primary focus of this book is on modern religious sites in China since 1911, examining religious sites for the five major religions in mainland China and comparing their significant changes during different historical periods between 1911 and 2004. This spans the Republican era (1911–1949), Mao Zedong era (1949–1976), Deng Xiaoping era (1978–1997), and Jiang Zemin era (1997–2004), analyzing fundamental characteristics, historical factors, government roles, and market-driving forces in the changes of religious sites. Notably, Chapter 13 specifically discusses the different characteristics and historical evolution of religious sites during the Cultural Revolution (1966–1976).

While the primary focus is on mainland China, this book also incorporates Taipei, Chicago, and religious sites in the United States for reference. It commences with individual city case studies that concentrate on Protestant churches, including Hangzhou (Chapter 2), Zhengzhou, Hefei, and Fuzhou (Chapter 3), and Taipei, Shanghai, Nanjing, and Guangzhou concerning Protestant religious sites (Chapter 4). Additionally, the book adopts a comparative perspective, examining both within China and between China and other countries. It compares 31 provincial capital cities in China, along with a comparison of Hangzhou and Chicago, as well as China and the United States (Chapters 2, 5 and 6). Furthermore, there is a comparison between Hangzhou in Zhejiang province and Taipei in Taiwan (Chapter 4), with the aim of identifying disparities, explaining the reasons for these discrepancies, and determining which cities experience a scarcity of religious sites. The book also introduces local socioeconomic elements such as population, education, and GDP as reference points, analyzing the correlation between the number of religious sites and the socioeconomic development status. It also conducts a cross-sectional comparison of religious sites for the five major religions, analyzing the current status, characteristics, and reasons for the inadequacy of religious sites for these religions (Chapters 8–12). Moreover, a dedicated chapter (Chapter 7) compares different conclusions regarding the shortage of Protestant churches obtained through multiple spatial research methods.

In addition to discussing the research methods, it is essential to clarify the sources and types of data used in this book. The primary data source for this book relies on publicly available information from the Chinese government. First, population data is derived mainly from the 2000 population census conducted by the National Bureau of Statistics of China, which reported a total population of 1,295,330,000 (National Bureau of Statistics of China, 2001). The reason for choosing the 2000 census as the population base, rather than the 2010 or 2020 census, is that the existing data on religious sites only extends up to 2004.

Second, the total number of believers in China is a key dataset. Due to the unavailability of precise figures for members of Protestant and Catholic house churches (Hong, 2011: 160; Hong, 2012a: 513–522; Hong, 2012b: 249–261), the data on the number of believers is primarily estimated based on official religious site statistics in China. The main source for this estimation is the statistical data published by the Institute of World Religions at the Chinese Academy of Social Sciences in 2010 (Research Project Team of the Institute of World Religious Studies in the Chinese Academy of Social Sciences, 2010: 191). Though many scholars believe that this figure significantly underestimates the actual number of believers, as of now, there are few, if any, alternative and convincing figures available to replace it. Therefore, this book has no choice but to rely on this official yet conservative data. For example, based on the ratio of Protestants to the total population in China, it can be inferred that Protestants make up approximately 1.8% of the total population (Hong and Zeng, 2012: 18), whereas in the United States, this figure is 21% (Hadaway, Marler and Chaves, 1993: 741–52; Hadaway and Marler, 2005: 307).

Third, the number of religious sites in China and its provinces and municipalities is determined primarily based on data published by the National Bureau of Statistics in 2004 (National Bureau of Statistics of China, 2004). From this data, the average number of believers per religious site in China is calculated. For example, according to official statistics in 2004, each Protestant church in China could accommodate an average of 1589 Protestant followers, whereas in the United States, the average church had 198 worshippers (Hadaway and Marler, 2005: 307–322).

Fourth, the number of religious sites in provinces and municipalities is another dataset used in this book. The Chinese government has not systematically released the number of believers in each province and municipality to date. However, the Amity Foundation in Hong Kong published the proportion of Protestants to the total population in various provinces and autonomous regions in China in 2004 (The Amity Foundation, 2004; Ying, 2009: 63–97). Nevertheless, they did not provide data for provincial capitals, which this book requires. Therefore, this book can

6 *Introduction*

only use the provincial ratios as a reference. Generally, provincial capital cities are expected to have more churches, and the scarcity of churches in these cities is relatively less severe. Using the provincial average to estimate the capital city's average is obviously more conservative.

Finally, spatial data for churches is another critical component. With support from the Henry Luce Foundation, the Center for Religion and Chinese Society at Purdue University (now Center on Religion and the Global East) and the China Data Center at the University of Michigan (now has been closed) jointly developed the *China Religion Explorer* (now *China Geo-Explore*) (The China Data Institute, 2012), which integrates Chinese religious data with various socioeconomic statistics. Many of the spatial maps and data used in this book benefit from this spatial network. However, the University of Michigan has since closed this website, but the China Data Institute still maintains it (https://www.chinageoexplorer.com/cge/) (China Data Institute, 2012). There is also the *Atlas of Religions in China* (https://chinadatacenter.net/Data/ServiceContent.aspx?id=1573) (China Data Institute, 2008), which can generate religious site data and maps along with other population and economic data. Additionally, we also referenced the *Online Spiritual Atlas of the Global East* (OSAGE) established by the Center on Religion and the Global East at Purdue University (https://www.globaleast.org/osage/index.html) (Center on Religion and the Global East at Purdue University, 2022). Finally, this book also relies on other statistical data and maps, including spatial street maps of cities, urban travel speeds, and empirical survey data, to provide essential data references for the study of shortage of religious sites. However, in response to suggestions from anonymous reviewers advocating for a reduction in tables, figures, and maps to prevent reader confusion, and considering the editor's recommendation to significantly cut down on all illustrations, the author has implemented a reduction of over 50% in illustrations, including tables, maps, and figures. Nevertheless, acknowledging the nature of spatial and digital studies explored in this book, it is essential to retain adequate illustrations to enhance the quality of analysis.

The book can be broadly divided into two main parts. Alongside the Introduction in Chapter 1, the first part, encompassing Chapters 2–7, primarily explores the shortage of Protestant churches. This part serves as the research foundation and model for studying scarcity in the other religious sites of four non-Protestant religions. The second part, spanning Chapters 8–13, focuses on the insufficiency of religious sites for Buddhism, Catholicism, Daoism, and Islam. Together, these two parts offer a comprehensive and systematic digital and spatial study of religious sites for the five major religions. The book's limitation stems from the inherent incompleteness of official Chinese data, as it does not encompass many underground churches and house churches. Protestant house churches in China are defined as Protestant churches that have not been registered and approved by the government. However, it's essential to recognize that incompleteness doesn't imply falsehood. It is natural to scrutinize and question existing official data. Nevertheless, in cases where we are unable to present more comprehensive, precise, and up-to-date data, it becomes necessary to accept the information conditionally and approach it critically.

In summary, the primary focus of this book is to introduce a research method. While the data may not be complete, precise, or entirely up to date, the main goal is to demonstrate this method's application, offering a new perspective, new approach, and new tools for the study of religious site. As for religious site data, it is hoped and believed that with collective efforts, it will continue to be improved and enriched.

References

The Amity Foundation. 2004. "How Many Sheep Are There in the Chinese Flock?," *Amity News Services*. Retrieved from: http://www.amitynewsservice.org

Bankston, C.L. 2003. "Rationality, Choice, and the Religious Economy: Individual and Collective Rationality in Supply and Demand," *Review of Religious Research*, 45 (2):155–171.

Center on Religion and the Global East at Purdue University. 2022. *The Online Spiritual Atlas of Global East (OSAGE)*. Retrieved from: https://www.globaleast.org/osage/index.html

China Data Institute. 2008. *Atlas of Religions in China*. Retrieved from: https://chinadatacenter.net/Data/ServiceContent.aspx?id=1573

China Data Institute. 2012. *China Geo-Explore*. Retrieved from: https://www.chinageoexplorer.com/cge/

Finke, R., and R. Stark. 2003. "The Dynamic of Religious Economies," *Handbook of the Sociology of Religion (96-109)*, M. Dillion, ed., pp. 96–109. New York: Cambridge University Press.

Finke, R., and R. Stark. 2005. *The Churching of America, 1776-2005. Winners and Losers in Our Religious Economy*. New Brunswick, NJ: Rutgers University Press.

Hadaway, C.K., and P.L. Marler. 2005. "How Many Americans Attend Worship Each Week? An Alternative Approach to Measurement," *Journal for the Scientific Study of Religion*, 44 (3):307–322.

Hadaway, C.K, P.L. Marler, and M. Chaves. 1993. "What the Polls Don't Show: A Closer Look at U.S. Church Attendance," *American Sociological Review*, 58 (6):741–752.

Hamberg, E.M., and T. Pettersson. 2003. "Religious Markets: Supply, Demand, and Rational Choices," *Sacred Markets, Sacred Canopies: Essays on Religious Markets and Religious Pluralism*, T.G. Jelen, ed., pp. 91–114. Lanham, MD: Rowman & Littlefield.

Hong, Z. 2011. "The Protestant House Church and Its Poverty of Rights in China," *Annual Review of the Sociology of Religion: Volume 2: Religion and Politics*, (2):160–176.

Hong, Z. 2012a. "In Search of Causes of the Poverty of Rights for Chinese Protestant House Church," *Asian Profile*, 40 (6):513–522.

Hong, Z. 2012b. "Protecting and Striving for the Rights to Religious Freedom: Case Studies on the Protestant House Churches in China," *Journal of Third World Studies*, XXIX (1):249–261.

Hong, Z. ed. 2023. *Digital and Spatial Studies of Religions*. Basel: MDPI.

Hong, Z., and L. Zeng. 2012. "Spatial Identification of the Christian Church Shortage: A Case Study in Hangzhou City," *American Review of China Studies*, 13 (1):17–36.

Jelen, T.G. ed. 2002. *Sacred Markets, Sacred Canopies: Essays on Religious Markets and Religious Pluralism*. Lanham, MD: Rowman & Littlefield.

Meng, X. 2011. "Study on Current 'Religious Fever' Phenomenon of China," *Canadian Social Science*, 7 (2):147–152.

National Bureau of Statistics of China. 2001. *2010 Renkou tongji* (2010 Population Census). Beijing: National Statistic Press.

National Bureau of Statistics of China. 2004. *Zhongguo renkou tongji nianjian* (The Chinese Population Statistical Yearbook, 2004). Beijing: National Statistic Press.

Research Project Team of the Institute of World Religious Studies in the Chinese Academy of Social Sciences. 2010. *Zhongguo jidujiao baokao, 2010* (The Survey Report on China's Christians, 2010), J. Ze and Q. Yonghui, eds., pp. 190–212. Beijing: Shehui kexue wenxian chubanshe.

Sherkat, D.E., and C.G. Ellison. 1999. "Recent Developments and Current Controversies in the Sociology of Religion," *Annual Review of Sociology*, 25 (1):363–394.

Sherkat, D.E., and J. Wilson. 1995. "Preferences, Constraints, and Choices in Religious Markets: An Examination of Religious Switching and Apostasy," *Social Forces*, 73 (3):993–1026.

Stark, R., and L. Iannaccone. 1994. "A Supply-side Reinterpretation of the 'Secularization' of Europe," *Journal for the Scientific Study of Religion*, 33 (3):230–252.

Stark, R., and R. Finke. 2000. *Acts of Faith: Explaining the Human Side of Religion*. Berkeley, CA: University of California Press.

Yang, F. 2006. "The Red, Black, and Gray Markets of Religion in China," *The Sociological Quarterly*, 47 (1):93–122.

Yang, F. 2010. "Religion in China under Communism: A Shortage Economy Explanation," *Journal of Church and State*, 52 (1):3–33.

Yang, F. 2018. *Atlas of Religion in China: Social and Geographical Contexts*. Boston, MA: Brill.

Ying, F.-t. 2009. "The Regional Development of Protestant Christianity in China: 1918, 1949 and 2004," *The China Review*, 9 (2):63–97.

2 The Shortage of Protestant Churches in Hangzhou City[1]

2.1 Introduction

The shortage of Protestant churches in China represents a critical issue that affects religious freedom and reflects administrative censorship. In the current "religious market," "overcrowded churches and temples are common scenes in today's China" (Yang, 2010: 23). Some scholars have explored political, economic, cultural, and social factors contributing to the shortage of Protestant churches or the scarcity of religious resources (Finke and Iannaccone, 1993; Stark and Iannaccone, 1994; Finke, 1997; Froese, 2001; Yang, 2010). Others have introduced innovative research methods for examining the relationship between geography and church availability (Welch and Balzell, 1984; Parr, 1985; Parr, O'Neill and Nairn, 1988; Zelinsky, 2001; Church and Marston, 2003; Xue and Zhu, 2008).

However, few, if any, scholars have harnessed the power of Geographic Information Systems (GIS) and spatial statistical analysis to address church availability and accessibility by quantifying the distance and driving time between the residences (demand points) and churches (supply points) in China. Hence, this chapter aims to provide a spatial perspective on the church shortage in Hangzhou City, China, while establishing practical and measurable criteria for identifying church shortages in China.

This chapter integrates data from diverse sources and formats into a unified system, facilitating the creation of dynamic spatial maps. The primary data for this case study are derived from official records released by the Chinese government and government-affiliated research institutes. For instance, the estimated number of Chinese Protestants stands at 23,050,000, based on an exhaustive survey conducted by the Chinese Academy of Social Sciences (CASS) in 2009 (Research Project Team of the Institute of World Religious Studies in the Chinese Academy of Social Sciences, 2010: 191). The estimated number of Protestant churches in China, 11,463, was disclosed in the *2004 China's Economic Census* (China Census Bureau, 2005), excluding house churches and new churches established after 2004. However, for Hangzhou, we have incorporated data on several new churches constructed after 2004, gathered through field research conducted by the author. Additionally, this study greatly benefited from the *Atlas of Religions in China* (China Data Institute, 2012), which offers a spatial exploration of religion based on the 2004 China Economic Census.

DOI: 10.4324/9781003495451-2

10   *The Shortage of Protestant Churches in Hangzhou City*

As for methodology, we employ ArcGIS and spatial statistical analysis to conduct comparative research on the state of Protestant churches in China and the United States, with a particular focus on Hangzhou and Chicago. Our methodology assesses the shortage of Protestant churches from four distinct angles: (1) A broad comparative perspective between China and the United States; (2) A historical examination spanning from 1855 to 2004 within China; (3) An analysis conducted on both macro and micro levels, encompassing national, regional, and local dimensions; and (4) Determining church availability and accessibility through the measurement of distances and driving times between residential areas (demand points) and church locations (supply points).

2.2   General overview of the Protestant church shortage in China

While it may not seem directly relevant to compare the differences in the number of Protestant churches between China and the United States, the significant numerical gap between these two countries conveys a striking image. According to Hadaway and Marler, "the best estimate for the total number of American congregations is 331,000, with 25 percent being mainline Protestants, 54 percent conservative/evangelical Protestants, 7 percent Catholic/Orthodox, 11 percent other Christian, and 3 percent non-Christian." In essence, this translates to 297,900 Protestant congregations in the United States, representing 90% of the total 331,000. With a US population of 281,421,906 in 2000, on average, 945 Americans attended a single Protestant congregation (Hadaway and Marler, 2005: 318). Similarly, based on the fact that 59 million Protestants were attending weekly worship, constituting 21% of the total population (calculated from a US population of 281,421,906 in 2000) (Hadaway and Marler, 2005: 318), each Protestant church, on average, had 198 participants (59 million Protestants and 297,900 Protestant churches).

In contrast, Chinese official records indicate that there were 23.05 million Chinese Protestants in 2010, which accounted for 1.8% of the total population (Research Project Team of the Institute of World Religious Studies in the Chinese Academy of Social Sciences, 2010: 191). As noted by Yang Fenggang, there were 85,000 religious congregations in China in 1997 (Yang, 2010: 28). However, the 2004 Economic Census Data with GIS Maps lists 71,292 religious sites identified by zip codes (China Census Bureau, 2005). On average, each religious site in China had 277 members. Nevertheless, when considering Chinese Protestants exclusively, there were 11,463 Protestant churches in 2004 (China Census Bureau, 2005). Consequently, on average, each Protestant church had 2,050 Chinese Protestants as participants. It becomes evident that Chinese Protestants may face a shortage of churches for their regular religious services. Table 2.1 provides a concise overview of the key disparities between Protestant churches in the United States and China. In this polished table, the author has adjusted the formatting to make it more visually appealing and easier to read.

After examining the comparative overview and the nationwide macro perspective in China, it becomes imperative to focus on Zhejiang Province, which stands

Table 2.1 Comparative Protestant Churches and Participants in China and the US.

	USA	China	Comparison (%)
Population of Protestant	59,000,000	23,050,000	+151 (US over China)
Percentages of Protestants in total population	21	1.8	+1,060 (US over China)
Numbers of Protestant churches (congregations)	297,900	11,463	+2,499 (US over China)
Average participants per church	198	2,050	−935 (China over US)

Source: C.K. Hadaway and Penny L. Marler, "How Many Americans Attend Worship Each Week? An Alternative Approach to Measurement," *Journal for the Scientific Study of Religion*, 44 (3) (2005):318; Research Project Team, *Zhongguo jidujiao diaocha baogao, 2010* (The Survey Report on China's Christians, in Annual Report on China's Religions, 2010), edited by Jin Ze and Qiu Yonghui (Beijing: Shehui kexue wenxian chubanshe, 2010), p. 191; Fenggang Yang, "Religion in China under Communism: A Shortage Economy Explanation," *Journal of Church and State*, 52 (1) (2010):28; China Census Bureau, *The 2004 China's Economic Census Data with GIS Maps* (Beijing: All China Market Research Co., LTD, 2005).

out as the most rapidly growing province in terms of the expansion of Protestantism. Additionally, Hangzhou, the capital city of Zhejiang Province, warrants particular attention. It is important in computing the ratio of churches per 1 million people, as it serves as a meaningful metric for assessing the concentration of churches in Zhejiang. The statistical data shows a remarkably uneven distribution of churches in Zhejiang, with Wenzhou City averaging just one church for every 10,149,000 people, in stark contrast to Jiaxing County where one church serves 1,200,000 people, despite the fact that only 1.8% of the Chinese population identifies as Protestant (China Census Bureau, 2005). For comparison, the United States maintains an average of one church for every 945 Americans.

In addition to the existing Protestant churches, a historical perspective can shed light on the evolving trends in church construction in Zhejiang since 1855, as depicted in Figure 2.1.

Figure 2.1 serves as a potential source of inspiration for religious scholars, offering a glimpse into the intricate interplay of political, social, economic, and cultural factors that may have contributed to significant events in China, notably the years 1983 and 1997. These figures also beckon scholars to investigate the spatial dynamics influencing new church construction across the nation. Equally thought-provoking are the sharp declines in new church construction evident in 1984 and 1998. Do these fluctuations follow discernible patterns, and what do they signify?

The continual increase in the cumulative number of churches in Zhejiang from 1978 to 2004 raises interesting questions. Has the region reached saturation in terms of church construction, or is there still room for further expansion? Does Zhejiang's experience represent an exceptional case, or does it mirror broader nationwide trends? These questions encourage religious scholars to embark on in-depth studies, exploring church shortages and comparing patterns with other Chinese provinces.

12 *The Shortage of Protestant Churches in Hangzhou City*

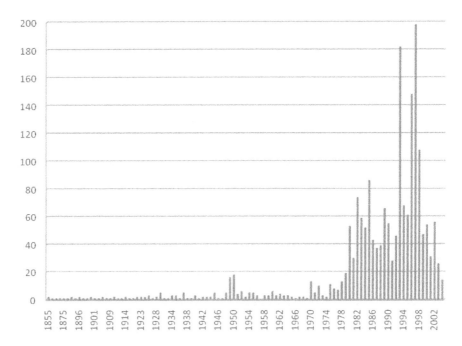

Figure 2.1 Evolution of New Protestant Church Construction in Zhejiang (1855–2004).
Source: China Census Bureau, *The 2004 China's Economic Census Data with GIS Maps* (Beijing: All China Market Research Co., LTD, 2005).

2.3 Spatial studies: A comparative perspective

A suitable case study for comparative analysis could involve Chicago City and Hangzhou City, the capital of Zhejiang Province. Both cities share similar population sizes (2,690,000 in Chicago and 2,080,000 in Hangzhou in 2010) and comparable territorial areas (606 square km in Chicago and 728.19 square km in Hangzhou). Hangzhou City comprises six districts: Shangcheng, Xiacheng, Xihu, Gongshu, Jianggai, and Bingjiang. Intriguingly, as of 2011, Hangzhou boasts a mere nine Protestant churches, while Chicago claims a staggering 1,329 Protestant churches. Map 2.1 provides a visual representation of Protestant churches in Chicago.

It's important to clarify that Hangzhou City should be different from the greater Hangzhou Area, which encompasses seven additional counties beyond Hangzhou City itself. These counties include Yuhang, Xiaoshan, Linan, Fuyang, Tonglu, Jiande, and Chunan. This study focuses on Hangzhou City only, excluding six districts, which have nine Protestant churches in total as of 2011. Leveraging the latitude and longitude data of nine churches within Hangzhou City, we can accurately pinpoint the geographic locations of these churches, represented by the nine dots in Map 2.2.

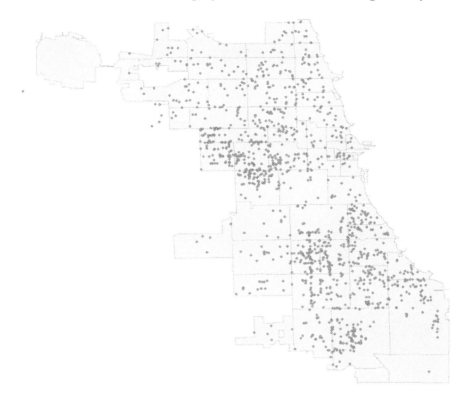

Map 2.1 Protestant Churches in Chicago: A Spatial Overview.

Source: Department of Innovation and Technology of the City of Chicago: New Interactive Chicago Map (http://www.cityofchicago.org/city/en/depts/doit/provdrs/gis.html).

While looking at the Chicago map (Map 2.3), the residents living in the gray areas can reach their nearest churches in the dark dots within 1.0 km. It covers 2,383,800 residents or 96.55% of the total residents. Those who are living in the white areas can't reach their churches within 1.0 km.

In the context of the Hangzhou case, each of the nine churches in Hangzhou serves as a central point, with a corresponding circle indicating an approximate radius of 1 km (as shown in Map 2.4). Within this 1-km radius, there resides a population of 270,026 individuals, constituting approximately 12.8% of the total population.

Expanding the perspective, the larger circle encompasses an area of approximately 10 km in radius (as depicted in Map 2.5). Within this extended radius, a substantial population of 2,044,030 individuals resides, accounting for approximately 96.87% of the total population.

Given the varying levels of church accessibility and availability in both Chicago and Hangzhou, the author has constructed a comparative table (Table 2.2). Due to the challenge of obtaining precise data on the number of Protestants in

14 *The Shortage of Protestant Churches in Hangzhou City*

Map 2.2 Nine Hangzhou Protestant Churches.
Source: China Census Bureau, *The 2004 China's Economic Census Data with GIS Maps* (Beijing: All China Market Research Co., LTD, 2005).

Hangzhou, this study employs the national average Protestant rate of 1.8% to estimate the number of Protestants in Hangzhou. Similarly, for Chicago, the study utilizes 21% of the American average Protestant rate to calculate the number of Protestants. Furthermore, in an effort to gain a more comprehensive understanding of church accessibility, the study employs an alternative approach to calculate the distance between residents' locations and church locations. Table 2.2 delineates the number of residents and Protestants who cannot reach their nearest churches within varying distances. Initially, the author considered a 0.5 km radius to assess church accessibility in Chicago. However, this same distance measurement cannot be applied to Hangzhou, as the *China Geo-Explorer* (China Data Institute, 2012) only permits a minimum distance measurement of 1 km. Consequently, the study

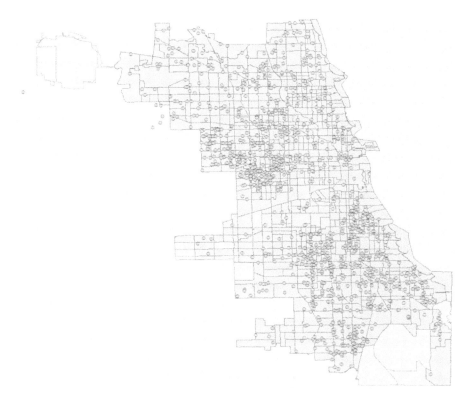

Map 2.3 Church Availability in Chicago (1 km) (2,383,800 residents or 96.55%).

Source: Department of Innovation and Technology of the City of Chicago: New Interactive Chicago Map (http://www.cityofchicago.org/city/en/depts/doit/provdrs/gis.html).

employs distance measurements of 2.5 km, 5 km, and 7.5 km for Hangzhou. This adjustment is necessary because, in the case of Chicago, a 1 km radius already encompasses 96% of its total population. As depicted in Table 2.2, the data reveals that more than 25% of Hangzhou residents are unable to reach their nearest church within 5 km, underscoring the disparities in church accessibility.

In addition to assessing the distance between residents' locations and churches, it is essential to incorporate spatial city street maps to calculate the driving time between residential areas and churches. As depicted in Map 2.6, the dots represent the locations of Protestant churches in Hangzhou, while the lines represent the streets.

However, due to the challenges of obtaining a comprehensive spatial street map covering the entire city, Map 2.7 provides a representation of only a portion of the streets.

With the aid of the street map, it becomes feasible to calculate driving distances in minutes. As illustrated in Map 2.6, varying colors such as inner circle (center), middle circle (between the center and outer), and outer circle represent driving distances of 20, 40, and 60 minutes to reach different churches, respectively, while

16 *The Shortage of Protestant Churches in Hangzhou City*

Map 2.4 Church Availability in Hangzhou (1 km) (270,026 residents or 12.8%).

Source: China Census Bureau, *The 2004 China's Economic Census Data with GIS Maps* (Beijing: All China Market Research Co., LTD, 2005).

question markers indicate instances where distance measurements couldn't be obtained due to the absence of street map data.

This pilot study underscores the need for further exploration in the realms of data selection, data analysis, and data accuracy. First, obtaining detailed spatial street maps for Hangzhou is imperative to accurately measure driving times while factoring in traffic variables. Additionally, it is essential to establish collaborative relationships with Chinese scholars who can provide invaluable spatial information on church accessibility and availability, ensuring the data remains updated and precise.

Furthermore, since the nine churches in Hangzhou vary in size and capacity, it becomes crucial to estimate the number of weekly attendees in each church. This can be achieved through various empirical methods, such as phone calls, email correspondence, and on-site observation. Moreover, enhancing the accuracy of driving time calculations from residential areas to the nearest church requires conducting

The Shortage of Protestant Churches in Hangzhou City 17

Map 2.5 Church Availability in Hangzhou (10 km) (2,044,030 residents or 96.87%).
Source: China Census Bureau, *The 2004 China's Economic Census Data with GIS Maps* (Beijing: All China Market Research Co., LTD, 2005).

surveys and interviews with church members. This will help identify the modes of transportation used and the time taken to travel from home to church, with particular attention to variations between Sundays and weekdays.

In addition, while the comparison between Chicago, with a significantly higher Protestant population, and Hangzhou, where residents primarily follow non-religious or Buddhist beliefs, may raise questions, it is essential to note that the methodology employed in this comparative spatial study can be adapted to explore

Table 2.2 Church Availability and Accessibility: Chicago vs. Hangzhou.

	Number of residents can't access their nearest church	Percentage of total population	Average number of Protestants per church
Chicago: 1 km	306,200	3.44	64,302
Hangzhou: 1 km	1,840,123	87.2	33,122
Hangzhou: 5 km	534,938	25.35	9,629
Hangzhou: 10 km	66,119	3.13	1,190

Source: China Data Institute, *China Geo-Explore, 2010*. Retrieved from: https://www.chinageoexplorer.com/cge/.

18   *The Shortage of Protestant Churches in Hangzhou City*

Map 2.6 Driving Times around the Churches in Hangzhou.
Source: China Census Bureau, *The 2004 China's Economic Census Data with GIS Maps* (Beijing: All China Market Research Co., LTD, 2005).

variations across different Chinese cities. The research can be extended to investigate causal relationships between new church construction and factors such as education, economics, culture, race, and politics in various regions of China. For example, comparing church accessibility between northern and southern regions, urban and rural areas, and the east coast and western regions of China can yield valuable insights. In essence, instead of solely comparing Chicago and Hangzhou, the approach can be applied to examine Hangzhou and Zhengzhou, Shanghai and Beijing, or even a township and a village. Moreover, field trip studies, combined with virtual maps and spatial analyses used in this project, can pinpoint specific areas requiring new church construction, akin to the selection and establishment of new gas stations and bank branches.

2.4   Conclusion

This pilot study offers a preliminary methodology for addressing the issue of church shortages in China. Through a comparative lens, it highlights disparities in church accessibility and availability between the United States and China, focusing

Map 2.7 Hangzhou Christian Church with Street Map.

Source: China Census Bureau, *The 2004 China's Economic Census Data with GIS Maps* (Beijing: All China Market Research Co., LTD, 2005).

on the number of Protestant churches, average congregation size, and churches per 1 million people. Additionally, the study measures the distance residents must travel to reach the nearest church and the population residing around each church. Street maps are employed to calculate driving times between churches and residential areas.

The three steps outlined herein provide a framework for establishing reasonable criteria to quantify church shortages in China. For instance, areas where residents must travel more than 5 km to reach the nearest church or where over 25% of residents live more than 5 km from a church can be considered to have a clear church shortage. Another important indicator is the one-way driving time of 30 minutes or more from one's home to the nearest church for weekly services, drawing inspiration from the US National Institute for Health, which uses a 30-minute driving time as a criterion for assessing medical clinic shortages. Employing these criteria, Hangzhou can be identified as an area with a church shortage, necessitating the construction of additional churches. It is worth noting that this study utilizes a nationwide average Protestant rate of 1.8% of the total population, even though

Zhejiang Province had a higher Protestant population of 3.92% in 2004, 217% more than the national average (Amity News Service, 2004; Ying, 2009: 83). Unfortunately, precise data on the number of Protestants in Hangzhou is challenging to obtain.

The issue of church shortages may prompt further scholarly inquiries regarding Protestant house churches in China (Hong, 2011). Critical questions may arise, including whether practical concerns related to transportation difficulties and overcrowding are more significant factors influencing individuals to join house churches than political and religious motivations. Besides, do house churches play a role in maintaining social stability by accommodating Protestants who cannot attend officially registered churches due to shortages? Given the Chinese government's concerns about social stability and harmony, will the construction of more officially registered churches effectively address these concerns?

Undoubtedly, the spatial study of church shortages faces numerous technical, statistical, and political obstacles due to incomplete spatial and imprecise church information in China. While this spatial study offers valuable insights and dimensions to religious studies, it should not replace traditional empirical religious research methods, such as surveys, interviews, and participant observation. The author hopes that this pilot study will inspire scholars to explore new information, enhance methodologies, and foster collaborations, thereby advancing spatial religious studies in China.

Note

1 With the publisher's permission, segments of this Chapter are excerpted from the article authored by Zhaohui Hong and co-authored by his graduate student, Le Zheng, "Spatial Identification of the Christian Church Shortage: A Case Study in Hangzhou City," *American Review of China Studies*, 13 (1) (2012):17–36. Mr. Zheng has granted permission and provided written consent to exclude his name as co-author of this book. The original work has been significantly revised and updated for this book.

References

The Amity Foundation. 2004. How Many Sheep Are There in the Chinese Flock? *Amity News Services*. Retrieved from: http://www.amitynewsservice.org

China Census Bureau. 2005. *Zhongguo jingji renkou shuju ji dili xinxi xitong didu, 2004* (The 2004 China's Economic Census Data with GIS Maps). Beijing: All China Market Research Co., LTD.

China Data Institute. 2012. *China Geo-Explore*. Retrieved from: https://www.chinageoexplorer.com/cge/

Church, R., and C. Marston. 2003. "Measuring Accessibility for People with a Disability," *Geographical Analysis*, 35 (1):83–96.

Finke, R. 1997. "The Consequences of Religious Competition: Supply-Side Explanations for Religious Change," *Rational Choice Theory and Religion: Summary and Assessment*, L. Young, ed., pp. 45–61. New York: Routledge.

Fink, R., and L. Iannaccone. 1993. "Supply-side Explanations for Religious Change," *The Annuals of the American Association for Political and Social Science*, 527:27–39.

Froese, P. 2001. "Hungary for Religion: A Supply-Side Interpretation of the Hungarian Religious Revival," *Journal for the Scientific Study of Religion*, 40 (2):251–268.

Hadaway, C.K., and P.L. Marler. 2005. "How Many Americans Attend Worship Each Week? An Alternative Approach to Measurement," *Journal for the Scientific Study of Religion*, 44 (3):307–322.

Hong, Z. 2011. "The Protestant House Church and Its Poverty of Rights in China," *Annual Review of the Sociology of Religion, Volume 2: Religion and Politics*, pp. 160–176. Beijing: China Census Bureau. 2005.

Parr, J. 1985. "A Population Density Approach to Regional Spatial Structure," *Urban Studies*, 22 (4):289–303.

Parr, J., G. O'Neill, and A. Nairn. 1988. "Metropolitan Density Functions: A Further Exploration," *Regional Science and Urban Economics*, 18 (4):463–478.

Research Project Team of the Institute of World Religious Studies in the Chinese Academy of Social Sciences. 2010. *Zhongguo jidujiao diaocha baogao, 2010* (The Survey Report on China's Christians, in Annual Report on China's Religions, 2010), J. Ze and Q. Yonghui, eds., pp. 190–212. Beijing: Shehui kexue wenxian chubanshe.

Stark, R., and L. Iannaccone. 1994. "A Supply-Side Reinterpretation of the 'Secularization' of Europe," *Journal for the Scientific Study of Religion*, 33 (3):230–252.

Welch, M., and J. Balzell. 1984. "Geographic Mobility and Church Attendance," *Journal for the Scientific Study of Religion*, 23:75–91.

Xue, X., and H. Zhu. 2008. "Guangdong jidujiao jiaoai de shikong yanbian" (Changing Time and Locations of the Christian Case in Guangdong, 1584–1910)," *Dili Yanjiu* (Geographic Studies), 9 (3):71–79.

Yang, F. 2010. "Religion in China under Communism: A Shortage Economy Explanation," *Journal of Church and State*, 52 (1):3–33.

Ying, F-t. 2009. "The Regional Development of Protestant Christianity in China: 1918, 1949 and 2004," *The China Review*, 9 (2):63–97.

Zelinsky, W. 2001. "The Uniqueness of the American Religious Landscape," *Geographical Review*, 91 (3):565–585.

3 Case Studies in Hangzhou, Zhengzhou, Hefei, and Fuzhou Cities[1]

3.1 Introduction

Having analyzed the cases in both Hangzhou and Chicago in Chapter 2, the logical progression is to now expand the study of the Hangzhou case to other provincial cities in China in this chapter. Actually, the shortage of Protestant churches stands as a critical factor in comprehending the dynamics of supply and demand within the "religious market" and the intricate correlations between religion and economic development. As Yang aptly defines it, the Chinese religious market can be likened to a socialist shortage economy, wherein demand always exceeds supply, and shortages of supply are chronic and systemic in the "socialist system" under Communist rule (Yang, 2012: 20). In this context, similar to the shortage material economy (Kornai, 1980), the church, serving as a supply-side entity, plays a pivotal role in addressing the demands of believers.

Broadly speaking, the Protestant church shortage reflects a situation where demand (Protestants) surpasses supply (Protestant churches). In the context of China's religious market today, this church shortage can be quantified through three measurable indicators: overcrowded church congregations, the significant distance between residential areas and the nearest church, and the extended travel time from home to the closest church.

In an endeavor to gauge these three indicators, the author has previously published research in collaboration with a graduate assistant, Zeng Le, outlining measurable, quantitative, and general criteria for defining the shortage of Protestant churches in China (Hong and Zeng, 2012: 17–26). This was accomplished through comparative studies between Chicago in the United States and Hangzhou in China. Recognizing that a direct comparison between Protestant-majority Chicago and Communist-led Hangzhou might not be entirely appropriate, this chapter extends its efforts to establish spatial and statistical measurements based on four Chinese provincial capital cities: Hangzhou (capital of Zhejiang province), Zhengzhou (capital of Henan province), Hefei (capital of Anhui province), and Fuzhou (capital of Fujian province). These cities represent the four most prominent Protestant provinces in China.

This study utilizes the advanced *Atlas of Religions in China* (China Data Institute, 2008) and *China Geo-Explore* (China Data Institute, 2012), the web-based spatial data service providing convenient access to religious site data and a rich repository of comprehensive information sourced from government statistics, censuses, economic data, and various other reliable sources. Additionally, it utilizes ArcGIS and other spatial and statistical analyses to conduct comparative studies on the four provincial capital cities in China.

It is worth noting that obtaining precise statistical and spatial information about Chinese Protestant house churches, which are not registered with the government (Hong, 2011, 2012a, 2012b), proves to be an insurmountable challenge. Consequently, this project predominantly relies on official data concerning registered Protestant churches, as released in 2010 by the Chinese Academy of Social Sciences (Research Project Team of the Institute of World Religious Studies in the Chinese Academy of Social Sciences, 2010: 190–212), and the 2004 China Economic Census (China Census Bureau, 2005), which has been incorporated into *China Geo-Explore* (China Data Institute, 2012). To complement this data, the project also undertakes field trips, interviews, and participatory observations, serving as indispensable supplements and value-added components to the spatial and statistical technology employed.

3.2 The density of Protestants per church in four Chinese cities

Chapter 2 conducts a comparative analysis of the spatial disparities between Chicago and Hangzhou concerning the availability and accessibility of churches. While it is essential to establish a reference point for the scarcity of churches through macro and general comparisons between the United States and China, it may be more meaningful to focus on comparing differences within representative Protestant regions in China exclusively, excluding the United States and other Western nations that are predominantly Protestant.

Fortunately, the Henry Luce project, spearheaded by this author and collaborating scholars, has successfully identified, located, verified, and documented 7,565 Protestant churches in the provinces of Zhejiang, Henan, Anhui, and Fujian. This achievement followed a thorough correction of numerous erroneous addresses and precise determination of the latitude and longitude coordinates of all Protestant churches. The project has successfully integrated official religious data, census data, and economic information pertaining to these four provinces into the *Atlas of Religions in China*. This spatial data has enabled dynamic and innovative comparative studies regarding the shortage of churches among the four provincial capital cities and their respective provinces.

The rationale behind choosing Hangzhou (Zhejiang), Zhengzhou (Henan), Hefei (Anhui), and Fuzhou (Fujian) as case studies for investigating the scarcity of Protestant churches merits attention. These four provinces enjoyed their prominence as the top regions in terms of accommodating Protestants. While the national average percentage of Chinese Protestants stands at 1.8% of the total population (Hong and Zeng, 2012: 18), Henan, Anhui, Zhejiang, and Fujian surpass this average with percentages of 5.4%, 5.01%, 3.92%, and 3.4%, respectively (Ying, 2009: 83). Significantly, these four provinces collectively harbor a substantial portion of

Table 3.1 Distribution of Protestants and Percentage of Protestants in the Total Population in Four Provinces, 2004.

Province	Protestant population	Percentage of total population (national average: 1.8%)	Percentage of Protestants in China
Henan	4,906,382	5.4	23.8
Anhui	2,943,550	5.01	14
Zhejiang	1,782,018	3.92	8.6
Fujian	1,148,042	3.4	5.6

Source: F.T. Ying, "The Regional Development of Protestant Christianity in China: 1918, 1949 and 2004," *The China Review* 2 (2009): 83; The Amity Foundation, "How Many Protestants Are There in China?" *Amity News Services* (September 1997): 27–28; The Amity Foundation, "How Many Sheep Are There in the Chinese Flock?" *Amity News Services* (December 2004) (http://www.amitynewsservice.org).

the total Protestant population in China, with their numbers accounting for 23.8%, 14%, 8.6%, and 5.6% of the national total, respectively. To put it differently, the combined population of Protestants in these four provinces alone represents a staggering 52% of the entire Protestant population in China (refer to Table 3.1). Moreover, the number of Protestant churches in these four provinces constitutes 56% of the total count, with 8,173 churches in contrast to the national total of 14,509 (Amity Foundation, 2004).

Additionally, according to the 2004 Economic Census Data with GIS Maps, there were a total of 14,509 Protestant churches in China in 2004 (China Census Bureau, 2005), serving a Protestant population of 23,050,000 in 2009. This data suggests that, on average, approximately 1,589 Chinese Protestants were affiliated with a single Protestant church, based on the 2000 census and the national average of 1.8% of the population identifying as Protestants. In stark contrast, the statistics for the United States reveal a significant difference. In 2004, there were 59 million Protestants attending 297,000 Protestant congregations, resulting in an average of about 198 participants per American Protestant church (Hong and Zeng, 2012: 18).

Using a similar methodology for calculation, we can deduce that, on average, there were approximately 17,660, 13,983, 8,763, and 2,675 Protestants in Anhui, Henan, Zhejiang, and Fujian, respectively, attending a single Protestant church (as shown in Table 3.2).

It is important to note that we were unable to obtain precise data on the number of Protestants in the four provincial capital cities or any other cities in China. Consequently, the percentage of Protestants at the provincial level has been applied to their respective capital cities, although it is likely that the shortage of churches is more severe in other regions within each province. Additionally, there may be slight discrepancies in the number of Protestants in the four provinces, as demonstrated in Tables 3.1 and 3.2, due to variations in data sources. Nevertheless, these numbers remain at a relatively similar level.

Understanding the shortage of Protestant churches in various regions, including the United States, China, and the four provincial capital cities, can be achieved by examining the average number of participants per church. While considering the size of each church's seating capacity is essential, obtaining accurate information

Table 3.2 Comparison of Protestants and Protestant Churches between the United States, China, and Four Chinese Provinces, 2004.

	United States	China	Zhengzhou	Hefei	Hangzhou	Fuzhou
Number of Protestants	59,000,000	23,050,000[b]	139,827	70,638	96,092	72,231
Percentage of Protestants	21[a]	1.8	5.4	5.01	3.92	3.4
Number of churches	297,900	14,509	10	4	11	27
Average participants per church	198	1,589	13,983	17,660	8,736	2,675

Source: *The 2004 China's Economic Census Data with GIS Maps* (Beijing: All China Market Research Co., LTD, 2005).

[a] C. Hadaway and Long Marler, "How many Americans attend worship each week? An alternative approach to measurement," *Journal for the Scientific Study of Religion* 44 (3) (2005): 307–322

[b] Research Project Team of the Institute of World Religious Studies in the Chinese Academy of Social Sciences, "The survey report on China's Protestants, 2010" (Zhongguo jidujiao ruhu wenjuan diaocha baogao), *Annual Report on China's Religions (2010)*, eds. Jin Ze and Qiu Yonghui (Beijing: Shehui kexue wenxian chubanshe, 2010), 190–212

on seat counts for every church in the four provinces and their capital cities is challenging due to limited available church data in China. As a result, we propose a sensible and reasonable criterion for labeling an area as experiencing a church shortage: an area should be designated as such if the number of regular church attendees exceeds the national average of 1,589. Applying this criterion, all four provincial capital cities should be classified as areas with a church shortage.

3.3 Availability of Protestant churches in the four Chinese cities

In addition to assessing the average number of participants per church, it is crucial to determine the average distance between residential areas and the nearest church. This measurement helps gauge how far residents must travel to attend their nearest church for weekly religious services. Leveraging geographic information systems (GISs), *Atlas of Religions in China* (China Data Institute, 2008), and *China Geo-Explore* (China Data Institute, 2012), we can establish different distance thresholds, measured in kilometers, to assess the accessibility of churches for varying percentages of the total population. For example, using a 2.5 km radius as the geographical coverage, the data reveals that 67.53% of Hefei's residents, 59.83% of Hangzhou's residents, 59.56% of Zhengzhou's residents, and 32.03% of Fuzhou's residents cannot reach their nearest church within this distance (see Table 3.3).

Utilizing the capabilities of the *Atlas of Religions in China*, Table 3.3 underscores a compelling conclusion: Hefei emerges as the city facing the most acute shortage of churches at 67.53%, closely trailed by Hangzhou at 59.83%, Zhengzhou at 59.56%, and Fuzhou at 32.03%, respectively. This pivotal finding lays the groundwork for a secondary criterion to define a Protestant church shortage, whereby any area where more than 50% of residents live more than 2.5 km from

Table 3.3 Comparison of Church Availability in the Four Cities (2.5 km Radius).

Cities	Number of residents who can't arrive at the nearest church	Percentage of the total population	Average Protestants	Total population
Fuzhou	680,423	32.03	23,134	2,124,435
Zhengzhou	1,542,350	59.56	83,287	2,589,387
Hangzhou	1,466,662	59.83	57,493	2,451,319
Hefei	952,136	67.53	47,702	1,409,950

Source: China Census Bureau, *The 2004 China's Economic Census Data with GIS Maps* (Beijing: All China Market Research Co., LTD, 2005).

the nearest church should be designated as experiencing a church shortage. In light of this criterion, Hefei, Hangzhou, and Zhengzhou would qualify under this classification.

3.4 Assessing Protestant church accessibility in the four cities

Following the analysis of the average number of participants per Protestant church and an examination of church availability in terms of proximity to residential areas, it is imperative to measure church accessibility by estimating the travel time from residential areas to the nearest church. For such an assessment, researchers must possess accurate spatial street maps, speed limit data, and traffic hour information for the selected cities. Regrettably, due to the confidential nature of many spatial street maps in Chinese cities, we have been unable to obtain comprehensive and up-to-date data on these subjects. Nevertheless, despite these limitations, we can still offer some spatial reference points to aid in comprehending church shortages based on empirical studies.

Regarding the methodology for calculating driving time, we rely on GIS to create a network dataset. After importing the necessary layers and coordinates, we perform network analysis following established procedures. Given the limited space, we select Fuzhou as a sample excluding the other three cities. Map 3.1 illustrates driving distances in minutes. Churches lacking spatial street information are denoted by question marks. While we lack sufficient speed limit data for all four provincial capital cities, we have chosen Hefei as a representative case. Using Google Maps, we calculated the driving time for five different routes around downtown Hefei, revealing the following speed limits: 21.85, 24.00, 25.41, 26.77, and 28.42 km/hour. Therefore, the average speed is approximately 25.29 km/hour, which we have rounded to 24 km/hour for ease of calculation in the context of the four cities.

As detailed street map layers with sufficient information for calculating population and area percentages are not available, we have had to make reasonable assumptions for this aspect of our analysis. Based on the assumption that each 5 km will take 12.5 minutes and each 10 km will take 24 minutes to drive, we have compiled Tables 3.4 and 3.5, respectively. We estimated driving times for increasing distances of 5 km and 10 km, respectively (refer to Tables 3.4 and 3.5).

Map 3.1 Driving Time around the Protestant Churches in Fuzhou.

Source: China Census Bureau, *The 2004 China's Economic Census Data with GIS Maps* (Beijing: All China Market Research Co., LTD, 2005).

As highlighted in Table 3.5, the data reveals that 51.2% of Hangzhou's total residents, 40.25% of Zhengzhou's population, 35.6% of Fuzhou's inhabitants, and 13.64% of Hefei's residents face the challenge of not being able to reach their nearest church within a 25-minute travel time.

To address the shortfall in spatial driving information, Lu Cao, one of my graduate students, conducted empirical studies. She selected Chongyi church in Hangzhou, the largest Protestant church in China, with the capacity to accommodate

Table 3.4 The Estimated Driving Time for the Four Cities (12.5 Minutes).

5km (12.5 minutes)	Fuzhou	Hangzhou	Hefei	Zhengzhou
Accumulated area (km²)	166.99	88.66	156.90	151.81
Population and area coverage (%)	16.10	12.20	21.59	14.94
Number of population in the area	400,771	359,203	304,397	386,783

Source: China Census Bureau, *The 2004 China's Economic Census Data with GIS Maps* (Beijing: All China Market Research Co., LTD, 2005).

Table 3.5 The Estimated Driving Time for the Four Cities (25 Minutes).

10km (25 minutes)	Fuzhou	Hangzhou	Hefei	Zhengzhou
Accumulated area (km^2)	667.96	354.64	627.60	607.23
Population and area coverage (%) (or residents can't reach the nearest church)	64.40 (35.6)	48.80 (51.2)	86.36 (13.64)	59.75 (40.25)
Number of population in the area	1,603,084	1,436,812	1,217,587	1,547,132

Source: China Census Bureau, *The 2004 China's Economic Census Data with GIS Maps* (Beijing: All China Market Research Co., LTD, 2005).

over 8,000 congregants. Between July 20 and 22, 2012, she randomly surveyed more than 20 church participants, posing two straightforward questions: (1) What means of transportation did you use today to travel from home to the church? (2) How long did your journey from home to the church take today? The responses revealed that 50% of the participants relied on public transportation, such as buses and subways, while the remaining 50% used private cars. Notably, 37.5% of participants completed their one-way trip in 30 minutes, another 37.5% took 45 minutes, and the remaining 25% required 60 minutes.

Furthermore, interviews conducted with members of the Chongyi church yielded valuable insights regarding church shortages. An overwhelming 75% of interviewees expressed the pressing need for Hangzhou to construct additional churches due to the current overcrowding. Equally noteworthy, another 75% of respondents voiced concerns about the considerable distance between their homes and the nearest church. Consequently, many churches in Hangzhou have resorted to offering multiple sessions, typically three to four, from 7 pm to 9 pm every Sunday to accommodate the substantial demand.

Taking into account both spatial travel time and empirical study findings, it is reasonable to introduce a third criterion for assessing church shortages, specifically concerning church accessibility. If over 35% of attendees must spend 25 minutes or more traveling from their homes to the nearest church for weekly services, this can serve as another indicator of church shortage. In light of this criterion, Hangzhou (51.2%), Zhengzhou (40.25%), and Fuzhou (35.6%) should be recognized as areas facing a church shortage with respect to church accessibility.

3.5 Conclusion

Based on the three criteria outlined above, Table 3.6 presents a comprehensive summary of the Protestant church shortage in the four provincial capital cities. We propose that a city falling within all three categories can be classified as one experiencing a shortage. Consequently, Hangzhou and Zhengzhou (meeting all three criteria) are cities deserving of attention for the construction of additional churches to address these shortages.

Given the current limitations in data availability concerning Protestant churches in the four cities, further research is imperative. It is essential to calculate the number of participants for selected churches to ascertain the average church size

Table 3.6 Comparison of the Three Criteria for Assessing Protestant Church Shortages among the Four Provincial Capital Cities.

Area	Average Protestant participants per church	Church availability (distance)	Church accessibility (travel time)	Overall conclusion
Hangzhou	Shortage	Shortage	Shortage	Shortage
Zhengzhou	Shortage	Shortage	Shortage	Shortage
Fuzhou	Shortage	Adequacy	Shortage	OK
Hefei	Shortage	Shortage	Adequacy	OK

accurately. Additionally, obtaining comprehensive data on speed limits per hour and traffic patterns is crucial for precise speed calculations. The acquisition of detailed and accurate spatial street maps for Chinese cities is of paramount importance to accurately determine the average driving time from residential areas to the nearest church.

Moreover, conventional interview and survey methodologies play a vital role in understanding the modes of transportation utilized by Chinese Protestants and the time it takes them to commute from their homes to the nearest church, both on Sundays and during the week. Urgently, extending the study of church shortage issues to encompass all 31 provincial capital cities in China, beyond the initial four cities, is necessary to establish national criteria for assessing church shortages. Lastly, it is imperative to identify specific areas requiring the construction of new churches, following a model akin to the selection and establishment of new gas stations and bank branches.

Note

1 With the publisher's permission, segments of this chapter are excerpted from the article authored by Zhaohui Hong and co-authored by his graduate students, Jiamin Yan and Lu Cao, "Spatial and Statistical Perspectives on the Protestant Church Shortage in China: Case Studies in Hangzhou, Zhengzhou, Hefei and Fuzhou Cities," *Journal of Third World Studies*, 31 (1) (2014):81–99. Mr. Yan and Ms. Cao have granted permission and provided written consent to exclude their names as co-authors of this book. The original work has been significantly revised and updated for this book.

References

The Amity Foundation. 1997. How to Count the Number of Christians in China? Questions and Answers. *Amity News Services*.

The Amity Foundation. 2004. How Many Sheep Are There in the Chinese Flock? *Amity News Services*. Retrieved from: http://www.amitynewsservice.org

China Census Bureau. 2005. *Zhongguo jingji renkou shuju ji dili xinxi xitong didu, 2004* (The 2004 China's Economic Census Data with GIS Maps). Beijing: All China Market Research Co., LTD.

China Data Institute. 2008. *Atlas of Religions in China*. Retrieved from: https://chinadatacenter.net/Data/ServiceContent.aspx?id=1573

China Data Institute. 2012. *China Geo-Explore*. Retrieved from: https://www.chinageoexplorer.com/cge/

Hadaway, C.K., and P.L. Marler. 2005. "How Many Americans Attend Worship Each Week? An Alternative Approach to Measurement," *Journal for the Scientific Study of Religion*, 44 (3):307–322.

Hong, Z. 2011. "The Protestant House Church and Its Poverty of Rights in China," *Annual Review of the Sociology of Religion, Volume 2: Religion and Politics*, pp.160–176.

Hong, Z. 2012a. "In Search of Causes of the Poverty of Rights for Chinese Protestant House Church," *Asian Profile*, 40 (6):513–522.

Hong, Z. 2012b. "Protecting and Striving for the Rights to Religious Freedom: Case Studies on the Protestant House Churches in China," *Journal of Third World Studies*, XXIX (1):249–261.

Hong, Z., and L. Zeng. 2012. "Spatial Identification of the Christian Church Shortage: A Case Study in Hangzhou City," *American Review of China Studies*, 13 (1):17–36.

Kornai, J. 1980. *Economics of Shortage*. Amsterdam, New York, and Oxford: North-Holland.

Research Project Team of the Institute of World Religious Studies in the Chinese Academy of Social Sciences. 2010. *"The Survey Report on China's Christians," Annual Report on China's Religions (2010)*, J. Ze and Q. Yonghui, eds., pp. 190–212. Beijing: Shehui kexue wenxian chubanshe.

Yang, F. 2012. *Religion in China: Survival and Revival under Communist Rule*. Oxford and New York: Oxford University Press.

Ying, F.-t. 2009. "The Regional Development of Protestant Christianity in China: 1918, 1949 and 2004," *The China Review*, 9 (2):63–97.

4 Taipei and Provincial Capital Cities on China's Southeast Coast[1]

4.1 Introduction

Taipei, the capital city of Taiwan, has exhibited significant growth in its Protestant market in recent years (Rubinstein, 1991; Lee and Sun, 1995; Chao, 2006). In this comparative study, we aim to enhance our understanding of Protestant churches and the Protestant community in Taipei, situated on China's southeast coast. The choice of Taipei as a case for comparison with similar regions in mainland China is intended to assess the impact of democratic governance and government regulations on religious matters. This research represents a meaningful and pioneering endeavor that utilizes digital and spatial data to include China's five additional provincial capital cities along the southeast coast: Guangzhou, Fuzhou, Hangzhou, Shanghai, and Nanjing (Dunch, 2001; Wu, 2003, 2005; Xue, Zhu and Tang, 2009; Keating, 2012).

The study employs digital and spatial methods to assess both the supply side (Protestant churches) and the demand side (Protestant population) in Taipei and the aforementioned Chinese capital cities. Presently, it is widely observed that due to current religious regulations and persecution, mainland Chinese Protestants face challenges in meeting the demand for Protestant churches (Leung and Liu, 2004; Grim and Finke, 2010). In contrast, Taipei, as a democratic society, benefits from religious freedom and government deregulation of religious affairs (Katz, 2003; Madsen, 2007). However, there has been limited research, if any, that provides a digital, spatial, and comparative perspective on measuring the Protestant density, accessibility, and availability of these six provincial capital cities on China's southeast coast. This chapter seeks to address these disparities and shed light on the distinctive characteristics of the Protestant market in Taiwan and mainland China.

4.2 Methodology and data

In this study, we utilize conventional statistical methods to calculate the density of Protestants, based on the number of Protestant members and churches in six cities: Taipei, Guangzhou, Fuzhou, Hangzhou, Shanghai, and Nanjing. Additionally, we employ three spatial and digital methods to validate and expand upon the findings obtained through statistical analysis. The first method, the Two-Step Floating

DOI: 10.4324/9781003495451-4

Catchment Area (2SFCA), calculates the accessibility score to Protestant churches, highlighting the varying distances from residential areas to the nearest church. The Network Analysis Method (NAM) complements this by estimating driving times for Protestants from their homes to the nearest church, addressing church availability. Last, the Location Analysis Method (LAM) is employed to compare and explain disparities in research findings obtained from different methodologies. Despite utilizing different time thresholds (30 minutes for NAM, 20 minutes for 2SFCA, and 15 minutes for LAM), these spatial methods are applied consistently and equally across all six cities.

Following the analysis of research findings, this chapter compares the rankings of church accessibility and availability among the six cities based on statistical and spatial methods, identifying the best and worst performing cities in terms of these metrics. This methodology can serve as a foundation for scholars to expand their research to other cities in both Taiwan and mainland China.

Regarding data on Protestant churches in mainland China's provincial capital cities, we rely on government data from the Chinese Baidu Map in 2015, supplemented by the 2004 China Economic Census Data with Geographic Information System (GIS) Maps, published by the China Census Bureau. Data on the Protestant population is sourced from statistics provided by city government agencies, census data, and scholarly research papers. Additionally, we leverage the *Atlas of Religions in China* (China Data Institute, 2008) and *China Geo-Explore* (China Data Institute, 2012), the spatial and digital platform supported by the Henry Luce Foundation and developed by the University of Michigan and Purdue University, to visualize and map church accessibility and availability in mainland China.

4.3 Overview and Protestant church density in Taiwan and mainland China

The selection of these six capital cities along China's southeast coast is grounded in several factors. Given their historical exposure to Westernization and Christianization since the Opium War of 1842, all six cities have a deep-rooted history of engagement with Western Christianity and civilization (Shen and Zhu, 1998; Bickers, 1999; Waley, 2013). They stand as the initial region in China to adopt Christianity, a trend that gained momentum in the late 17th century and significantly accelerated after the Opium War. Additionally, substantial Western investments from the mid-19th century to the mid-20th century and the subsequent period of revolutionary reform and opening since 1978 have laid the economic, social, and cultural foundations for Protestant development (Dees, 1998). As a result, the southeast coast region has earned a reputation for being the most economically developed, culturally open-minded, and socially diverse region in China (Johnson, 1992; Goodman, 1997). Consequently, choosing these six major cities in the East Coast region as a cohort offers a unique window into observing the Protestant market in both Taiwan and mainland China.

In the initial step of analysis, the primary challenge lies in calculating the density of Protestants within each city. This challenge primarily stems from the limited availability of data related to the Protestant population in all six cities under study. As a result, we must carefully select years for data collection that are as close as possible for each of these cities. While we possess data on the Protestant population for Taiwan, Taipei, Guangzhou, and Nanjing from the year 2015, information for the other cities, including the data for the national Protestant population in mainland China, spans from the years 2004 to 2015. As indicated in Table 4.1, mainland China had a 1.8% Protestant membership rate in 2010, whereas Taiwan exhibited a 5.61% Protestant presence in 2015. Interestingly, Taipei reported its highest percentage of Protestants at 13.07% in 2015, while Guangzhou recorded its lowest rate at 0.72%. Table 4.1 further includes estimates of the Protestant population based on the latest available census data. Moreover, it provides reference information related to Protestant data.

In the second step of our process to estimate the density of Protestants, a critical aspect involves determining the count of Protestant churches within the selected cities. Table 4.2 offers an overview by presenting the number of Protestant churches in both mainland China and Taiwan. Furthermore, Table 4.2 highlights that in 2015, Taipei boasted a total of 543 churches, while the other five mainland Chinese cities saw an increase in the number of churches, ranging from 16 to 35, as evidenced by data from Baidu Map, often referred to as the "Chinese Google Map."

In our efforts to gather church information through Baidu, the initial step involves extracting data related to the churches' coordinates, including altitude and latitude, via the following link: http://api.map.baidu.com/lbsapi/getpoint/index.html. Following this, after conducting searches within each city district, we proceeded to input the acquired data into an Excel spreadsheet to integrate it into the ArcGIS system.

Table 4.1 Protestant Population in Mainland China, Taiwan, and the Six Capital Cities (2010–2015).

Location	Protestant population	Percentage of Protestant	Sources
Mainland China	23,050,000	1.8	Research Project Team of the Institute of World Religious Studies in the Chinese Academy of Social Sciences (2010)
Taiwan	1,307,842	5.61	Mitchell (2015)
Hangzhou	33,594	1.50	Hangzhou Statistical Bureau (2010)
Taipei	288,793	13.07	Mitchell (2015)
Guangzhou	45,308	0.72	Guangzhou Municipal Bureau of Ethnic and Religious Affairs (2015)
Fuzhou	72,231	2.47	The Amity Foundation (2004)
Shanghai	97,869	1.58	Shanghai Bureau of Ethnic and Religious Affairs (2012)
Nanjing	57,106	2.35	Nanjing Bureau of Ethnic and Religious Affairs (2015)

Source: See column 4 of Table 4.1.

Table 4.2 The Number of Protestant Churches in Mainland China, Taiwan, and the Six Capital Cities.

Location	Number of Protestant churches	Sources
Mainland China	11,463	China Census Bureau (2005)
Taiwan	4,101	Mitchell (2015)
Hangzhou	35 (includes all greater Hangzhou Area instead of Hangzhou City only)	Baidu Map (2015)
Taipei	543	Mitchell (2015)
Guangzhou	22	Baidu Map (2015)
Fuzhou	25	Baidu Map (2015)
Shanghai	23	Baidu Map (2015)
Nanjing	16	Baidu Map (2015)

Source: See the column 3 of Table 4.2.

Taking into consideration the data regarding the Protestant population and churches, we are able to compile an overview of the Protestant density across all six cities, including mainland China and Taiwan. Table 4.3 outlines the Protestant density in both mainland China and Taiwan, revealing a substantial disparity in the average number of Protestants per church. Notably, in 2010, mainland China had an average of 2,011 Protestants per church, whereas Taiwan boasted a significantly lower but positive figure, with an average of 319 Protestants per church—approximately 6.3 times better than that of mainland China.

Turning our focus to the selected six cities, we observe that Taipei accommodated an average of 532 Protestants per church. In contrast, the other five provincial capital cities surpassed the national average, with the exception of Hangzhou, which reported an average of 960 Protestants per church. Table 4.3 also presents rankings of Protestant density, highlighting Taipei as the city with the highest density, while Shanghai ranks as the city with the lowest Protestant density. These findings provide valuable insights into the distribution of Protestants across the selected cities, shedding light on variations in Protestant density.

Table 4.3 Protestant Density Rankings.

Location	Number of Protestants	Percentage of Protestants	Number of Protestant churches	Average number of Protestants per church	Rankings of density
Taiwan	1,307,842	5.61	4,101	319	1
Taipei	288,793	13.07	543	532	2
Hangzhou	33,594	1.50	35	960	3
Mainland China	23,050,000	1.74	11,463	2,011	4
Guangzhou	45,308	0.72	22	2,059	5
Fuzhou	72,123	2.47	31	2,327	6
Nanjing	57,106	2.35	16	3,569	7
Shanghai	97,869	1.58	23	4,255	8

Source: Compiled from column 4 of Table 4.1 and column 3 of Table 4.2.

4.4 Spatial measurement of the Protestant market

Leveraging GIS technology, this study has employed three spatial methodologies to assess Protestant accessibility and availability within the six selected cities. The 2SFCA method proves effective in calculating the driving time required for a Protestant residing in a specific area to reach the nearest church. Utilizing available mapping techniques, we have established a 20-minute one-way driving threshold to illustrate the church's accessibility score through 2SFCA (refer to Map 4.1). Given the space limitation, Taipei and Guangzhou have been listed.

Regarding Map 4.1, the black color signifies areas where the ratio (r) is greater than 1/10,000, indicating that Protestants can access their nearest church within a 20-minute one-way drive. Conversely, the gray areas, where 1/10,000 > r > 1/15,000, imply that Protestants residing there would require more than 20 minutes to reach their closest church on a regular basis. A larger expanse covered in white signifies poorer accessibility for Protestants and, consequently, more significant challenges regarding the Protestant demand for church supply in the Protestant market.

Following the export of data based on the 2SFCA method, Table 4.4 provides statistical insights into church accessibility across the six cities. Evidently, Taipei boasts the best church accessibility, aligning with the density of church information, as all Protestants in Taipei can reach their nearest church within a 20-minute

Taipei   Guangzhou

Map 4.1 The Protestant Church Accessibility Scores in Taipei and Guangzhou by the 2SFCA.

Source: Compiled from column 4 of Table 4.1 and column 3 of Table 4.2.

Table 4.4 Church Accessibility Statistics.

Cities	Percentage of Protestant population taking more than 20 minutes to the nearest church	Ranking
Taipei	0	1
Nanjing	10.88	2
Shanghai	19.01	3
Guangzhou	33.62	4
Hangzhou	38.45	5
Fuzhou	55.92	6

Source: China Data Institute. 2012. *China Geo-Explore*. Retrieved from: https://www.chinageoexplorer.com/cge/.

one-way drive. In contrast, 10.88% of Protestants in Nanjing, 19.01% in Shanghai, 33.62% in Guangzhou, 35.45% in Hangzhou, and 55.92% in Fuzhou would need more than 20 minutes to reach their nearest churches.

In addition, the NAM has been employed to verify the driving time required for a Protestant to reach the nearest churches from their residential areas. In this verification process, the study has adopted a driving time of 30 minutes, extending the distance from a Protestant's home to the nearest church to 12 km. Across all six cities, this adjustment has been made to ensure the consistency of the NAM approach. Map 4.2 illustrates the results of these three different measurements: the areas marked in the inner circle represent a range of 6 km and 15 minutes of one-way driving, the middle circle signify 12 km and 30 minutes of driving, and the outer circle symbolize 18 km and 45 minutes of driving from a Protestant's residential area to the closest church.

Table 4.5 provides a clear representation of each city's cumulative area and Protestant coverage, taking into account a distance of 12 km and a driving time of 30 minutes. Specifically, the table presents the percentage of Protestants unable to access their nearest church, as well as the total number of Protestants unable to reach the nearest church within a 12 km and 30-minute one-way drive. The higher the number of Protestants who cannot reach their nearest church, the lower the accessibility and availability of church services in that area.

Table 4.5 offers a ranking of the six cities based on their church accessibility. Notably, Taipei stands out as the most accessible area for churchgoers, with 36.73% of Protestants able to reach their nearest church within the specified time and distance. Conversely, Guangzhou ranks as the least accessible area, as 46.44% of Protestants in the city are unable to reach their nearest church within 30 minutes and 12 km.

Additionally, it is worthwhile to consider the LAM as a supplementary tool to further explore the spatial aspects of church availability and accessibility within the six cities. Due to the constraints of mapping and visualization, the designated driving time and distance in this method must be limited to 3 km and 15 minutes. While this may not be the ideal scenario, it should be noted that uniformity is maintained across all six cities, ensuring consistency and acceptability. On Map 4.3, the center of each circle represents the location of a church, with the circle encompassing the

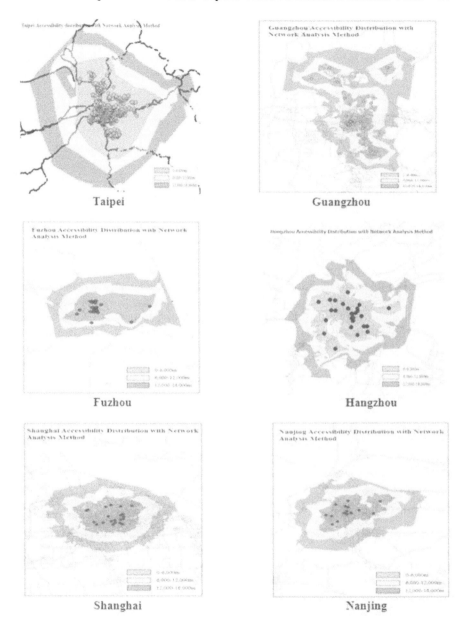

Map 4.2 The Protestant Church Availability and Accessibility by the NAM.
Source: Compiled from column 4 of Table 4.1 and column 3 of Table 4.2.

Table 4.5 Protestant Church Accessibility in the Six Cities by the NAM (30 Minutes).

12 km (30 minutes)	Accumulated area (km²)	Protestant area coverage (km²)	Percentage of Protestant who can't reach the nearest church	Number of Protestants who can't reach	Ranking
Taipei	946.169	182,397	36.73	105,887	1
Hangzhou	1,562.837	20,909	37.76	12,685	2
Fuzhou	1,417.048	856.525	39.56	6,497	3
Shanghai	1,964.430	1,138.450	42.05	97,869	4
Nanjing	1,864.611	1,058.757	43.22	24,680	5
Guangzhou	3,717.82	1,991.308	46.44	21,040	6

Source: Compiled from column 4 of Table 4.1 and column 3 of Table 4.2.

area where each Protestant can access the nearest church within 3 km and 10 minutes of driving.

Table 4.6 illustrates that all Protestants in both Taipei and Shanghai can conveniently access their nearest churches within a mere 10 minutes and within a 3 km distance. In contrast, more than 30% of Protestants in Guangzhou and Fuzhou face challenges in meeting the same time and distance criteria, while both Nanjing and Hangzhou fall in the middle ground when it comes to rankings for Protestant church availability and accessibility.

Having examined Protestant church availability and accessibility in the six cities through statistical analysis and the three spatial methods (2SFCA, NAM, and LAM), it is crucial to offer an overall perspective by comparing their average rankings based on these diverse research methodologies. Table 4.7 reveals that Taipei consistently holds the top position in terms of Protestant church accessibility, as evidenced by the digital density and spatial measurements of 2SFCA, NAM, and LAM. On the other hand, Fuzhou and Guangzhou consistently rank at the bottom in terms of church accessibility, while Hangzhou, Shanghai, and Nanjing maintain intermediate positions among the six cities.

4.5 Conclusion

This spatial study has ventured into new research territories that conventional quantitative research methods struggle to address. Nevertheless, due to incomplete and inaccurate data concerning Protestant churches and congregants in mainland China, scholars must recognize the limitations in obtaining a comprehensive understanding of the Chinese Protestant market. Additionally, spatial methodologies cannot entirely replace traditional empirical surveys, interviews, and participant observations, which offer detailed micro-level insights and in-depth qualitative interpretations.

Furthermore, upon comparing the diverse Protestant landscapes in the six capital cities through digital and spatial analyses, it becomes evident that Taipei, as a democratic society, exemplifies the significance of religious freedom in nurturing a thriving Protestant market, characterized by superior church density, accessibility,

Taipei and Provincial Capital Cities on China's Southeast Coast 39

Map 4.3 The Protestant Church's Availability and Accessibility in the Six Cities by the NAM.

Source: Compiled from column 4 of Table 4.1 and column 3 of Table 4.2.

Table 4.6 Protestant Church Availability and Accessibility in the Six Cities by the LAM (10 Minutes and 3 km).

3 km (10 minutes)	Number of people in the city	Percentage of Protestants who can't arrive at the nearest church	Ranking
Taipei	2,618,383	0.00	1
Shanghai	6,181,683	0.00	2
Nanjing	2,430,729	3.46	3
Hangzhou	2,239,600	7.88	4
Guangzhou	6,285,000	32.30	5
Fuzhou	2,921,763	48.56	6

Source: Compiled from column 4 of Table 4.1 and column 3 of Table 4.2.

Table 4.7 The Combined Rankings of Protestant Church Accessibility in the Six Cities.

	Density rankings	Rankings by LAM	Rankings by NAM	Rankings by 2SFCA	Combined rankings
Taipei	1	1	1	1	1.00
Hangzhou	2	4	2	5	3.25
Shanghai	6	2	4	3	3.75
Nanjing	5	3	5	2	3.75
Fuzhou	4	6	3	6	4.75
Guangzhou	3	5	6	4	4.75

Source: Compiled from column 4 of Table 4.1 and column 3 of Table 4.2.

and availability. However, it is important to acknowledge that there may be additional factors contributing to Taipei's favorable Protestant market. The key takeaway is that regions and nations practicing religious persecution and stringent religious regulations may inadvertently undermine both the supply and demand aspects of the Protestant market.

Note

1 With the publisher's permission, segments of this chapter are excerpted from the article authored by Zhaohui Hong and co-authored by his graduate student, Jianfeng Jin, "Digital Study of the Protestant Market: Taipei and Provincial Capital Cities in China's Southeast Coast as Case Studies," *Asian Journal of Social Sciences and Management Studies*, 5 (1) (2014):23–31. Mr. Jin has granted permission and provided written consent to exclude his name as co-author of this book. The original work has been significantly revised and updated for this book.

References

The Amity Foundation. 2004. How Many Sheep Are There in the Chinese Flock? *Amity News Services*. Retrieved from: http://www.amitynewsservice.org

Baidu Map. 2015. "Christian Churches in Fuzhou," Baidu Online Network Technology Co., Ltd. Retrieved from: https://map.baidu.com/search/%E7%A6%8F%E5%B7%9E%E5%

9F%BA%E7%9D%A3%E6%95%99%E6%95%99%E5%A0%82/@13280060,2989611
.9000000004,11z?querytype=s&c=300&wd=%E7%A6%8F%E5%B7%9E%E5%9F%B
A%E7%9D%A3%E6%95%99%E6%95%99%E5%A0%82&da_src=shareurl&on_gel=
1&l=11&gr=2&b=(13181756,2944107.9000000004;13378364,3035115.9000000004)&
pn=0&device_ratio=2

Bickers, R. 1999. *Britain in China: Community, Culture and Colonialism, 1900-49.* Manchester: Manchester University Press.

Chao, H.K. 2006. "Conversion to Protestantism among Urban Immigrants in Taiwan," *Sociology of Religion*, 67 (2):193–204.

China Census Bureau. 2005. *The 2004 China's Economic Census Data with GIS Maps.* Beijing: All China Market Research Co., LTD.

China Data Institute. 2008. *Atlas of Religions in China.* Retrieved from: https://chinadatacenter.net/Data/ServiceContent.aspx?id=1573

China Data Institute. 2012. *China Geo-Explore.* Retrieved from: https://www.chinageoexplorer.com/cge/

Dees, S. 1998. "Foreign Direct Investment in China: Determinants and Effects," *Economics of Planning*, 31 (2–3):175–194.

Dunch, R. 2001. "Protestant Christianity in China Today: Fragile, Fragmented, Flourishing," *China and Christianity: Burdened Past, Hopeful Future*, U. Stephen and W. Xiaoxin, eds., pp. 195–216. New York: M.E. Sharpe, Inc.

Goodman, D.S. 1997. *China's Provinces in Reform: Class, Community, and Political Culture.* London: Taylor & Francis.

Grim, B.J., and R. Finke. 2010. *The Price of Freedom Denied: Religious Persecution and Conflict in the Twenty-First Century.* New York: Cambridge University Press.

Guangzhou Municipal Bureau of Ethnic and Religious Affairs. 2015. "Guangzhoushi jidu jiaotang qingkuan" (An Overview of the Christian Church in Guangzhou). Retrieved from: http://mzzjj.gz.gov.cn/zwfw/gzcx/zjjzrycx/index.html

Hangzhou Statistical Bureau. 2010. *2010 Hangzhou tongji nianjian* (2010 Yearbook of Hangzhou). Retrieved from: http://tjj.hangzhou.gov.cn/art/2010/11/2/art_1229453592_3819403.html

Hong, Z., and J. Jin. 2014. "Digital Study of the Protestant Market: Taipei and Provincial Capital Cities in China's Southeast Coast as Case Studies," *Asian Journal of Social Sciences and Management Studies*, 5 (1):23–31.

Johnson, G.E. 1992. *The Political Economy of Chinese Urbanization: Guangdong and the Pearl River Delta Region.* Westport, CT: Greenwood Press.

Katz, P.R. 2003. "Religion and the State in Post-War Taiwan," *China Quarterly*, 174 (1):395–341.

Keating, J.C.W. 2012. *A Protestant Church in Communist China: Moore Memorial Church Shanghai, 1949–1989.* Bethlehem, PA: Lehigh University Press..

Madsen, R. 2007. *Democracy's Dharma: Religious Renaissance and Political Development in Taiwan.* Berkeley, California: University of California Press.

Mitchell, R., 2015. *Taiwan Church Growth Report 2015.* Retrieved from: One Challenge's Global Research Team.

Nanjing Bureau of Ethnic and Religious Affairs. 2015. *Nanjing Shi jidu jiaotang qingkuan* (An Overview of the Christian Church in Nanjing). Retrieved from: http://mzzjj.nanjing.gov.cn/.

Lee, M.L., and T.H. Sun. 1995. "The Family and Demography in Contemporary Taiwan," *Journal of Comparative Family Studies*, 26 (1):101–115.

Leung, B., and W.T. Liu. 2004. *Chinese Catholic Church in Conflict: 1949–2001.* Boca Raton, Florida: Universal-Publishers.

Research Project Team of the Institute of World Religious Studies in the Chinese Academy of Social Sciences. 2010. "*The Survey Report on China's Christians*," *Annual Report on China's Religions (2010)*, J. Ze and Q. Yonghui, eds., pp. 190–212. Beijing: Shehui kexue wenxian chubanshe.

Rubinstein, M.A. 1991. *The Protestant Community on Modern Taiwan: Mission, Seminary, and Church*. New York: M.E. Sharpe.

Shanghai Bureau of Ethnic and Religious Affairs. 2012. *Shanghai shi jidu jiaohui qingkuan* (An Overview of the Christian Church in Shanghai). Retrieved from: https://mzzj.sh.gov.cn/

Shen, D.P., and W.F. Zhu. 1998. "Western Missionary Influence on the People's Republic of China: A Survey of Chinese Scholarly Opinion between 1980 and 1990," *International Bulletin of Missionary Research*, 22 (4):154–158.

Waley, A. 2013. *The Opium War Through Chinese Eyes*. Oxfordshire: Routledge.

Wu, X.T. 2003. "Religious Reconstruction after 1949: A Case Study in Jiangsu," *Journal of Southern Yangtze University Humanities & Social Edition*, 4 (1):1–10.

Wu, X.T. 2005. "On the Propagation of Protestantism in Guangzhou," *Journal of Hanshan Teachers College*, 1 (1):1–5.

Xue, X.M., H. Zhu, and X.Q. Tang. 2009. "Spatial Distribution and Evolution of Urban Religious Landscape–A Case Study of the Protestant Churches in Guangzhou after 1842," *Human Geography*, 1 (1):1–13.

5 Growth of Officially Registered Protestant Churches since 1949[1]

5.1 Introduction

Following the examination of individual cities in Chapters 2, 3, and 4 as microstudies of religious sites, it is essential to broaden the scope from local to nationwide to comprehend the macro-level picture of the shortage of Protestant churches. Notable, the Chinese Protestant market has undergone several pivotal transformations since the establishment of the People's Republic of China in 1949, marking the victory of the atheist Communist Party. However, Deng Xiaoping's era, characterized by the "reform and opening" policy since 1978, sparked a period of "Christianity Fever" and the reopening of Protestant churches in 1979. These changing political regimes and religious regulations have significantly impacted the supply and demand dynamics of the Protestant market. Analyzing these dynamics can serve as a window into understanding Chinese religion and society since 1949.

To gain a comprehensive understanding of the Chinese religious market, it is essential to first compare the differences between churches (supply side) and Protestants (demand side) within the same period. Additionally, a historical perspective is valuable to map the development of the Protestant market in different historical periods since 1949, examining variations in growth rates. Moreover, integrating other relevant data, such as population growth and information about major religions in China, provides supplemental references for understanding church supply and Protestant demand.

This chapter will begin by discussing three provincial capital cities representing the three major regions of China, East, Central, and West, as case studies. These cities will help us examine the changing numbers of Protestant members and churches since 1949. Building on similar research methods, we will expand our analysis from these three representative cities to encompass all 31 provincial capital cities in China. This expanded research will focus on the growth rates of both Protestant members and church numbers from 1949 to 2004. Furthermore, it is critical to broaden the geographic scope from the 31 provincial capital cities to include all 31 provinces across the eastern, central, and western regions of China. This expansion aims to identify any different patterns of Protestant development between provincial capital cities and provinces. Finally, it is necessary to summarize the national characteristics of the Chinese Protestant market, mapping the supply

DOI: 10.4324/9781003495451-5

of Protestant churches and the demand of the Protestant population. The goal is to provide a statistical and spatial study of Chinese Protestantism to enhance our understanding of religious markets and religious economies in China.

5.2 Data

Acquiring reliable and comprehensive data on the changing numbers of Protestants since 1949 has been a significant challenge. While many scholars have skepticism regarding Chinese official data, we must cautiously and selectively utilize it as the second-best option. This is because, to date, scholars have not reached a consensus on, or identified the best source for, non-official data concerning Chinese Protestants. Despite recognizing this dilemma and the limitations of official data, this project relies on the following data sources as key references for Chinese Protestants: (1) Chinese official census data since 1949; (2) the total number of Chinese Protestants reported by an official research institute, the Chinese Academy of Social Sciences, in 2009 (Research Project Team of the Institute of World Religious Studies in the Chinese Academy of Social Sciences, 2010); (3) the number of Protestants in each province and their average percentages of the total population, as reported by the Hong Kong-based religious organization, The Amity Foundation (2004), and Ying's article (2009); and (4) the number of Protestants in specific cities and provinces, as documented in county and city Gazetteers (fang zhi).

Regarding the data on Chinese Protestant churches, we have leveraged the 2004 China's Economic Census Data with Geographic Information System (GIS) Maps (China Census Bureau, 2005), the *Atlas of Religions in China* (China Data Institute, 2008), and *China Geo-Explore* (China Data Institute, 2012). Relatively speaking, the data on Protestant churches from 1852 to 2004 is more accurate, comprehensive, and consistent compared to the data on the Protestants. It's important to note that all church and Protestant information in this chapter excludes non-registered house churches and their congregations, as it is nearly impossible to collect accurate information about these "underground" churches at the present stage. Additionally, we have benefited from various official information concerning Buddhism, Islamism, Daoism, and economic data as supplemental resources.

5.3 Literature review

The theory of the religious market, introduced by Stark and Bainbridge (1985), has inspired numerous scholars to investigate the relationship between the supply of religious sites and the demand for religious believers. This theory has generated considerable research interest (Iannaccone, 1991; Stark and Iannaccone, 1994; Sherkat and Wilson, 1995; Stark and Finke, 2000; Jelen, 2002; Bankston, 2003; Finke and Stark, 2005; Yang, 2006). Defined by Finke and Stark, the religious market and economy consist of "all the religious activity going on in any society, including 'market' of current and potential adherents, a set of one or more organizations seeking to attract or maintain adherents, and the religious culture offered by the organization(s)" (Finke and Stark, 2003: 100).

The fundamental contribution of the religious market theory lies in its delineation of religious development along two dimensions: demand and supply, akin to conventional economic theory. As articulated by Paldam and Gundlach (2012: 33), "Religion is demanded as a factor of production and for consumption. Religion is supplied by institutions, which are termed churches for brevity." This underscores the emphasis of the religious market theory on the causal relationship between the supply of religious goods (provided by churches) and the demand for these goods (by congregations or individuals seeking religion). The theory posits that in a healthy and competitive religious market, with an increased demand for religious goods, the supply of these goods (religious services and institutions) will also rise. This conceptual framework applies to both Western and Chinese religious contexts. In instances of heightened demand for religious goods, multiple churches are expected to supply them, preventing any single church from accruing substantial profits. Moreover, the theory suggests that greater religious diversity contributes to an overall increase in religiosity. Li (2008: 59) extends this understanding to the Chinese religious market, characterizing it as comprising two structures: "One is the supplier structure formed by institutional religion, and the other is the demander structure formed by private belief."

In addition, the religious market theory addresses the invisible adjustment and adaptation of religious demand and supply. One fact is that "when the relative number of churches began to rise, the rates for church membership, Sunday school enrollment, church attendance, and local church expenditures sharply increased" (Finke, 1997: 122). McBride (2010: 261) argues that "Some anecdotal evidence indicates that suppliers are adapting to meet changing religious demand" although they often have dysfunctional patterns in China. The key driving force for the religious market, in McBride's view, is economic growth which "potentially affects both the demand and supply sides of an open religious market, and it can do so in a manner that produces countervailing influences" (McBride, 2010: 161). Indeed, "more supply side adaptations are required to keep pace with changing demand" (McBride, 2010: 162). However, the key condition for the function of self-adaptation is to have an open religious market with competitive forces that "can lead denominations to adapt to changing demand and supply conditions, thereby keeping religion alive despite forces leading to secularization" (McBride, 2010: 167).

Moreover, the passage underscores the significance of religious regulations in shaping the religious market. State regulations are considered crucial in influencing religious supply, and alterations in regulations, opportunities, and incentives can have repercussions on religious practices (Chaves, Schraeder and Sprindys, 1994; Iannaccone, Finke and Stark, 1997: 351; Yang, 2006: 1088). For example, according to Finke, "Whether the religious change involves private practice or public expression, supply-side explanations seek changes in regulations, opportunities, and incentives" (Finke, 1997: 124). Klein and Meyer (2011: 532) argue that China's marketization of religion is counteracted by the growth of religious movements and groups explicitly offering "non-market forms of sociality." In other words, "religious change must be attributed not to changes in religious demands, but, on the contrary, to shifts in religious supply." The cases in China appear to affirm that regulations played a vital role in constraining the growth of new church constructions, particularly for officially registered churches in 1949, 1985, 1997, and 2004, during which government regulations played either positive or negative roles in the supply side of the religious market. As McBride (2010: 149) suggests, religious regulations, including the prohibition of religious entry, "can yield high participation for religious monopolies even in the face of possible negative effects of economic growth on religion."

It appears that there is a notable gap in the application of religious market theory, particularly in the quantitative examination of the supply-side dynamics within the Protestant market in China. Clearly, a primary imperative in the study of the Chinese Protestant market is to compile comprehensive and statistically sound data pertaining to Protestant churches and the Protestants since 1949. This data-driven approach is crucial as it avoids relying solely on the application of religious market theory without adequate quantitative analysis.

To gain a comprehensive understanding of the Protestant market in China, we must first comprehend its structure before delving into the reasons behind its dynamics. Therefore, in addition to employing historical and comparative methodologies, this chapter places significant emphasis on the statistical, spatial, and digital aspects when exploring the Protestant church as the supply-side component of the market and Protestant congregations as the demand side. Furthermore, it is vital to embark on additional research projects that incorporate qualitative analysis into this subject matter.

5.4 Case studies in three selected Chinese cities

To measure the disparity between demand and supply within the Chinese Protestant market, it becomes imperative to discern the distinct growth patterns exhibited by both Protestant membership and the number of Protestant churches. When the growth rate of Protestant congregations (representing demand) outpaces that of Protestant churches (representing supply), it is reasonable to infer that the demand exceeds supply within the Chinese Protestant market, leading to an evident shortage of church facilities.

Adopting a bottom-up perspective, it is crucial to focus on one provincial capital city in each of the three major regions of China: the eastern, Central, and western regions. Meanwhile, it is necessary to compare the varying growth rates between Protestants and Protestant churches at four pivotal time points: 1949, 1985, 1997, and 2004.

Taking Hangzhou, the provincial capital of Zhejiang province, as a representative example for the eastern region, it is worth noting that Hangzhou's city boundaries have undergone several changes since 1949, making it challenging to visualize the precise locations of churches within the city throughout that period. After identifying the number of Protestant churches, Protestants, and their growth rates in Hangzhou since 1949,[2] Table 5.1 highlights the density of Protestants per church within Hangzhou city across the four distinct periods.

Table 5.1 reveals several noteworthy insights. First, when considering the density of Protestants, the year 1985 emerges as a significant point of interest. In that

Table 5.1 The Density of Protestants per Church in Hangzhou.

Year	1949	1985	1997	2004
Hangzhou	8,154	857	5,077	14,311
Growth rate (%)	0	−89.5	492	182

Source: Fuk-tsang Ying, "The Regional Development of Protestant Christianity in China: 1918, 1949 and 2004," *The China Review*, 9 (2) (2009):63–97; The Amity Foundation, "How Many Sheep Are There in the Chinese Flock?" Amity News Services, 2004.

year, there were 857 Protestants per church in Hangzhou, despite having 63% fewer church members compared to 1949. This suggests an improvement in bridging the gap between supply and demand, with church supply increasing by 250% from 1949 to 1985. Second, the year 1989 appears to be a pivotal moment regarding the relative decline in church supply and the relative growth of Protestant demand. This is evident from the first intersection point on the growth rate curve between the number of churches and the number of Protestants in 1989. Third, considering the continuous increase in the Protestant population since 1989, it is apparent that the growth of Protestants consistently outpaced that of churches. However, it's noteworthy that the expansion of the Protestant population began to slow down after 1997. Fourth, the year 1997 can be seen as the peak in terms of the growth rate of Protestants, with a remarkable 746% increase between 1985 and 1997. Subsequently, the growth rate witnessed a dramatic decline.

In summary, it can be inferred that since the 1990s, the Protestant market in Hangzhou has been characterized by demand surpassing supply. This conclusion is supported by the substantial increase in the density of Protestants by 1,569.9% (from 857 to 14,311) and a staggering 2,524% growth in the Protestant population (from 6,000 to 157,423) between 1985 and 2004, while the number of churches only rose by 57% (from 7 to 11).

In addition to examining an eastern region city, let's turn our attention to Harbin, the capital of Heilongjiang province, as a representative example from the central region. It is necessary to explore whether similar patterns as observed in Hangzhou can be identified. Following a similar method and data calculation, Table 5.2 based

Table 5.2 Density of Protestants per Church in Harbin.

Year	1949	1985	1997	2004
Harbin	1,575	1,050	3,953	4,594
Growth rate (%)	0	−33.33	276.45	16.22

Source: Fuk-tsang Ying, "The Regional Development of Protestant Christianity in China: 1918, 1949 and 2004," *The China Review*, 9 (2) (2009):63–97; The Amity Foundation, "How Many Sheep Are There in the Chinese Flock?" Amity News Services, 2004.

on the changing Protestants and churches since 1949 in Harbin summarizes the density of Protestants per church.

Harbin City has yielded findings akin to those of Hangzhou City, as presented in Table 5.2. First, when examining the density of Protestants, the year 1985 stands out as significant. During this year, Harbin boasted 1,050 Protestants per church, despite having 33% more church members in 1985 compared to 1949. This points to an amelioration in the disparity between religious supply and demand, with church supply increasing by 100% from 1949 to 1985. Second, the year 1986, rather than 1989, might serve as the pivotal moment concerning the relative decline in church supply and the corresponding growth in Protestant demand. It was in 1986 that we observed a turning point in the growth rates between the number of churches and the number of Protestants. Third, since 1986, the growth of the Protestant population consistently outstripped that of the churches, although the expansion of the Protestant population began to decelerate after 1997. Fourth, the year 1997 emerges as a noteworthy peak in terms of the growth rate of Protestants, with the Protestant population surging by 1,218% between 1985 and 1997 (from 2,100 to 27,668). However, this growth rate experienced a sharp decline after 1997.

In summary, we can tentatively conclude that the Protestant market in Harbin has been characterized by a demand for a Protestant population surpassing the supply of Protestant churches since 1985. This conclusion is supported by the fact that while the number of Protestants increased by more than 13 times (from 2,100 to 27,668), the number of churches only grew by 7 times (from 2 to 14), resulting in the density of Protestants increasing by 337.5% (from 1,050 to 4,594).

Having examined two provincial capital cities in the eastern and central regions, we now need to select one more city from the western region. Chengdu, the provincial capital city of Sichuan province, serves as an apt example representing Western China. Although we lack data on the Protestant population in 1985 for Sichuan, we can focus on the years 1949, 1997, and 2004 for insights into Protestant membership and church numbers. Additionally, detailed information regarding the density of the Protestant population can be found in Table 5.3 based on the church numbers, Protestant members, and their growth rates.

Table 5.3 presents crucial data that sets the stage for further discussion. First, when assessing the density of Protestant members, the year 1949 emerges as noteworthy. In that year, the average density was 2,871 Protestants per church in

Table 5.3 Density of Protestants per Church in Chengdu.

Year	1949	1997	2004
Chengdu	2,871	5,728	14,633
Growth rate (%)	0	99.51	155.46

Source: Fuk-tsang Ying, "The Regional Development of Protestant Christianity in China: 1918, 1949 and 2004," *The China Review*, 9 (2) (2009):63–97; The Amity Foundation, "How Many Sheep Are There in the Chinese Flock?" Amity News Services, 2004.

Chengdu. However, since 1949, the churches in Chengdu have become increasingly crowded, with the density soaring from 2,871 members per church in 1949 to 14,633 members per church in 2004. Second, as consistently observed, the growth rate of Protestant members has consistently outpaced that of church numbers since 1949, although the growth of the Protestant population began to decelerate after 1997. Third, the year 1997 stands as a historical peak in terms of the growth rate of Protestant members, experiencing a 299% increase between 1949 and 1997. However, this growth rate saw a significant decline after 1997.

In conclusion, the Protestant market in Chengdu can also be characterized by a demand for Protestant members surpassing the supply of Protestant church numbers. This conclusion is supported by the fact that while the number of Protestant members increased by nearly ten times (from 2,871 to 29,266), the number of churches only doubled (from one to two) from 1949 to 2004.

5.5 Protestant members and Protestant churches in 31 provincial capital cities

Having explored three distinct cities in three different regions of China, it is imperative to expand our study to encompass all 31 provincial capital cities and their respective provinces. This broader analysis will determine whether the findings observed in the three cities can be corroborated at the national, regional, and provincial levels of Protestant development. Excluding Taiwan, Hong Kong, and Macau, mainland China comprises three major regions: Eastern China (11 provinces), Central China (8 provinces), and Western China (12 provinces), totaling 31 provinces and municipalities.

Due to limited data availability for nationwide Protestantism in 1985 and 1997, the analysis focuses exclusively on data from 1949 and 2004. The comprehensive dataset comprising the Protestant population and church numbers in 31 provincial capital cities provides us with the means to compare average growth rates across the three regions. Table 5.4 enhances our understanding by presenting the total number of churches in each region for both 1949 and 2004, highlighting their overall growth rates. Remarkably, the central region stands out as the leader in terms of the growth rate of Protestant churches, experiencing an amazing increase of 622%. It's worth noting that this growth rate is particularly impressive, considering that much of the church information from 1949 was unavailable.

Table 5.4 Comparison of the Growth Rates of Protestant Churches in the 31 Provincial Capital Cities of the Three Regions, 1949 and 2004.

Region	Church numbers in 1949	Church numbers in 2004	Growth rate (%)
East	18	83	361
Central	9	65	622
West	12	46	283

Source: Fuk-tsang Ying, "The Regional Development of Protestant Christianity in China: 1918, 1949 and 2004," *The China Review*, 9 (2) (2009):63–97; The Amity Foundation, "How Many Sheep Are There in the Chinese Flock?" Amity News Services, 2004.

Table 5.5 Comparison of the Growth Rates of Protestant Members in the 31 Provincial Capital Cities of the Three Regions, 1949 and 2004.

Region	Protestant numbers in 1949	Protestant numbers in 2004	Growth rate (%)
East	49,398	519,697	952
Central	10,603	432,498	3,979
West	14,481	241,660	1,569

Source: Fuk-tsang Ying, "The Regional Development of Protestant Christianity in China: 1918, 1949 and 2004," *The China Review*, 9 (2) (2009):63–97; The Amity Foundation, "How Many Sheep Are There in the Chinese Flock?" Amity News Services, 2004.

Moreover, it is intriguing to note that, despite the fact that the capital cities in Eastern China had the highest number of churches in both 1949 (18) and 2004 (83), their growth rate was relatively lower at 361%. This can be attributed to the higher baseline number of churches in 1949 (18) in the region. Similarly, as shown in Table 5.5, concerning the Protestant population, capital cities in Eastern China recorded the highest number of congregants in both 1949 (49,398) and 2004 (519,697). However, their growth rate was comparatively lower at 952%. These findings shed light on the regional variations in the growth of Protestant churches and populations, underscoring the distinct trajectories and historical contexts within each region.

In our endeavor to assess the disparity between supply and demand within the Chinese Protestant market, it becomes imperative to juxtapose the growth rates of the Protestant population and the number of Protestant churches across different regions from 1949 to 2004. As elucidated in Table 5.6, across all three regions, the growth rate of the Protestant population consistently outpaced that of the Protestant churches.

Specifically, central capital cities exhibited the most substantial negative gap (−3,357%), while eastern capital cities registered a gap of −591%. These negative disparities unequivocally signify that the growth rate of demand among Protestant members exceeded the growth rate of supply among Protestant churches in all Chinese provincial capital cities. These findings underscore the acute shortage of Protestant churches in contemporary China, substantiating the existence of a substantial gap between supply and demand within the Chinese Protestant market.

Table 5.6 Density of Protestants per Church in the 31 Provincial Capital Cities of the Three Regions, 1949 and 2004.

Region	Protestants per church in 1949	Protestants per church in 2004
East	2,744	6,261
Central	1,178	6,654
West	1,207	5,253

Source: Fuk-tsang Ying, "The Regional Development of Protestant Christianity in China: 1918, 1949 and 2004," *The China Review*, 9 (2) (2009):63–97; The Amity Foundation, "How Many Sheep Are There in the Chinese Flock?" Amity News Services, 2004.

Table 5.7 Regional Province Comparison of the Church Growth Rates.

Church	Church number in 1949	Church number in 2004	Growth rate (%)
East	272	6,535	2,303
Central	39	6,220	15,849
West	58	1,754	2,924

Source: Fuk-tsang Ying, "The Regional Development of Protestant Christianity in China: 1918, 1949 and 2004," *The China Review*, 9 (2) (2009):63–97; The Amity Foundation, "How Many Sheep Are There in the Chinese Flock?" Amity News Services, 2004.

5.6 Changing trends in Protestants and Protestant churches across 31 provinces

In our quest to comprehensively gauge the dynamics of the Chinese Protestant market in terms of demand and supply, we can extend our analysis from the 31 provincial capital cities to encompass all 31 provinces. By evaluating the evolving patterns of Protestant members and church numbers since 1949 at the provincial level, we can benefit from a more comprehensive understanding of the demand and supply dynamics within the Chinese Protestant market. Given the wealth of information available at the provincial level compared to that of provincial capital cities, we can achieve a more complete illustration of the demand and supply dynamics characterizing the Chinese Protestant market.

Employing similar methodologies as those used in our examination of provincial capital cities, it is possible to evaluate the development of Protestantism in eastern, central, and western provinces since 1949. In summarizing the patterns of Protestant development across the three regions of China, Tables 5.7 and 5.8 reveal several notable similarities between the 31 provincial capital cities and the 31 provinces. First, the eastern region consistently boasts the highest number of Protestant churches, both in 1949 (272) and in 2004 (6,535), surpassing the other two regions. Second, the central region exhibits the most substantial growth rate of Protestant churches, experiencing an impressive increase of 15,849% from 1949 to 2004 (39 churches to 6,220 churches). Third, with regard to information concerning the Protestant population, Central China emerged as the region with the largest number of Protestant congregations in 2004 (10,350,000) and also the fastest growth rate of Protestants, recording a remarkable 4,054% increase. These findings highlight the regional dynamics and trends within the development of

Table 5.8 Regional Province Comparison of the Protestant Growth Rates.

Protestant	Protestant in 1949	Protestant in 2004	Growth rate (%)
East	681,163	7,275,718	968
Central	249,131	10,350,000	4,054
West	220,945	3,654,190	1,554

Source: Fuk-tsang Ying, "The Regional Development of Protestant Christianity in China: 1918, 1949 and 2004," *The China Review*, 9 (2) (2009):63–97; The Amity Foundation, "How Many Sheep Are There in the Chinese Flock?" Amity News Services, 2004.

Table 5.9 Density of Protestants in Regional Provinces, 1949 and 2004.

Region	1949	2004
East	2,504	1,113
Central	6,388	1,664
West	3,809	2,083

Source: Fuk-tsang Ying, "The Regional Development of Protestant Christianity in China: 1918, 1949 and 2004," *The China Review*, 9 (2) (2009):63–97; The Amity Foundation, "How Many Sheep Are There in the Chinese Flock?" Amity News Services, 2004.

Protestantism across China, shedding light on the varying patterns of growth and expansion in different parts of the country.

In addition, examining the Protestant density, as indicated in Table 5.9, it becomes apparent that there are fewer Protestant members per church on average across the 31 provinces during the same period. The shortage of churches appears to have improved since 1949.

5.7 National trends in the supply and demand of the Chinese Protestant market

Having conducted a comprehensive study encompassing three distinct cities across three different regions, the 31 provincial capital cities divided into three regions, and all 31 provinces in China, it is now both necessary and feasible to delve into a discussion regarding the national landscape of church supply and Protestant demand in China.

By employing both median and mean methods to compute the average growth rates of Protestant churches and congregations, Table 5.10 provides us with the means to corroborate our earlier assessment. It confirms that the growth of Protestant churches, representing the supply side of the market, was 843% slower in the median calculation and 1,636% slower in the mean calculation compared to the growth of the Protestant population, which represents the demand side of the market.

As a result, Figure 5.1 provides valuable insight into the Chinese Protestant market's evolution since 1949. First, before 1982, the growth of Protestant churches

Table 5.10 The Growth Rate of Churches and Protestants in the 31 Provincial Capital Cities.

Growth rate	Church number (%)	Protestant population (%)	Growth rate difference (%)
Median	250	1,093	−843
Mean	383	2,018	−1,636

Source: Fuk-tsang Ying, "The Regional Development of Protestant Christianity in China: 1918, 1949 and 2004," *The China Review*, 9 (2) (2009):63–97; The Amity Foundation, "How Many Sheep Are There in the Chinese Flock?" Amity News Services, 2004.

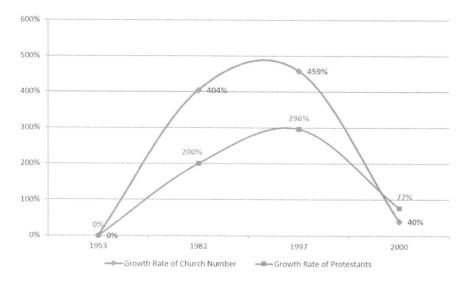

Figure 5.1 Comparison of the National Growth Rates between Protestant Members and Church Numbers.

Source: Fuk-tsang Ying, "The Regional Development of Protestant Christianity in China: 1918, 1949 and 2004," *The China Review*, 9 (2) (2009):63–97; The Amity Foundation, "How Many Sheep Are There in the Chinese Flock?" Amity News Services, 2004.

outpaced the growth of the Protestant population, with a 280% growth rate for churches compared to 200% for Protestants. Second, the growth rate of church numbers peaked in 1997 at 459%, surpassing the growth rate of Protestants, which stood at 296%. Third, 1999 marked a significant turning point when the growth rate of Protestants exceeded that of Protestant churches for the first time. Finally, by the year 2000, the growth on the supply side (churches) at 21% couldn't keep up with the growth on the demand side of the market (Protestants) at 77%.

Furthermore, it is of great significance to compare the growth rate of Protestant churches with the expansion of other prominent religious sites in China. Table 5.11

Table 5.11 Comparison between Protestant Church and Other Chinese Religious Sites.

Year	1949	2004	Growth rate (%)
Protestant church	369	14,509	3,832
Buddhist temple	2,357	16,248	589
Daoist abbey	493	4,938	902
Islamic mosque	9,014	34,306	281

Source: China Data Institute. *China Geo-Explore, 2012*. Retrieved from: https://www.chinageoexplorer.com/cge/; Fuk-tsang Ying, "The Regional Development of Protestant Christianity in China: 1918, 1949 and 2004," *The China Review*, 9 (2) (2009):63–97; The Amity Foundation, "How Many Sheep Are There in the Chinese Flock?" Amity News Services, 2004.

Table 5.12 Comparison on the Growth Rates between Protestantism and Population.

Subjects	Numbers in 1949	Numbers in 2004	Growth rate (%)
Population	541,670,000	1,299,880,000	140
Protestants	700,000[3]	21,000,000	2,900
Church	369	14,509	3,832

Source: Fuk-tsang Ying, "The Regional Development of Protestant Christianity in China: 1918, 1949 and 2004," *The China Review*, 9 (2) (2009):63–97; The Amity Foundation, "How Many Sheep Are There in the Chinese Flock?" Amity News Services, 2004.

clearly illustrates that Protestant churches experienced an extraordinarily high growth rate when compared to Buddhist temples (6.5 times), Daoist temples (4.2 times), and Islamic Mosques (13.6 times) from 1949 to 2004.

Additionally, when contrasting the growth rate of the Chinese population during the same period, Table 5.12 reveals that the growth rate of Chinese Protestants and their churches was 20.7 times higher and 27.4 times higher, respectively.

5.8 Conclusion

Recognizing that both demand and supply are pivotal facets of the religious market, it becomes imperative to scrutinize the evolving dynamics of Protestant church numbers and Protestants from historical, comparative, statistical, and spatial vantage points. As revealed through examinations of three representative provincial capital cities, all 31 provincial capitals, 31 provinces, and various census and religious sources, this chapter offers a general conclusion: the demand side of the Protestant market has exhibited notably swifter growth compared to the supply side. Consequently, the scarcity of Protestant churches has become increasingly conspicuous in contemporary China.

In pursuit of cultivating a healthy and equitable Protestant market in China, government regulations are poised to play an essential role. This role entails expanding the supply side by erecting more churches, mitigating restrictive controls on religious freedoms, and fostering religious pluralism. Undoubtedly, achieving equilibrium between the demand and supply within the religious market constitutes one of the critical factors influencing social ecology and social harmony in China.

Notes

1 With the publisher's permission, segments of this chapter are excerpted from the article authored by Zhaohui Hong and co-authored by his graduate students (with Jiamin Yan and Lu Cao), "The Growth Trend of Officially Registered Protestant Churches in China since 1949," *Journal of Social Sciences Research*, 2 (2015):14–41. Mr. Yan and Ms. Cao have granted permission and provided written consent to exclude their names as co-authors of this book. The original work has been significantly revised and updated for this book.
2 Except for special notes, all information about Protestant population in this article are from Ying (2009) and The Amity Foundation (2004).

3 Prior to the establishment of People's Republic of China in 1949, the official statistical data indicated that "there were 700,000 Protestants in China." See the Central Committee of the Chinese Communist Party, "Zhonggong zhongyang guanyu tianzhujiao, jidujiao wenti de tishi" [Presentation on Catholics and Protestant by the Central Committee of the Chinese Communist Party, August 19, 1950], *Xinhua Web, http://news.xinhuanet.com/ziliao/2004-12/13/content_2328881.htm* (Assessed December 1, 2013).

References

The Amity Foundation. 2004. How Many Sheep Are There in the Chinese Flock? *Amity News Services*.

Bankston, C.L. 2003. "Rationality, Choice, and the Religious Economy: Individual and Collective Rationality in Supply and Demand," *Review of Religious Research*, 45 (2):155–171.

Chaves, M., P.J. Schraeder, and M. Sprindys. 1994. "State Regulation of Religion and Muslim Religious Vitality in the Industrialized West," *Journal of Politics*, 56 (4):1087–1097.

China Census Bureau. 2005. *The 2004 China's Economic Census Data with GIS Maps*. Beijing: All China Market Research Co., LTD.

China Data Institute. 2008. *Atlas of Religions in China*. Retrieved from: https://chinadatacenter.net/Data/ServiceContent.aspx?id=1573

China Data Institute. 2012. *China Geo-Explore*. Retrieved from: https://www.chinageoexplorer.com/cge/

Finke, R. 1997. "The Consequences of Religious Competition: Supply-side Explanations for Religious Change," *Rational Choice Theory and Religion: Summary and Assessment*, L. Young, ed., pp. 45–61. New York: Routledge.

Fink, R., and R. Stark. 2003. "The Dynamic of Religious Economies," *Handbook of the Sociology of Religion*, M. Dillion, ed., pp. 96–109. New York: Cambridge University Press.

Fink, R., and R. Stark. 2005. *The Churching of America, 1776-2005. Winners and Losers in Our Religious Economy*. New Brunswick, NJ: Rutgers University Press.

Hong, Z., J. Yan, and L. Cao. 2015. "The Growth Trend of Officially Registered Protestant Churches in China since 1949," *Journal of Social Sciences Research*, 2 (1):14–41.

Iannaccone, L.R. 1991. "The Consequences of Religious Market Structure: Adam Smith and the Economics of Religion," *Rationality and Society*, 3 (2):156–177.

Iannaccone, L.R., R. Finke, and R. Stark. 1997. "Deregulating Religion: The Economics of Church and State," *Economic Inquiry*, 35 (2):350–64.

Jelen, T.G., ed., 2002. *Sacred Markets, Sacred Canopies: Essays on Religious Markets and Religious Pluralism*. Lanham, MD: Rowman & Littlefield Publishers, Inc.

Klein, T., and C. Meyer. 2011. "Beyond the Market: Exploring the Religious Field in Modern China," *Religion*, 41 (4):529–534.

Li, F. 2008. "Jidujiao he Zhongguo zhengzhi fazhan" (Christianity and China's Political Development). Retrieved from: https://www.aisixiang.com/data/28334.html

McBride, M. 2010. "Religious Market Competition in a Richer World," *Economics*, 77 (305):148–171.

Paldam, M., and E. Gundlach. 2012. "The Religious Transition. A Long-Run Perspective," *Public Choice*, 3 (3):1–19.

Research Project Team of the Institute of World Religious Studies in the Chinese Academy of Social Sciences. 2010. *The Survey Report on China's Christians*, in *Annual Report on China's Religions (2010)*, J. Ze and Q. Yonghui, eds., pp. 190–212. Beijing: Shehui kexue wenxian chubanshe.

Sherkat, D.E., and J. Wilson. 1995. "Preferences, Constraints, and Choices in Religious Markets: An Examination of Religious Switching and Apostasy," *Social Forces*, 73 (3):993–1026.

Stark R., and W. Brainbridge. 1985. *The Future of Religion: Secularization, Revival, and Cult Formation*. Berkeley, CA: University of California Press.

Stark, R., and R. Finke. 2000. *Acts of Faith: Explaining the Human Side of Religion*. Berkeley, CA: University of California Press.

Stark, R., and L. Iannaccone. 1994. "A Supply-side Reinterpretation of the 'Secularization' of Europe," *Journal for the Scientific Study of Religion*, 33 (3):230–52.

Yang, F. 2006. "The Red, Black, and Gray Markets of Religion in China," *The Sociological Quarterly*, 47 (1):93–122.

Ying, F.-t. 2009. "The Regional Development of Protestant Christianity in China: 1918, 1949 and 2004," *The China Review*, 9 (2):63–97.

6 The Nationwide Shortage of Chinese Protestant Churches[1]

6.1 Introduction

While Chapter 5 has discussed digital and statistical information concerning nationwide church data, the present chapter extends its quantitative analysis to map the nationwide shortage of Protestant churches in China, encompassing all 31 provinces or the three major regions (east, central, and west) through spatial insight.

The shortage of churches, as an academic topic, straddles the disciplines of religious market analysis and religious economy. As Yang (2010: 3) aptly notes, "The religious economy is driven by the interactions of demand, supply, and regulation." In this context, church shortage signifies the supply side of the religious market and religious economy, reflecting the demand of Protestants exceeding the supply of church organizations. While the shortage of religion and Protestantism in China can be attributed to various intangible factors, such as government regulations (Yang, 2006) and the prevailing atheist ideology (Hamberg and Pettersson, 2003; Yang, 2010), it is vital to study one of the visible factors: organized churches. Given the assertion that "the Chinese religious market is seriously underdeveloped" (Yang, 2006: 114), it is essential to compile measurable data and spatial maps to quantify the levels of "underdevelopment" or the statistical shortage of churches. While some scholars emphasize the demand side of the religious market (Yang, 2010), and others concur that the supply of Chinese churches cannot meet the demand of Chinese Protestants, their conclusions, to some extent, rely on theoretical perspectives or empirical observations without comprehensive digital and spatial calculations (Sherkat and Ellison, 1999).

It is necessary to note that this study relies on the following data as key references: (1) population data from the 2000 China census (National Bureau of Statistics of China, 2001); (2) the total number of Chinese Protestants from the Chinese Academy of Social Sciences (Research Project Team of the Institute of World Religious Studies in the Chinese Academy of Social Sciences, 2010); (3) the number of Chinese Protestant churches from the 2004 China Economic Census Data with GIS Maps (China Census Bureau, 2005); (4) the number of Protestants in each province from The Amity Foundation (2004); and (5) spatial religious information from *Atlas of Religions in China* (China Data Institute, 2008) and *China Geo-Explore*

58 The Nationwide Shortage of Chinese Protestant Churches

(China Data Institute, 2012). Additionally, it is necessary to incorporate various official economic data as supplementary information.

This chapter primarily focuses on two variables to assess the shortage of Protestant churches in China. The first is the density of congregations, designed to measure the average number of Protestant participants per church. A higher congregation density indicates a more severe church shortage. The second measurement is church availability, aimed at mapping the distance between residential areas and the nearest church in a specific city. Longer travel times from home to the nearest church signify a worse experience regarding church shortage. The chapter selects 31 provincial capital cities as case study sites to demonstrate church shortages in each province or municipality. After discussing the density of congregations and church availability in each city, it is critical to compare church shortages between the three regions in China and identify the top 14 cities with the most acute church shortages. It is also critical to examine the correlations between church shortage and residents' economic income, using GDP per capita data for each city.

6.2 The density of congregations and church availability in Eastern China

Before we evaluate the national pattern, let's delve into the density of congregations and church shortages within each region. Based on data obtained from the 2000 China census and studies conducted by The Amity Foundation (2004) and F.t. Ying (2009) regarding the percentage of the Protestant population, Table 6.1 provides a summary of information pertaining to the Protestant community and its representation as a percentage of the total population in 11 provincial capital cities in Eastern China.

Furthermore, it is imperative to incorporate data on the number of Protestant churches in order to assess the density of the Protestant population per church in

Table 6.1 Protestant Congregations in Eastern China, 2004.

City	*Protestant population*	*Percentage of total population (national average: 1.8%)*	*Percentage of Protestants in China*
Hangzhou	96,092	3.92	0.42
Fuzhou	72,231	3.40	0.31
Shanghai	69,616	1.12	0.30
Shenyang	47,434	1.42	0.21
Nanjing	37,231	2.11	0.16
Jinan	27,468	1.30	0.12
Beijing	18,605	0.28	0.08
Shijiazhuang	10,986	0.59	0.05
Guangzhou	10,657	0.30	0.05
Tianjin	7,661	0.20	0.03
Haikou	4,151	0.50	0.02

Source: Fuk-tsang Ying, "The Regional Development of Protestant Christianity in China: 1918, 1949 and 2004," *The China Review*, 9 (2) (2009):63–97; The Amity Foundation, "How Many Sheep Are There in the Chinese Flock?" Amity News Services, 2004.

Table 6.2 Protestant Population Density in Eastern China, 2004.

	Number of Protestants	Percentage of Protestants	Number of churches	Average participants per church	Rankings of shortage
United States	59,000,000	21[2]	297,900	198	
China	23,050,000[3]	1.8	14,509	1,589	
Nanjing	37,231	2.11	2	18,616	1
Beijing	18,605	0.82	2	9,303	2
Jinan	27,468	1.30	3	9,156	3
Hangzhou	96,092	3.92	11	8,736	4
Shenyang	47,434	1.42	7	6,776	5
Shanghai	69,616	1.12	12	5,801	6
Shijiazhuang	10,986	0.59	2	5,493	7
Haikou	4,151	0.50	1	4,151	8
Fuzhou	72,231	3.4	27	2,675	9
Guangzhou	10,657	0.30	7	1,522	10
Tianjin	7,661	0.20	9	851	11

Source: Fuk-tsang Ying, "The Regional Development of Protestant Christianity in China: 1918, 1949 and 2004," *The China Review*, 9 (2) (2009):63–97; The Amity Foundation, "How Many Sheep Are There in the Chinese Flock?" Amity News Services, 2004.

Eastern China, relative to the national averages in both China and the United States. As depicted in Table 6.2, the rankings of church shortages become readily apparent. Notably, only Guangzhou (1,522) and Tianjin (851) demonstrate an average number of Protestant participants per church below the national average of 1,589. In stark contrast, Nanjing, Beijing, Jinan, Hangzhou, and Shenyang each have over 5,000 Protestant participants per church, respectively.

As the second measurable indicator of church shortage, church availability should be addressed by measuring the distance between the residential area and the nearest church in a specific city. Relying on the information concerning the overall population and that of the Protestants, it is possible to determine the spatial data about church availability. Table 6.3 indicates that more than 50% of Protestants in seven of the 11 capital cities (63%) in Eastern China, such as Beijing, Haikou, Shijiazhuang, Hangzhou, Jinan, Nanjing, and Tianjin, can't reach their nearest churches within a 2.5 km radius.

Based on the comparison of the Protestant population density and the availability of churches in Eastern China, Table 6.4 amalgamates these two variables to present the rankings of church shortages in 11 provincial capital cities in Eastern China. Clearly, these two distinct rankings highlight disparities across many cities, with exceptions, including Hangzhou (ranked fourth in both categories), Beijing (ranked second in one and first in the other), and Fuzhou (ranked ninth in one and tenth in the other). It's worth noting that church availability is influenced by the proximity between churches. When churches are nearby, the covered areas for these spatial churches become smaller, potentially resulting in more Protestants being unable to reach their nearest church within a reasonable timeframe. Consequently, the rankings can vary when considering both the number of Protestant participants per church and the number of Protestants who cannot access their nearest church in each city.

Table 6.3 Comparative Church Availability in Eastern China, 2004.

2.5 km	Number of Protestants who can't arrive at the nearest church	Percentage of the total Protestants	Rankings of church shortage
Beijing	17,067	91.73	1
Haikou	3,295	79.37	2
Shijiazhuang	6,940	63.17	3
Hangzhou	57,493	59.83	4
Jinan	16,364	59.57	5
Nanjing	19,288	51.81	6
Tianjin	3,832	50.02	7
Guangzhou	4,923	46.20	8
Shenyang	15,869	33.46	9
Fuzhou	23,134	32.03	10
Shanghai	12,680	18.21	11

Source: Fuk-tsang Ying, "The Regional Development of Protestant Christianity in China: 1918, 1949 and 2004," *The China Review*, 9 (2) (2009):63–97; The Amity Foundation, "How Many Sheep Are There in the Chinese Flock?" Amity News Services, 2004.

After combining the rankings of the two categories and dividing the result by 2, column 4 of Table 6.4 presents the average points and rankings for all 11 cities. Consequently, the top six cities, which account for approximately 50% of all cities in Eastern China and have scores of 5 points or less, include Beijing, Nanjing, Jinan, Hangzhou, Shijiazhuang, and Haikou. These cities can be identified as areas with a significant church shortage. Remarkably, this closely aligns with the top six rankings for church shortage in both categories. Beijing, Nanjing, Jinan, and Hangzhou maintain their top positions concerning both Protestant density and church availability. While Shijiazhuang and Haikou rank seventh and eighth, respectively, in terms of Protestant density, their overall church shortage scores remain within the top six.

Table 6.4 Rankings of Church Shortages in Provincial Capital Cities in Eastern China, 2004.

City	Ranking of average participants per church	Ranking of comparative church availability	Average rankings of church shortage
Nanjing	1	6	2 (3.5 points)
Beijing	2	1	1 (1.5 points)
Jinan	3	5	3 (4 points)
Hangzhou	4	4	3 (4 points)
Shenyang	5	9	7 (7 points)
Shanghai	6	11	8 (8.6 points)
Shijiazhuang	7	3	5 (5 points)
Haikou	8	2	5 (5 points)
Fuzhou	9	10	11 (9.5 points)
Guangzhou	10	8	9 (9 points)
Tianjin	11	7	9 (9 points)

Source: Fuk-tsang Ying, "The Regional Development of Protestant Christianity in China: 1918, 1949 and 2004," *The China Review*, 9 (2) (2009):63–97; The Amity Foundation, "How Many Sheep Are There in the Chinese Flock?" Amity News Services, 2004.

Table 6.5 Protestant Congregations in Central China, 2004.

City	Protestant population	Percentage of total population (national average: 1.8%)	Percentage of Protestants in China
Zhengzhou	139,827	5.40	0.61
Hefei	70,638	5.01	0.31
Harbin	53,481	1.63	0.23
Changchun	41,287	1.28	0.18
Wuhan	32,652	0.83	0.14
Taiyuan	15,606	0.61	0.07
Nanchang	11,882	0.97	0.05
Changsha	9,978	0.47	0.04

Source: Fuk-tsang Ying, "The Regional Development of Protestant Christianity in China: 1918, 1949 and 2004," *The China Review*, 9 (2) (2009):63–97; The Amity Foundation, "How Many Sheep Are There in the Chinese Flock?" Amity News Services, 2004.

6.3 The density of congregations and availability of churches in Central China

Using a similar methodology as described previously, it is feasible to assess the density of Protestant congregations and the availability of Protestant churches in eight provincial capital cities in Central China. Table 6.5 provides a visual representation of data pertaining to the Protestant population and its percentage within the total population in eight provincial capital cities in Central China.

Table 6.6 showcases data on the density of Protestants in Central China, incorporating average church-related information. In terms of the average number of Protestant congregations per church, all eight capital cities exceed the national average of 1,589, with three of them—Hefei, Zhengzhou, and Nanchang—reporting more than 5,000 participants per church.

Table 6.6 The Density of Protestants in Central China, 2004.

	Number of Protestants	Percentage of Protestants	Number of churches	Average participants per church	Rankings of shortage
United States	59,000,000	21	297,900	198	
China	23,050,000	1.8	14,509	1,589	
Hefei	70,638	5.01	4	17,660	1
Zhengzhou	139,827	5.40	12	13,983	2
Nanchang	11,882	0.97	2	5,941	3
Changsha	9,978	0.47	2	4,989	4
Wuhan	32,652	0.83		4,665	5
Taiyuan	15,606	0.61	4	3,902	6
Harbin	53,481	1.63	14	3,820	7
Changchun	41,287	1.28	21	1,966	8

Source: Fuk-tsang Ying, "The Regional Development of Protestant Christianity in China: 1918, 1949 and 2004," *The China Review*, 9 (2) (2009):63–97; The Amity Foundation, "How Many Sheep Are There in the Chinese Flock?" Amity News Services, 2004.

Table 6.7 Comparative Church Availability in Central China, 2004.

2.5 km	Number of Protestants who can't arrive at the nearest church	Percentage of the total Protestants	Rankings of church shortage
Taiyuan	12,355	79.17	1
Changsha	7,292	73.09	2
Hefei	47,702	67.53	3
Wuhan	20,891	63.98	4
Zhengzhou	83,287	59.56	5
Harbin	30,346	56.74	6
Nanchang	4,817	40.54	7
Changchun	14,957	36.23	8

Source: Fuk-tsang Ying, "The Regional Development of Protestant Christianity in China: 1918, 1949 and 2004," *The China Review*, 9 (2) (2009):63–97; The Amity Foundation, "How Many Sheep Are There in the Chinese Flock?" Amity News Services, 2004.

When considering church availability, Table 6.7 substantiates that in six out of the eight capital cities (75%) in Central China, over 50% of the Protestant population cannot access their nearest churches within a 2.5 km radius from their residences. This percentage is 12% higher than that observed in Eastern China (75% vs. 63%). Notably, Nanchang (45.54%) and Changchun (36.23%) are the only two cities where fewer than 50% of the Protestants face difficulties reaching their nearest churches within a 2.5 km distance from their homes.

To draw comparisons between the rankings of Protestant density and church availability in Central China, Table 6.8 provides an overview of these rankings and their averages across all eight cities in the region. Once again, disparities are evident, but the overall rankings align closely. Particularly, Harbin and Changchun maintain consistent rankings in terms of their average number of participants per church and church availability. Half of the selected cities in Central China, precisely the top four cities (50%), have an average ranking of four points or lower. These cities include Hefei, Zhengzhou, Changsha, and Taiyuan, which should be recognized as areas experiencing a church shortage.

Table 6.8 Rankings of Church Shortage in Provincial Capital Cities in Central China, 2004.

City	Ranking of average participants per church	Ranking of comparative church availability	Average rankings of church shortage
Hefei	1	3	1 (2 points)
Zhengzhou	2	5	3 (3.5 points)
Nanchang	3	7	6 (5 points)
Changsha	4	2	2 (3 points)
Wuhan	5	4	5 (4.5 points)
Taiyuan	6	1	3 (3.5 points)
Harbin	7	6	7 (6.5 points)
Changchun	8	8	8 (8 points)

Source: Fuk-tsang Ying, "The Regional Development of Protestant Christianity in China: 1918, 1949 and 2004," *The China Review*, 9 (2) (2009):63–97; The Amity Foundation, "How Many Sheep Are There in the Chinese Flock?" Amity News Services, 2004.

6.4 The density of congregations and availability of churches in Western China

Exploring the context of 12 provincial capital cities in Western China, investigating the density of Protestant congregations and the availability of churches using analogous research methodologies is critical. Likewise, Table 6.9 showcases data concerning the Protestant congregations and the total population in Western China.

Regarding the number of Protestants, the percentage of Protestants, the number of churches, and the average number of Protestants per church in western cities, Table 6.10 presents their rankings concerning church shortage. These rankings are closely tied to the density of the Protestant population in Western China.

Obviously, when considering the density of Protestant churches, all western provincial capital cities, with the exception of Nanning, surpass the national average of 1,589 congregations per church. Furthermore, 4 out of the 12 cities have an average of more than 5,000 congregations per church, which is quite noteworthy. Interestingly, current information regarding religious sites does not indicate the presence of any Protestant churches in Lhasa, Tibet.

To gain insight into the average number of residents unable to reach their nearest churches within a 2.5 km radius, Table 6.11 presents comparative church availability data for Western China. Remarkably, 8 out of the 12 cities (67%) have over 50% of their Protestant population unable to access the nearest churches located within 2.5 km of their residences. This overall situation in Western China aligns with the situation in Eastern China (67%) and fares better than that in Central China (75%). It's worth noting that both Xian and Nanning exhibit a remarkable 100% accessibility rate to the nearest churches within a 2.5 km radius for all Protestants in those cities.

Table 6.9 Protestant Congregations in Western China, 2004.

City	Protestant population	Percentage of total population (national average: 1.8%)	Percentage of Protestants in China
Kunming	75,896	2.75	0.33
Chongqing	36,688	0.97	0.16
Xi'an	23,580	1.27	0.10
Chengdu	21,864	0.63	0.09
Lanzhou	16,433	1.02	0.07
Guiyang	15,671	1.13	0.07
Urumqi	10,292	0.68	0.04
Hohhot	10,130	0.72	0.04
Yinchuan	9,448	1.17	0.04
Xining	6,494	0.76	0.03
Nanning	1,451	0.26	0.01
Lhasa	0	0.00	0.00

Source: Fuk-tsang Ying, "The Regional Development of Protestant Christianity in China: 1918, 1949 and 2004," *The China Review*, 9 (2) (2009):63–97; The Amity Foundation, "How Many Sheep Are There in the Chinese Flock?" Amity News Services, 2004.

Table 6.10 The Density of Protestants in Western China, 2004.

	Number of Protestants	Percentage of Protestants	Number of churches	Average participants per church	Rankings of shortage
United States	59,000,000	21	297,900	198	
China	23,050,000	1.8	14,509	1,589	
Kunming	75,896	2.75	4	18,974	1
Guiyang	15,671	1.13	1	15,671	2
Chengdu	21,864	0.63	2	10,932	3
Xi'an	23,580	1.27	4	5,895	4
Yinchuan	9,448	1.17	2	4,724	5
Hohhot	10,130	0.72	3	3,377	6
Xining	6,494	0.76	2	3,247	7
Chongqing	36,688	0.97	14	2,621	8
Lanzhou	16,433	1.02	7	2,348	9
Urumqi	10,292	0.68	6	1,715	10
Nanning	1,451	0.26	2	726	11
Lhasa	N/A	N/A	0	0	12

Source: Fuk-tsang Ying, "The Regional Development of Protestant Christianity in China: 1918, 1949 and 2004," *The China Review*, 9 (2) (2009):63–97; The Amity Foundation, "How Many Sheep Are There in the Chinese Flock?" Amity News Services, 2004.

To determine the average rankings for church shortage in Western China, Table 6.12 consolidates ranking data pertaining to the density of Protestant congregations and church availability. When focusing on the top 50% of cities in Western China, areas experiencing a church shortage include Chengdu, Kunming, Yinchuan, Guiyang, and Hohhot.

Table 6.11 Comparative Church Availability in Western China, 2004.

2.5 km	Number of Protestants who can't arrive at the nearest church	Percentage of the total Protestants	Rankings of church shortage
Chengdu	19,057	87.16	1
Yinchuan	7,702	81.52	2
Kunming	61,277	80.74	3
Hohhot	7,719	76.20	4
Lanzhou	12,371	75.28	5
Guiyang	10,848	69.23	6
Xining	4,140	63.76	7
Chongqing	18,513	50.46	8
Urumqi	3,633	35.30	9
Xi'an	0	0.00	10
Nanning	0	0.00	11
Lhasa	N/A	N/A	12

Source: Fuk-tsang Ying, "The Regional Development of Protestant Christianity in China: 1918, 1949 and 2004," *The China Review*, 9 (2) (2009):63–97; The Amity Foundation, "How Many Sheep Are There in the Chinese Flock?" Amity News Services, 2004.

Table 6.12 Rankings of Church Shortage in Provincial Capital Cities of Western China, 2004.

City	Ranking of average participants per church	Ranking of comparative church availability	Average rankings of church shortage
Kunming	1	3	1 (2 points)
Guiyang	2	6	4 (4 points)
Chengdu	3	1	1 (2 points)
Xi'an	4	10	6 (7 points)
Yinchuan	5	2	3 (3.5 points)
Hohhot	6	4	5 (5 points)
Xining	7	7	6 (7 points)
Chongqing	8	8	9 (8 points)
Lanzhou	9	5	6 (7 points)
Urumqi	10	9	10 (9.5 points)
Nanning	11	11	11 (11 points)
Lhasa	12	12	12 (12 points)

Source: Fuk-tsang Ying, "The Regional Development of Protestant Christianity in China: 1918, 1949 and 2004," *The China Review*, 9 (2) (2009):63–97; The Amity Foundation, "How Many Sheep Are There in the Chinese Flock?" Amity News Services, 2004.

6.5 National comparisons of Protestant church shortage

Following the computation of data related to the density of the Protestant population and church availability in 31 provincial capital cities spanning Eastern, Central, and Western China, it becomes imperative to assess the distinctions between these three regions from a national standpoint. Upon calculating the median of Protestant congregation density in three regions, it becomes evident that the average number of participants per church in Eastern China exceeds that in Central China by 20% (5,801 vs. 4,827) and surpasses that in Western China by 75% (5,801 vs. 3,312), as depicted in Table 6.13, column 2.

Remarkably, when incorporating GDP per capita in 2000 for each region as a reference to investigate potential correlations between church shortages and individuals' income levels, an intriguing trend emerges. It reveals that regions with higher income levels tend to have more residents living in areas characterized by church shortages. For instance, in 2000, the per capita income in Eastern China was 66% higher than that

Table 6.13 Correlations between Church Shortage and GDP Per Capita in Three Regions.

Region	Average participants per church	GDP per capita (Chinese Yuan)
Eastern China	5,801	30,575.00
Central China	4,827	18,420.00
Western China	3,312	15,280.00

Source: National Bureau of Statistics of China, *China Statistical Yearbook, 2000* (Beijing: China Statistical Publisher, 2000); Fuk-tsang Ying, "The Regional Development of Protestant Christianity in China: 1918, 1949 and 2004," *The China Review*, 9 (2) (2009):63–97; The Amity Foundation, "How Many Sheep Are There in the Chinese Flock?" Amity News Services, 2004.

Table 6.14 The Nationwide Density of Protestants in Provincial Capital Cities, 2004.

City	Number of Protestants	Average participants per church
Kunming (West)	75,896	18,974
Nanjing (East)	37,231	18,616
Hefei (Central)	70,638	17,660
Guiyang (West)	15,671	15,671
Zhengzhou (Central)	139,827	13,983
Chengdu (West)	21,864	10,932
Beijing (East)	18,605	9,303
Jinan (East)	27,468	9,156
Hangzhou (East)	96,092	8,736
Shenyang (East)	47,434	6,776
Nanchang (Central)	11,882	5,941
Xi'an (West)	23,580	5,895
Shanghai (East)	69,616	5,801
Shijiazhuang (East)	10,986	5,493

Source: Fuk-tsang Ying, "The Regional Development of Protestant Christianity in China: 1918, 1949 and 2004," *The China Review*, 9 (2) (2009):63–97; The Amity Foundation, "How Many Sheep Are There in the Chinese Flock?" Amity News Services, 2004.

in Central China (30,575 yuan vs. 18,420 yuan) and 100% higher than that in Western China (30,575 yuan vs. 15,280 yuan), as shown in Table 6.13, column 3.

Paradoxically, despite the higher income levels in Eastern China, the church shortage situation in this region was more pronounced compared to the other two regions. For example, when considering provincial capital cities with an average of more than 5,000 Protestant congregations per church, Eastern China alone had seven cities, constituting 64% of the total, while both Central and Western China collectively shared the remaining seven cities, as indicated in Table 6.14.

Moreover, by amalgamating the two categories of congregational density and church availability, a more comprehensive understanding of areas experiencing church shortages in the three distinct regions—six cities in Eastern China, four cities in Central China, and five cities in Western China—becomes apparent through Table 6.15. The numbers within parentheses in columns 2 and 3 denote the rankings of church shortages in China. In column 4 of Table 6.15, the numbers within parentheses signify the points assigned after combining the rankings of both church availability and congregational density from columns 2 and 3. The numbers without parentheses in column 4 represent the national rankings of church shortages. For example, Kunming is identified as the region with the most pronounced church shortage, while both Beijing and Chengdu are ranked as the second most affected cities. This underscores the clear necessity for constructing more churches to bolster the supply within the religious market.

6.6 Conclusion

The examination of the density of Protestant congregations and the availability of Protestant churches in China has shed light on a significant shortage in the supply of churches within the Chinese religious market. This scarcity becomes even more

Table 6.15 National Comparisons on Church Shortage, 2004.

Name of cities	Percentages of the total Protestants who couldn't arrive at the nearest church within 2.5 km and national rankings (column 2)	Average participants per church and rankings (column 3)	Average rankings (column 4)
Kunming (west)	80.74% (4)	18,974 (1)	1 (5 points)
Beijing (east)	91.73% (1)	9,303 (7)	2 (8 points)
Chengdu (west)	87.16 (2)	10,932 (6)	2 (8 points)
Taiyuan (central)	79.17 (6)	3,902 (14)	4 (10 points)
Hefei (central)	67.53 (10)	17,660 (3)	5 (13 points)
Guiyang (west)	69.23 (9)	15,671 (4)	5 (13 points)
Yinchuan (west)	81.52 (3)	4,724 (12)	7 (15 points)
Nanjing (east)	51.81 (15)	18,616 (2)	8 (17 points)
Haikou (east)	79.37 (5)	4,151 (13)	9 (18 points)
Zhengzhou (central)	59.56 (14)	13,983 (5)	10 (19 points)
Changsha (central)	73.09 (8)	4,989 (11)	10 (19 points)
Jinan (east)	59.57 (13)	9,156 (8)	12 (21 points)
Hangzhou (east)	59.83 (12)	8,736 (9)	12 (21 points)
Shijiazhuang (east)	63.17 (11)	5,493 (10)	12 (21 points)
Hohhot (west)	76.20 (7)	3,377 (15)	15 (22 points)

Source: Fuk-tsang Ying, "The Regional Development of Protestant Christianity in China: 1918, 1949 and 2004," *The China Review*, 9 (2) (2009):63–97; The Amity Foundation, "How Many Sheep Are There in the Chinese Flock?" Amity News Services, 2004.

pronounced in the context of the rapid growth in demand, exemplified by the remarkable expansion of the Chinese Protestant population. Obviously, the supply of churches lags behind the burgeoning demand from church members.

The objective of this chapter has been to offer a digital and statistical analysis of Protestant churches in China. The aim is to provide scholars interested in studying the Chinese religious market and economy with quantitative methods and data to further their research in this field.

Notes

1 With the publisher's permission, segments of this chapter are excerpted from the article authored by Zhaohui Hong and co-authored by his graduate students, Lu Cao and Jiamin Yan, "The Protestant Church Shortage and Religious Market in China: Spatial and Statistical Perspectives," in Xiaobing Li and Patrick Shan, eds., *Ethnic China—Identity, Assimilation, and Resistance* (New York: Lexington Books, 2014), pp. 139–150. Ms. Cao and Mr. Yan have granted permission and provided written consent to exclude their names as co-authors of this book. The original work has been significantly revised and updated for this book.
2 According to C. Kirk Hadaway and Penny Long Marler, there are only 21% of Americans participating in the weekly Christian church activities. See C. Kirk Hadaway and Penny L. Marler, "How Many Americans Attend Worship Each Week? An Alternative Approach to Measurement," *Journal for the Scientific Study of Religion*, 44 (3) (2005):307–322.
3 The total Protestant population, 23,050,000, was estimated by a research team sponsored by the Chinese Academy of Social Sciences in 2010. See Research Project Team

of the Institute of World Religious Studies in the Chinese Academy of Social Sciences, "The Survey Report on China's Christians" (Zhongguo jidujiao ruhu wenjuan diaocha baogao), in Jin Ze and Qiu Yonghui, eds., *Annual Report on China's Religions (2010)* (Beijing: Shehui kexue wenxian chubanshe, 2010), pp. 190–212.

References

The Amity Foundation. 2004. How Many Sheep Are There in the Chinese Flock? *Amity News Services*. Retrieved from: http://www.amitynewsservice.org

China Census Bureau. 2005. *The 2004 China's Economic Census Data with GIS Maps*. Beijing: All China Market Research Co., LTD.

China Data Institute. 2008. *Atlas of Religions in China*. Retrieved from: https://chinadatacenter.net/Data/ServiceContent.aspx?id=1573

China Data Institute. 2012. *China Geo-Explore*. Retrieved from: https://www.chinageoexplorer.com/cge/

Hadaway, C.K., and P.L. Marler. 2005. "How Many Americans Attend Worship Each Week? An Alternative Approach to Measurement," *Journal for the Scientific Study of Religion*, 44 (3):307–322.

Hamberg, E.M., and T. Pettersson. 2003. "Religious Markets: Supply, Demand, and Rational Choices," *Sacred Markets, Sacred Canopies: Essays on Religious Markets and Religious Pluralism*, T.G. Jelen, ed., pp. 91–114. Lanham, MD: Rowman & Littlefield.

Hong, Z., L. Cao, and J. Yan. 2014. "The Protestant Church Shortage and Religious Market in China: Spatial and Statistical Perspectives," *Ethnic China—Identity, Assimilation, and Resistance*, Xiaobing Li and Patrick Shan, ed., pp. 139–150. New York: Lexington Books.

National Bureau of Statistics of China. 2001. *China Statistical Yearbook, 2000*. Beijing: China Statistical Publisher

National Bureau of Statistics of China. 2010. *2010 Population Census*. Beijing: National Statistic Press.

Research Project Team of the Institute of World Religious Studies in the Chinese Academy of Social Sciences. 2010. *The Survey Report on China's Christians, Annual Report on China's Religions (2010)*, J. Ze and Q. Yonghui, eds., pp. 190–212. Beijing: Shehui kexue wenxian chubanshe.

Sherkat, D.E., and C.G. Ellison. 1999. "Recent Developments and Current Controversies in the Sociology of Religion," *Annual Review of Sociology*, 25 (1):363–394.

Yang, F. 2006. "The Red, Black, and Gray Markets of Religion in China," *The Sociological Quarterly*, 47 (1):93–122.

Yang, F. 2010. "Religion in China under Communism: A Shortage Economy Explanation," *Journal of Church and State*, 52 (1):3–33.

Ying, F.-t. 2009. "The Regional Development of Protestant Christianity in China: 1918, 1949 and 2004," *The China Review*, 9 (2):63–97.

7 Multi-Methods Research Design[1]

7.1 Introduction

This chapter builds upon those endeavors by employing methods to address church accessibility and driving distances between the demand side (residential areas of Protestant members) and the supply side (Protestant churches). Evaluating the driving distances between churches and Protestant residential zones is pivotal when examining church accessibility and shortages in specific regions. With the assistance of a geographic information system (GIS), spatial analysis adds temporal and geographical dimensions to the study of supply and demand disparities in a religious market.

The methodologies include the Two-Step Floating Catchment Area (2SFCA) method and the Network Analysis Method (NAM), designed to assess 31 provincial capital cities across three Chinese regions (east, central, and west) to estimate the percentage of Chinese Protestants unable to reach their nearest churches within specified time and distance constraints. The congruent and distinctive results yielded by these two methods will enhance our research methodology and uncover additional insights into the Protestant market and religious economy in China.

7.2 Methodology

This project utilizes ArcGIS 10.1 to calculate the driving time from Protestant residential areas to Protestant churches in specific locations, with the aim of estimating the percentage of Protestants who cannot reach their nearest church within a designated time frame. Both the 2SFCA and NAM are applied to measure and compare driving times and geographic areas between these designated locations, providing insights into church accessibility and shortages.

To begin, it is vital to employ the 2SFCA method as the primary tool for examining church accessibility. Originally developed by John Radke and Lan Mu, the 2SFCA was designed to "develop a method which measures access to social services for each household and makes adjustments among service providers to better accommodate under-served regions" (2000: 111). While initially intended for measuring spatial accessibility to primary-care physicians, the 2SFCA method is adaptable for measuring accessibility to various other services, including working

DOI: 10.4324/9781003495451-7

locations, gas stations, bank branches, and more (Luo and Wang, 2003a). It quantifies spatial accessibility as a ratio of primary-care physicians to population, achieved through two steps. First, it evaluates "physician availability" at physician locations (supply) as the physician-to-population ratio within a specified travel time. Second, it aggregates these ratios (derived in the first step) around each resident location (demand) within the same travel time threshold (Luo and Wang, 2003b).

Rather than relying on detailed street maps for travel time calculations, this chapter adopts a simplified 2SFCA approach, which employs straight-line distance for travel time estimation due to the limited availability of street map data in Chinese cities. The analysis unit combines polygon-integrated census information with church locations. Given the data constraints, we assume an equal distribution of the population across each district.

It's important to understand that the maps created using the 2SFCA represent varying church accessibility scores within a specific city. Darker colors indicate higher church accessibility scores. In the context of church accessibility, areas without color or shown in white represent a score of zero, signifying that there are no churches reachable within a 30-minute one-way drive. To interpret the distribution of these accessibility scores, we refer to Wang and Luo's methodology of defining Health Professional Shortage Areas (HPSA) by assessing both spatial and non-spatial factors for healthcare access (2005: 131). They identify areas with scores lower than 1/3,500, approximately 0.00028571, as HPSA, based on HPSA criteria. Specifically, HPSA defines an area as a health professional shortage if residents cannot reach their nearest health clinic within a 30-minute drive (U.S. Department of Health and Human Services, 2013). Building on this definition, we have chosen to use a 30-minute one-way driving criterion to estimate church shortages in large Chinese cities.

However, it's central to consider that the threshold score for church shortages may need to be redefined, as it differs in characteristics from healthcare. As demonstrated in Map 7.1, areas marked in white represent church accessibility scores lower than 1/10,000. This indicates that Protestants residing in these areas would need more than 30 minutes of one-way driving to reach the nearest church or that a single church may not sufficiently serve the Protestant population. In contrast, the shaded areas symbolize the best or highest church accessibility scores, signifying that Protestants in these regions can access their nearest churches within 30 minutes of one-way driving, and one church may adequately serve the local Protestant community.

To complement and support the 2SFCA method, it's essential to incorporate another spatial research technique known as the NAM into the study of church shortages in China. The NAM leverages network data, maps, and spatial information through GIS and other spatial statistical methods to assess church availability and accessibility. Unlike the 2SFCA, the NAM can display a street layer that includes information like road type, distance, and permitted travel speeds (miles or kilometers per hour) from the underlying data table within GIS. This feature allows users to pinpoint station locations, specify travel times, and conduct network analyzes.

Multi-Methods Research Design 71

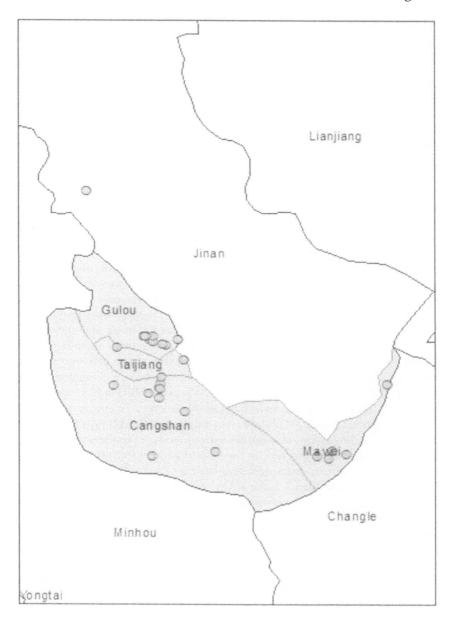

Map 7.1 The Sample by the Two-Step Floating Catchment Area (2SFCA).

Sources: Compiled from Research Project Team, *The Survey Report on China's Christians, Annual Report on China's Religions (2010)*, edited by Jin Ze and Qiu Yonghui, Beijing: Shehui kexue wenxian chubanshe, pp. 190–212; China Census Bureau, *The 2004 China's Economic Census Data with GIS Maps.* (Beijing: All China Market Research Co., LTD, 2004); China Data Institute, *China Geo-Explore*, 2012, retrieved from: https://www.chinageoexplorer.com/cge/; The Boya Diming Website, 2005, retrieved from http://www.tcmap.com.cn/.

72   *Multi-Methods Research Design*

The NAM involves several key steps. First, it performs map transformation to convert raw online map data into the appropriate format for analysis. This includes changing the map format to a coverage format and exporting the coverage data back to a shapefile format editable through ArcGIS software. The second step entails creating a network dataset, a critical component for network analysis when working with shapefiles obtained from online maps. The third step involves importing church point coordinates, including longitude and latitude, to establish these locations as service facilities within the network.

Next comes the network analysis itself, where church points and maps are imported into the software. This analysis enables the calculation of driving times for selected areas using three different time intervals: 15 minutes, 30 minutes, and 45 minutes, corresponding to distances of 6 km, 12 km, and 18 km, respectively. Additionally, the network analysis provides the means to determine coverage areas using built-in functions, organize resulting data in Excel, and ascertain the percentage or number of Protestants unable to reach their nearest church within the specified time.

An added advantage of the NAM is its capability to determine average driving speeds in cities based on selected samples. Assuming that provincial capital cities in China share similar traffic conditions, three representative cities—Beijing, Shanghai, and Xi'an—were chosen for sampling. Google Maps proves effective in calculating routes between randomly selected starting and ending locations within these cities, such as from the city center to its boundary. Given designated distances and driving times, it is critical to obtain driving speed data for these cities: Beijing—14.71, 25.85, and 38.54 km/hour; Shanghai—18.00, 21.4, and 25.89 km/h; and Xi'an—32.40, 32.88, and 39.00 km/h. Consequently, the average driving speed was calculated as 27.63 km/h. To ensure consistency, an average driving speed of 24 km/h was established for all provincial capital cities. Certainly, Protestants may opt for various modes of transportation to reach their nearest churches. However, for the sake of general statistics, we have chosen to use private cars as a representative sample.

As demonstrated in Map 7.2, the NAM effectively visualizes various driving times (in minutes) and distances within designated locations. The inner circle represents 15 minutes of driving time, the middle circle corresponds to 30 minutes of driving, and the outer circle signifies 45 minutes of driving. Each point on the map indicates the location of a Protestant church. To maintain consistency with the 2SFCA, our study selected 30 minutes as the standard time unit for assessing church accessibility and shortages in China, aligning with the NIH's definition of HPSA.

7.3 Data

Gathering and verifying data related to Chinese Protestants presents an exceptionally daunting challenge due to the lack of transparency within religious institutions. This opacity is observed in both official Protestant churches and non-official religious gatherings, such as house churches. Despite acknowledging the inherent

Map 7.2 Sample by the Network Analysis Method (NAM).

Sources: Compiled from Research Project Team, *The Survey Report on China's Christians, Annual Report on China's Religions (2010)*, edited by Jin Ze and Qiu Yonghui, Beijing: Shehui kexue wenxian chubanshe, pp. 190–212; China Census Bureau, *The 2004 China's Economic Census Data with GIS Maps*. (Beijing: All China Market Research Co., LTD, 2004); China Data Institute, *China Geo-Explore*, 2012, retrieved from: https://www.chinageoexplorer.com/cge/; The Boya Diming Website, 2005, retrieved from http://www.tcmap.com.cn/.

inaccuracies and gaps in our measurement of church accessibility and shortages in China using the 2SFCA and the NAM, we've made diligent efforts to rely on the following data as key references for our project.

The first one is the total number of Chinese Protestants. While various sources present differing estimates of the number of Chinese Protestants, such as Pew data indicating 58 million (Pew Research Center, 2010), we have chosen to reference the Chinese official data, which reported 23,050,000 Chinese Protestants in 2009 (Research Project Team of the Institute of World Religious Studies in the Chinese Academy of Social Sciences, 2010). We recognize that official data likely underestimates the true number of Protestant members in China, but we lack sufficient empirical evidence and capacity to contest this estimate.

The second one is the total number of Chinese Protestant Churches. Following a meticulous analysis of *the 2004 China's Economic Census Data with GIS Maps* released by the Chinese government, we've opted to adhere to this official estimate, which reported 14,509 Chinese Protestant churches in 2004, excluding Catholic churches and non-official Protestant house churches (China Census Bureau, 2004). Furthermore, the *Atlas of Religions in China* (China Data Institute, 2008) and *China Geo-Explore* (China Data Institute, 2012) incorporate the aforementioned 14,509 churches through spatial information technology. While we acknowledge the time disparity between the number of Protestants in 2009 and the number of churches in 2004, we are constrained by limited data and must use estimates from similar periods as our reference.

The next one is the number of Protestants at the provincial and provincial capital city levels. Unfortunately, we have been unable to locate any official information regarding the number of Protestants at the provincial and city levels. Consequently, we have selectively relied on the following sources: (1) Data released by the Amity Foundation (2004); (2) County and City Gazetteers (Fang Zhi); (3) Fuk-tsang Ying's article (2009).

The last one is the spatial street and district maps at the city level. To calculate church accessibility scores and identify shortages, we've utilized the following resources: (1) The "CloudMade" website to access spatial street maps for the 31 provincial capital cities; (2) The "Boya Diming" website (博雅地名网) (2005) (http://www.tcmap.com.cn/) to retrieve district map information for these cities; and (3) Google Maps at the country, province, and city levels. Despite the limitations and challenges posed by the availability and reliability of data, we've strived to use the best available information to conduct our analysis of church accessibility and shortages in China.

7.4 Spatial church accessibility in Eastern China

Mainland China comprises three regions, eastern, central and western regions, and 31 provinces and municipalities in addition to Taiwan, Hong Kong, and Macau. Eastern China includes 11 provinces and municipalities, such as Zhejiang, Fujian, Shanghai, Liaoning, Jiangsu, Beijing, Shandong, Hebei, Guangdong, Tianjin, and Hainan.

In applying the aforementioned 2SFCA method to the study of church accessibility in Eastern China, we selected 30 minutes or 12 km as the reference to figure out the church accessibility score in 11 provincial capital cities in Eastern China. In other words, we define the areas in which the Protestant population cannot reach their nearest churches within 30 minutes through either driving or public transportation as the church shortage or low-church accessibility.

Table 7.1 summarizes the church accessibility scores in the 11 cities above and concludes that some percentages of the Protestants in nine cities need to take more than 30 minutes of one-way or 60 minutes of round-trip transportation to arrive at the nearest churches. It is worth noting that the calculation of the percentages of Protestants who must take more than 30 minutes to reach the nearest church is based on the assumption that the density of Protestants (ρ) is the same in different districts. Then, the percentage of Protestants can be calculated by using the following formula: [(area that can be reached in 30 minutes)× ρ]/[(total area of the city)× ρ] = (area that can be reached in 30 minutes)/(total area of the city).

Furthermore, it holds significance to employ the NAM as a cross-reference to validate the reliability of the 2SFCA method in assessing church accessibility and identifying church shortages. Following the same driving time of 30 minutes across the 11 provincial capital cities in Eastern China, it is necessary to conduct an analysis using the NAM. Table 7.2 presents the outcomes, encompassing: (1) the

Table 7.1 Church Accessibility in Eastern China by the 2SFCA.

Provincial capital cities	Percentage of Protestants that have lower accessibility score than 1/10,000
Nanjing	100.0
Haikou	94.8
Beijing	83.8
Jinan	73.7
Shenyang	69.4
Fuzhou	67.7
Hangzhou	64.9
Guangzhou	42.8
Shanghai	10.4
Shijiazhuang	0.0
Tianjin	0.0

Sources: Compiled from Pew Research Center, "Report 1: Religious Affiliation," *Pew Research Center's Religion & Public Life Project, 2010*, retrieved from https://www.pewresearch.org/topic/religion/; Research Project Team, *The Survey Report on China's Christians, Annual Report on China's Religions (2010)*, edited by Jin Ze and Qiu Yonghui, Beijing: Shehui kexue wenxian chubanshe, pp. 190–212; China Census Bureau, *The 2004 China's Economic Census Data with GIS Maps*. (Beijing: All China Market Research Co., LTD, 2004); China Data Institute, *China Geo-Explore*, 2012, retrieved from: https://www.chinageoexplorer.com/cge/; The Boya Diming Website, 2005, retrieved from http://www.tcmap.com.cn/.

Table 7.2 Church Accessibility in Eastern China by the NAM (30 Minutes).

12 km (30 minutes)	Accumulated area (km²)	Protestants and area coverage (%)	Protestants can't reach the nearest church (%)	Number of Protestants in the area
Haikou	153.1992	6.53	93.47	467
Beijing	593.2156	60.61	39.39	18,625
Jinan	568.0469	71.76	28.24	31,881
Fuzhou	1,097.782	105.80	0.00	58,089
Guangzhou	512.6185	138.33	0.00	17,998
Hangzhou	974.5984	133.84	0.00	157,423
Nanjing	464.8829	178.66	0.00	105,760
Shanghai	1,297.462	448.95	0.00	151,468
Shenyang	1,097.721	142.75	0.00	69,912
Shijiazhuang	435.4794	108.51	0.00	12,820
Tianjin	1,101.038	636.44	0.00	15,385

Sources: Compiled from Pew Research Center, "Report 1: Religious Affiliation," *Pew Research Center's Religion & Public Life Project, 2010*, retrieved from https://www.pewresearch.org/topic/religion/; Research Project Team, *The Survey Report on China's Christians, Annual Report on China's Religions (2010)*, edited by Jin Ze and Qiu Yonghui, Beijing: Shehui kexue wenxian chubanshe, pp. 190–212; China Census Bureau, *The 2004 China's Economic Census Data with GIS Maps*. (Beijing: All China Market Research Co., LTD, 2004); China Data Institute, *China Geo-Explore*, 2012, retrieved from: https://www.chinageoexplorer.com/cge/; The Boya Diming Website, 2005, retrieved from http://www.tcmap.com.cn/.

76   *Multi-Methods Research Design*

aggregated areas; (2) the count of Protestant members; (3) the coverage area; (4) the count of Protestants unable to reach their nearest church within 30 minutes; and (5) the total number of Protestants residing in the respective areas.

Table 7.2 provides a compelling illustration of the church shortage challenge in specific regions. Haikou, Beijing, and Jinan stand out as areas facing significant issues, with 93.47%, 39.39%, and 28.24% of their Protestant populations enduring more than a 30-minute one-way commute to reach their nearest churches. In contrast, the remaining eight cities in Eastern China enjoy better accessibility, with all Protestants able to access their nearest churches within a 30-minute drive.

Interestingly, both the NAM and the 2SFCA methodologies concur in identifying Haikou, Beijing, and Jinan as areas with severe church shortages, where accessibility to churches is virtually non-existent. It's worth noting, however, that the rankings for church shortages and the percentages of Protestants facing extended travel times differ among these three cities, depending on the research method used, owing to variations in their analysis databases.

To address these disparities, employing more detailed district maps through the 2SFCA method is a potential solution. Regrettably, obtaining and developing such comprehensive maps is a challenging endeavor in China due to the limited availability of data infrastructure and spatial resources. Consequently, we can conclude that the NAM proves more effective than the 2SFCA in regions with a scarcity of district maps and spatial data.

7.5 Spatial church accessibility in Central China

Central China encompasses eight provinces: Henan, Anhui, Heilongjiang, Jilin, Hubei, Shanxi, Jiangxi, and Hunan. Employing the 2FSCA method to assess the accessibility of eight provincial capital cities in the region reveals that Harbin, Changsha, Taiyuan, and Hefei exhibit the most extensive areas with a zero accessibility score. Table 7.3 offers a statistical overview that aids in pinpointing the rankings of cities facing church shortages and in computing the percentages of Protestants enduring over 30 minutes of one-way travel to reach their nearest churches.

In a similar vein, we must also incorporate the NAM as an additional tool for comparing the outcomes generated by various spatial research methods. As illustrated in Table 7.4, there are instances where certain percentages of Protestants residing in Hefei, Harbin, Zhengzhou, Changsha, and Taiyuan find it impossible to reach their nearest churches within a 30-minute timeframe. Conversely, Protestants residing in the remaining three cities within the region can reach their nearest churches in under 30 minutes. Consequently, Hefei, Harbin, Zhengzhou, Changsha, and Taiyuan can be classified as regions experiencing a church shortage according to the results obtained through the NAM.

A deeper examination of the comparative data derived from the 2SFCA and the NAM yields intriguing findings. On one hand, both methodologies concur in identifying Changsha, Taiyuan, and Harbin as regions experiencing a church shortage,

Table 7.3 Church Accessibility in Central China by the 2SFCA.

Provincial capital cities	Percentage of Protestants that have lower accessibility score than 1/10,000
Hefei	95.7
Harbin	76.9
Zhengzhou	70.5
Changsha	44.6
Taiyuan	15.8
Changchun	0.0
Nanchang	0.0
Wuhan	0.0

Sources: Compiled from Pew Research Center, "Report 1: Religious Affiliation," *Pew Research Center's Religion & Public Life Project, 2010,* retrieved from https://www.pewresearch.org/topic/religion/; Research Project Team, *The Survey Report on China's Christians, Annual Report on China's Religions (2010),* edited by Jin Ze and Qiu Yonghui, Beijing: Shehui kexue wenxian chubanshe, pp. 190–212; China Census Bureau, *The 2004 China's Economic Census Data with GIS Maps.* (Beijing: All China Market Research Co., LTD, 2004); China Data Institute, *China Geo-Explore,* 2012, retrieved from: https://www.chinageoexplorer.com/cge/; The Boya Diming Website, 2005, retrieved from http://www.tcmap.com.cn/.

albeit with differing rankings within these cities. On the other hand, they exhibit disparities: while the NAM designates Nanchang as an area with limited church accessibility, the 2SFCA points to Hefei and Zhengzhou as regions facing church shortages. Once again, it's worth noting that these divergent outcomes could be mitigated by utilizing more detailed and precise district maps through the 2SFCA method.

Table 7.4 Church Accessibility in Central China by the NAM (30 Minutes).

12 km (30 minutes)	Accumulated area (km²)	Protestants and area coverage (%)	Protestants can't reach the nearest church (%)	Number of Protestants in the area
Changsha	350.5395	36.18	63.82	3,442
Taiyuan	923.2529	65.21	34.79	10,134
Nanchang	75.44191	88.76	11.24	17,540
Harbin	4,620.649	99.42	0.58	63,940
Changchun	3,601.888	124.16	0.00	40,287
Hefei	774.0141	106.50	0.00	81,924
Wuhan	860.9509	304.36	0.00	65,230
Zhengzhou	1,102.777	108.51	0.00	135,929

Sources: Compiled from Pew Research Center, "Report 1: Religious Affiliation," *Pew Research Center's Religion & Public Life Project, 2010,* retrieved from https://www.pewresearch.org/topic/religion/; Research Project Team, *The Survey Report on China's Christians, Annual Report on China's Religions (2010),* edited by Jin Ze and Qiu Yonghui, Beijing: Shehui kexue wenxian chubanshe, pp. 190–212; China Census Bureau, *The 2004 China's Economic Census Data with GIS Maps.* (Beijing: All China Market Research Co., LTD, 2004); China Data Institute, *China Geo-Explore,* 2012, retrieved from: https://www.chinageoexplorer.com/cge/; The Boya Diming Website, 2005, retrieved from http://www.tcmap.com.cn/.

7.6 Spatial church accessibility in Western China

Expanding beyond east and Central China, it is vital to encompass 12 provinces and municipalities in Western China: Yunnan, Chongqing, Shaanxi, Sichuan, Gansu, Guizhou, Xinjiang, Inner Mongolia (Neimenggu), Ningxia, Qinghai, Guangxi, and Tibet (Xizang). However, it's worth noting that our project does not encompass Tibet and Yinchuan, as we were unable to obtain any church-related information from official data sources. Fortunately, through the use of GIS, the 2SFCA method allows us to evaluate church accessibility in ten other cities in Western China.

Table 7.5 provides a straightforward depiction of the church shortage scenario in Western China. Notably, it highlights that in Chengdu, Kunming, Nanning, Huhhot, Urumqi, and Chongqing, a portion of the Protestant population must endure travel times exceeding 30 minutes to reach their nearest churches. Consequently, these six cities can be classified as areas with low accessibility scores and a significant church shortage, as indicated by the 2SFCA method.

Similarly, it is imperative to assess church accessibility in Western China using the NAM methodology to verify its alignment with the findings obtained from the 2SFCA. Employing the same research approach, the NAM enables the determination of the percentage of Protestants who are unable to reach their nearest church within a 30-minute one-way drive or within a distance of 12 km (as detailed in Table 7.6).

Table 7.5 Church Accessibility in Western China by the 2SFCA.

Provincial capital cities	Percentage of Protestants that have lower accessibility score than 1/10,000
Chengdu	100.0
Kunming	100.0
Nanning	90.8
Huhhot	84.8
Urumqi	43.6
Chongqing	37.9
Guiyang	0.0
Lanzhou	0.0
Xi'an	0.0
Xining	0.0
Lasa	N/A
Yinchuan	N/A

Sources: Compiled from Pew Research Center, "Report 1: Religious Affiliation," *Pew Research Center's Religion & Public Life Project, 2010*, retrieved from https://www.pewresearch.org/topic/religion/; Research Project Team, *The Survey Report on China's Christians, Annual Report on China's Religions (2010)*, edited by Jin Ze and Qiu Yonghui, Beijing: Shehui kexue wenxian chubanshe, pp. 190–212; China Census Bureau, *The 2004 China's Economic Census Data with GIS Maps*. (Beijing: All China Market Research Co., LTD, 2004); China Data Institute, *China Geo-Explore*, 2012, retrieved from: https://www.chinageoexplorer.com/cge/; The Boya Diming Website, 2005, retrieved from http://www.tcmap.com.cn/.

Table 7.6 Church Accessibility in Western China by the NAM (30 Minutes).

12 km (30 minutes)	Accumulated area (km²)	Protestants and area coverage (%)	Protestants can't reach the nearest church (%)	Number of Protestants in the area
Nanning	330.5973	20.37	79.63	1,292
Kunming	501.8277	23.13	76.87	14,398
Huhhot	697.2991	33.19	66.81	2,623
Chongqing	1,183.309	82.40	17.60	251,322
Chengdu	466.7656	110.87	0.00	29,266
Guiyang	466.7656	154.09	0.00	22,981
Lanzhou	1,383.937	196.86	0.00	22,981
Urumqi	1,150.604	138.96	0.00	22,981
Xi'an	557.8924	613.07	0.00	65,570
Xining	633.3008	130.07	0.00	65,570
Lasa	N/A	N/A	N/A	N/A
Yinchuan	N/A	N/A	N/A	N/A

Sources: Compiled from Pew Research Center, "Report 1: Religious Affiliation," *Pew Research Center's Religion & Public Life Project, 2010*, retrieved from https://www.pewresearch.org/topic/religion/; Research Project Team, *The Survey Report on China's Christians, Annual Report on China's Religions (2010)*, edited by Jin Ze and Qiu Yonghui, Beijing: Shehui kexue wenxian chubanshe, pp. 190–212; China Census Bureau, *The 2004 China's Economic Census Data with GIS Maps*. (Beijing: All China Market Research Co., LTD, 2004); China Data Institute, *China Geo-Explore*, 2012, retrieved from: https://www.chinageoexplorer.com/cge/; The Boya Diming Website, 2005, retrieved from http://www.tcmap.com.cn/.

In line with the results from the NAM analysis presented in Table 7.6, it becomes evident that Nanning, Kunming, Huhhot, and Chongqing can be identified as regions grappling with church shortages. This conclusion arises from the fact that a significant proportion, ranging from 18% to 80%, of Protestants in these four cities are unable to access their nearest churches within a 30-minute drive from their residential locations.

Evidently, both the NAM and the 2SFCA methodologies are in agreement when it comes to identifying Nanning, Kunming, Huhhot, and Chongqing as regions facing a church shortage. However, the 2SFCA analysis underscores Chengdu and Urumqi as places with limited church accessibility.

To paint a comprehensive national picture of the shortage of Protestant churches and church accessibility across the 31 provincial capital cities in China, it is crucial to consolidate and compare the outcomes obtained through the NAM and the 2SFCA methods (see Table 7.7). In general, both methods concur that the following ten provincial capital cities should be designated as regions experiencing church shortages: Haikou, Beijing, and Jinan in the east; Changsha, Taiyuan, and Harbin in the central region; and Nanning, Kunming, Huhhot, and Chongqing in the west. However, they diverge in their assessments of several other cities within these three regions. While the NAM designates Nanchang as an area with limited church accessibility, the 2SFCA method classifies an additional ten cities as regions with church shortages.

To provide an overarching perspective on the average percentages of Protestants unable to reach their nearest church within 30 minutes, column 4 in Table 7.7 combines the average percentages calculated by both the NAM and the 2SFCA

80 Multi-Methods Research Design

Table 7.7 Provincial Capital Cities with the Shortage of Protestant Church in China.

Name of city	Percentage of Protestants can't reach the nearest church: NAM	Percentage of Protestants can't reach the nearest church: 2SFCA	Average percentages and rankings (%)
1. Haikou	93.47	94.8	94.14
2. Kunming	76.87	100	88.44
3. Nanning	79.63	90.8	85.22
4. Huhhot	66.81	84.8	75.8
5. Beijing	39.39	83.8	61.60
6. Changsha	63.82	44.6	54.2
7. Jinan	28.24	73.7	50.97
8. Harbin	0.58	76.9	38.74
9. Chongqing	17.6	37.9	27.75
10. Taiyuan	34.79	15.8	25.3

Sources: Compiled from Pew Research Center, "Report 1: Religious Affiliation," *Pew Research Center's Religion & Public Life Project, 2010*, retrieved from https://www.pewresearch.org/topic/religion/; Research Project Team, *The Survey Report on China's Christians, Annual Report on China's Religions (2010)*, edited by Jin Ze and Qiu Yonghui, Beijing: Shehui kexue wenxian chubanshe, pp. 190–212; China Census Bureau, *The 2004 China's Economic Census Data with GIS Maps*. (Beijing: All China Market Research Co., LTD, 2004); China Data Institute, *China Geo-Explore*, 2012, retrieved from: https://www.chinageoexplorer.com/cge/; The Boya Diming Website, 2005, retrieved from http://www.tcmap.com.cn/.

and ranks them accordingly. As a result, among the ten cities facing a church shortage in China, Haikou exhibits the lowest church accessibility, with the highest percentage of Protestants needing over 30 minutes to reach their nearest churches (94.15%). In contrast, Taiyuan has the relatively lowest percentage of Protestants (25.3%) requiring more than 30 minutes of travel to attend church services.

7.7 Conclusion: Comparative analysis of two spatial methods

Leveraging GIS, our study represents an innovative approach that harnesses both the 2SFCA and the NAM methodologies to address issues related to Protestant church accessibility, church shortages, and the religious landscape in China. Our research has demonstrated the advantage of combining these methods, highlighting that the synergy of both approaches enhances the spatial analysis of religious phenomena.

A pivotal distinction between these two methods lies in their reliance on different types of maps. The NAM relies on spatial street maps, whereas the 2SFCA employs district maps that are often segmented into several small districts instead of detailed street-level granularity. This difference impacts measurement accuracy significantly.

It's important to highlight that while the 2SFCA method may exhibit some minor accuracy limitations compared to the NAM, this drawback can be substantially mitigated by utilizing more detailed district maps. Both methodologies prove valuable for investigating church shortages and religious market dynamics; however, the 2SFCA stands out for its ability to compute accessibility scores for smaller geographic areas, providing nuanced insights into varying levels of church accessibility within a given region. Nevertheless, it's essential to acknowledge that due to the incomplete district maps and spatial data available in China, applying the 2SFCA method for a precise assessment of church accessibility based on accurate and comprehensive district maps is currently challenging, if not unfeasible.

Consequently, employing both methods to examine the same research topic can yield complementary effects and added value based on their convergent and divergent findings. On one hand, their shared conclusions bolster each other's credibility, providing a solid foundation for studying church shortages in China. On the other hand, their differing findings spark further in-depth exploration and may even inspire the development of new research methods that leverage the strengths of each approach.

In summary, while theory-driven and qualitative research on Chinese religious markets remains crucial, innovative research methodologies supported by qualitative analysis play a vital role in enhancing the quality of religious studies. Clearly, alongside spatial investigations of Chinese Protestantism, it is imperative to integrate conventional research methods such as surveys, interviews, observations, and statistics. Given the intricate nature of religious studies, interdisciplinary approaches are necessary to deepen our comprehension of religion and society in China, as well as in other regions around the world.

Note

1 With the publisher's permission, segments of this chapter are excerpted from the article authored by Zhaohui Hong and co-authored by his graduate student, Jiamin Yan, "Mapping Accessibility and Shortage of the Protestant Church in China: Applying Two Spatial Research Methods," *Asian Journal of Social Sciences and Management Studies*, 2 (1) (2015):1–16. Mr. Yan has granted permission and provided written consent to exclude his name as co-author of this book. The original work has been significantly revised and updated for this book.

References

The Amity Foundation. 2004. How Many Sheep Are There in the Chinese Flock? *Amity News Services*.
The Boya Diming Website. 2005. Retrieved from http://www.tcmap.com.cn/
China Census Bureau. 2004. *The 2004 China's Economic Census Data with GIS Maps*. Beijing: All China Market Research Co., LTD.
China Data Institute. 2008. *Atlas of Religions in China*. Retrieved from: https://chinadatacenter.net/Data/ServiceContent.aspx?id=1573
China Data Institute. 2012. *China Geo-Explore*. Retrieved from: https://www.chinageoexplorer.com/cge/
Hong, Z., and J. Yan. 2015. "Mapping Accessibility and Shortage of the Protestant Church in China: Applying Two Spatial Research Methods," *Asian Journal of Social Science and Management Studies*, 2 (1):8–22.
Luo, W., and F. Wang. 2003a. "Spatial Accessibility to Primary Care and Physician Shortage Area Designation: A Case Study in Illinois with GIS Approaches," *Geographic Information Systems and Health Applications*, R. Skinner and O. Khan, eds., pp. 260–278. Hershey, PA: Idea Group Publishing.

Luo, W., and F. Wang. 2003b. "Measures of Spatial Accessibility to Healthcare in a GIS Environment: Synthesis and a Case Study in Chicago Region," *Environment and Planning B: Planning and Design*, 30 (6):865–884.

Pew Research Center. 2010. "Report 1: Religious Affiliation," *Pew Research Center's Religion & Public Life Project*. Retrieved from https://www.pewresearch.org/topic/religion/

Radke, J., and L. Mu. 2000. "Spatial Decomposition, Modeling and Mapping Service Regions to Predict Access to Social Programs," *Geographic Information Sciences*, 6 (2):105–112.

Research Project Team of the Institute of World Religious Studies in the Chinese Academy of Social Sciences. 2010. "The Survey Report on China's Christians," Annual Report on China's Religions (2010), J. Ze and Q. Yonghui, eds., pp. 190–212. Beijing: Shehui kexue wenxian chubanshe.

Wang, F., and W. Luo. 2005. "Assessing Spatial and Nonspatial Factors for Healthcare Access: Towards an Integrated Approach to Defining Health Professional Shortage Areas," *Health & Place*, 11:131–146.

Ying, F.t. 2009. "The Regional Development of Protestant Christianity in China: 1918, 1949 and 2004," *The China Review*, 9 (2):63–97.

8 The Evolution of Buddhist Temples[1]

8.1 Introduction

Chapters 2–7 have primarily centered on the Protestant churches, serving as the foundational framework for the research methodology applied to four other non-Protestant religions in China: Buddhism, Catholicism, Daoism, and Islam. This particular chapter delves into the exploration of Buddhism, the predominant religion in China, which has undergone remarkable growth since 1911.

Over the past century, Chinese Buddhism has witnessed six significant historical phases that have shaped its development. The first phase occurred from 1911 to 1949 during the Republic of China's rule, characterized by impressive and stable temple growth. The subsequent phase, from 1949 to 1966, coincided with the Communist Party's governance, leading to tight regulation of all religious activities, including Buddhism. The Chinese Cultural Revolution (1966–1976), the third phase, marked nationwide anti-religious persecutions aimed at purifying ideological beliefs. In 1978, Deng Xiaoping initiated economic reforms, leading to a resurgence of religious interest. Deng's 1992 southern tour further boosted market-oriented reforms, fostering temple construction. Finally, this study extends up to 2004, when the availability of government religious data ended, marking the conclusion of its timeline.

Studying Buddhist temples provides essential insights into understanding the supply side of the Chinese Buddhist market, offering a unique perspective. While data on Chinese Buddhists or the market's demand side over the past century is lacking, changes in Buddhist temple supply offer clues regarding the fluctuation of Buddhist demand, following market theory. Temples hold profound significance for Buddhists, serving as holy sites for worship and financial contributions. The Buddhist market has also mirrored China's political and socioeconomic transitions over the past century.

8.2 Data and methodology

This chapter primarily relies on official data released by the China Census Bureau, specifically *the 2004 China's Economic Census Data with GIS Maps* (China Census Bureau, 2004). Supported by the Henry Luce Foundation, a research team

84 *The Evolution of Buddhist Temples*

from Purdue University and the University of Michigan developed the *Atlas of Religions in China* (China Data Institute, 2008) and *China Geo-Explore* (China Data Institute, 2012), the online spatial information explorer that contains spatial data on religious sites for five major religions in China. This official data provides information on Buddhist temples from 210 to 2004, including details at various administrative levels, such as township, county, city, and province.

In addition to this comprehensive dataset, the chapter draws upon supplementary data sources, including the 2000 China census for population data, official urbanization and urban population ratio data, official GDP and GDP per capita statistics, data on the number of Chinese universities and colleges, and empirical research on famous Chinese Buddhist mountains conducted by the author. While official data may have limitations in accuracy and completeness, this study does not challenge its authenticity. Instead, it employs official data to discern the general trends and patterns in Chinese Buddhist temple development since 1911.

The methodology combines spatial analysis, statistical examination, correlation coefficient calculations, and a bottom-up research approach to explore the evolution of Buddhist temples. It begins with a case study of four renowned Buddhist holy mountains and expands to regional and national examinations. Additionally, the chapter uses comparative perspectives to explore differences and similarities between Buddhist temples, other religious sites, and socioeconomic factors.

8.3 Case studies of the four famous Buddhist mountain areas

To gain a comprehensive understanding of the development of Buddhist temples in China, this study adopts a bottom-up research method. It starts by investigating individual cases, cities, and regions before summarizing national patterns. The chapter reflects the four famous Buddhist Mountains in China as representative cases, each having a significant impact on Chinese Buddhism: (1) Mount Wutai in Xinzhou City of Shanxi province; (2) Mount Emei in Leshan City of Sichuan province; (3) Mount Putuo in Zhoushan City of Zhejiang province; and (4) Mount Jiuhua in Chizhou City of Anhui province. Serving as the critical hubs of Chinese Buddhism, these four sacred Buddhist mountains wield significant influence in enhancing the prominence of Buddhist sites within their respective regions (China Data Institute, 2012).

The locations of Buddhist temples in Xinzhou City have experienced gradual expansion since 1911 when the city had only 16 temples. Between 1911 and 1949, the number of temples increased by 69% (from 16 to 27). However, temple growth slowed from 1949 to 1978, with only a 15% increase (from 27 to 31). The most significant changes occurred between 1978 and 2004 when the number of temples surged by 255% (from 31 to 110) (refer to Table 8.1).

Consequently, it is crucial to make statistical comparisons of the varying numbers and growth rates of Buddhist sites. As shown in Table 8.1, concerning the number of temples, Mount Jiuhua and Chizhou City held the highest rank with 138 temples in 2004, while Mount Emei and Leshan City were ranked the lowest with 38 temples in 2004. However, when considering the growth rate from 1966 to 2004, Mount Putuo

Table 8.1 Evolution of the Number of Buddhist Temples in the Four Cities Surrounding the Four Famous Mountains (1911–2004).

City	Year 1911	1949	1966	1978	1992	2004
Xinzhou City (Mount Wutai)	16	27	30	31	87	110
Chizhou City (Mount Jiuhua)	43	69	72	74	101	133
Leshan City (Mount Emei)	N/A	N/A	11	11	14	38
Zhoushan City (Mount Putuo)	N/A	N/A	2	3	59	121

Sources: Compiled from China Census Bureau, *The 2004 China's Economic Census Data with GIS Maps* (Beijing: All China Market Research Co., LTD, 2004); China Data Institute, *China Geo-Explore*, 2012, retrieved from: https://www.chinageoexplorer.com/cge/; China Data Institute, *Atlas of Religions in China*, 2008, retrieved from: https://chinadatacenter.net/Data/ServiceContent.aspx?id=1573.

and Zhoushan City exhibited the fastest growth rate at 59.5 times (from 2 to 121 temples). Meanwhile, Mount Wutai and Xinzhou City, Mount Emei and Leshan City, and Mount Jiuhua and Chizhou City increased by 2.67 times, 2.45 times, and 85%, respectively, during the same period (refer to Table 8.1).

As seen in Figure 8.1, the Buddhist temples in Mount Putuo and Zhoushan City experienced significant growth from 1978 to 2004. This expansion can be attributed in part to their proximity to the east coast and Shanghai, China's largest city, while the other three Buddhist Mountains are situated in either Central (Mount

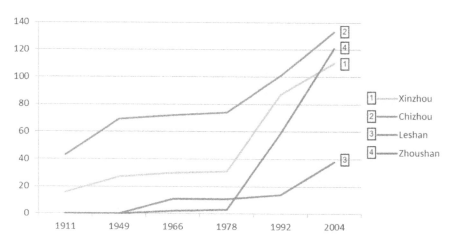

Figure 8.1 Evolution of Buddhist Temples in the Four Cities Surrounding the Four Famous Mountains (1911–2004).

Sources: Compiled from China Census Bureau, *The 2004 China's Economic Census Data with GIS Maps* (Beijing: All China Market Research Co., LTD, 2004); China Data Institute, *China Geo-Explore*, 2012, retrieved from: https://www.chinageoexplorer.com/cge/; China Data Institute, *Atlas of Religions in China*, 2008, retrieved from: https://chinadatacenter.net/Data/ServiceContent.aspx?id=1573.

Wutai and Mount Jiuhua) or Western China (Mount Emei). This favorable location on the East Coast not only attracted support from affluent Chinese entrepreneurs for temple construction but also made it a focal point for regular worship by overseas Chinese and Japanese Buddhists (Darian, 1977; Daniels, 1998; He, 2007).

Additionally, as part of Zhejiang Province, Zhoushan City is one of China's economically developed regions, with both high GDP and GDP per capita, ranking among the highest in the country (Zhejiang Statistic Bureau, 2013). Clearly, local economic development plays a crucial role in fostering the growth of Buddhist temples. Notably, the local government actively encourages and even subsidizes temple construction, while discouraging and prohibiting the construction of Christian churches (Harris, 1999; Ashiwa and Wank, 2006; Fisher, 2008).

However, as revealed in Table 8.2, the four Buddhist Mountain areas exhibited similar trends. First, the years between 1966 and 1978 marked a challenging period for Buddhist temple construction. It's noteworthy that despite the closure of numerous temples by the Red Guard during the Cultural Revolution and extensive damage to the interiors of these temples (1966–1978), all four Mountain areas maintained a relatively stagnant growth rate because the physical structures of the temples still stood and remained visible (FitzGerald, 1967; Welch, 1969; Kieschnick, 2003). Second, the period from 1978 to 1992 witnessed the most significant growth in Buddhist temples, mainly due to Deng Xiaoping's reforms that encouraged the development of Buddhism (Lancashire, 1977; Kulessa, 1990; Jing, 2006). Consequently, Buddhist temples in Zhoushan, Xinzhou, Chizhou, and Leshan cities experienced growth rates of 1,870%, 180%, 36%, and 27%, respectively. Third, after 1992, the ongoing momentum of Chinese economic development continued to stimulate temple construction until 2004. During the period from 1992 to 2004, the growth rate in Zhoushan was 105%, 26% in Xinzhou, 32% in Chizhou, and 171% in Leshan. While Zhoushan and Xinzhou exhibited slower growth compared to the 1978–1992 period, both Chizhou and Leshan continued to experience dynamic development (see Table 8.2).

Table 8.2 Growth Rates of Buddhist Temples in the Four Cities from 1978 to 2004.

City	1978–1992 (%)	1992–2004 (%)
Zhoushan	1,870	105
Xinzhou	180	26
Chizhou	36	32
Leshan	27	171

Sources: Compiled from China Census Bureau, *The 2004 China's Economic Census Data with GIS Maps* (Beijing: All China Market Research Co., LTD, 2004); China Data Institute, *China Geo-Explore*, 2012, retrieved from: https://www.chinageoexplorer.com/cge/; China Data Institute, *Atlas of Religions in China*, 2008, retrieved from: https://chinadatacenter.net/Data/ServiceContent.aspx?id=1573.

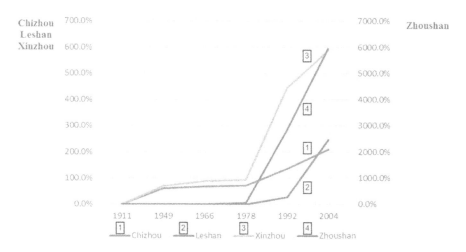

Figure 8.2 Trends in the Growth Rates of Buddhist Temples in Zhoushan, Xinzhou, Chizhou, and Leshan Cities (1911–2004).

Sources: Compiled from China Census Bureau, *The 2004 China's Economic Census Data with GIS Maps* (Beijing: All China Market Research Co., LTD, 2004); China Data Institute, *China Geo-Explore*, 2012, retrieved from: https://www.chinageoexplorer.com/cge/; China Data Institute, *Atlas of Religions in China*, 2008, retrieved from: https://chinadatacenter.net/Data/ServiceContent.aspx?id=1573.

Temple construction exhibited continuous and dynamic growth until 2004. As depicted in Figure 8.2, the growth rates of temples in Chizhou and Xinzhou span from 1911 to 2004, while those in Leshan and Zhoushan only cover the period from 1966 to 2004. This limitation arises from the availability of incomplete data, which resulted in less accurate representations.

8.4 Evolving patterns of Buddhist Temples at regional and national levels

The case studies of the four renowned Buddhist Mountain areas have yielded valuable insights into changing trends and trajectories since 1911. The next logical step is to examine the regional and national developments of Chinese Buddhist temples, along with the supply-side dynamics of the Buddhist market.

Before delving into the national characteristics of Buddhist temples, it's crucial to explore the regional landscape of Buddhism. As per the current administrative divisions of the Chinese government, mainland China is divided into three major regions: Eastern China (comprising 11 provinces), Central China (with 8 provinces), and Western China (encompassing 12 provinces), making a total of 31 provinces and municipalities. The presence of the four famous Buddhist Mountains spanning all three regions allows us to comprehensively represent regional Buddhist development.

In addition to the visual representation of Buddhist temples, Table 8.3 presents statistical data on the changing temple counts across the three regions. Remarkably,

Table 8.3 Number of Buddhist Temples in Eastern, Central, and Western China (1911–2004).

Year / Region	1911	1949	1966	1978	1992	2004	Growth rate (1911–2004) (%)
Eastern China	489	835	1,153	1,413	3,171	7,243	1,381.2
Central China	118	301	450	611	1,783	3,969	3,263.6
Western China	1,043	1,221	1,429	1,571	3,670	5,464	423.9

Sources: Compiled from China Census Bureau, *The 2004 China's Economic Census Data with GIS Maps* (Beijing: All China Market Research Co., LTD, 2004); China Data Institute, *China Geo-Explore*, 2012, retrieved from: https://www.chinageoexplorer.com/cge/; China Data Institute, *Atlas of Religions in China*, 2008, retrieved from: https://chinadatacenter.net/Data/ServiceContent.aspx?id=1573.

in 2004, Eastern China boasted the highest number of Buddhist temples, reaching 7,243. However, Central China experienced the most substantial growth rate, expanding by a remarkable 32.63 times from 1911 to 2004. This suggests that the demand in the Buddhist market in Eastern China was notably strong, likely propelled by its advanced economic development, which stimulated both demand and support for Buddhist temple construction, particularly after 1992.

In terms of temple numbers, Western China consistently held the top position in 1911, 1949, 1966, 1978, and 1992, with the exception of the year 2004 (see Table 8.3). This indicates that local economic development, increased wealth, and attractive tourist destinations played a significant role in promoting temple construction, particularly after 1992 when Deng Xiaoping's southern tour reignited economic reform dynamics in the region (Uprety, 1996; Birnbaum, 2003; Jing, 2006; Obadia, 2011). However, the rapid growth of temples in the Central region (almost 32 times from 1911 to 2004) (see Table 8.3) may be attributed to the presence of two of the four famous Buddhist Mountains in this area (Anhui and Shanxi provinces). This factor likely contributed to the influential and stimulating effects on temple construction in Central China, particularly between 1978 and 2004 when the growth rate of Buddhist temples surged to 5.5 times, while Eastern China increased by 4.13 times during the same period. It's important to note that while the size of a temple is significant, this study lacks precise evidence regarding the size of each temple in China.

Regarding the developmental trends and momentum of Buddhist temples since 1911, Table 8.4 highlights some key findings. First, the growth of Buddhist temples remained consistently robust from 1911 to 2004, even during the challenging period of religious persecution from 1949 to 1978. This underscores a persistent demand for Buddhist temples within Chinese society. Second, the period from 1966 to 1978 (as shown in Table 8.4) recorded the lowest growth rate, indicating a negative impact of the Cultural Revolution (1966–1976) across all three regions. Third, 1978 marked a significant turning point, facilitating explosive growth in Buddhist temple construction. This surge can be attributed in large part to economic reforms and political decentralization, playing critical roles in fostering what can be termed "the Buddhist fever" since 1978. Last, 1992 represents another milestone in Buddhist temple construction, although the growth rate from 1992 to 2004 was slightly lower compared to the period from 1978 to 1992 (as indicated in Table 8.4).

Table 8.4 Growth Rate of Buddhist Temples in Eastern, Central, and Western China (1911–2004).

Region / Year	1911	1949 (%)	1966 (%)	1978 (%)	1992 (%)	2004 (%)
Eastern China	N/A	70.8	38.1	22.5	124.4	128.4
Central China	N/A	155.1	49.5	35.8	191.8	122.6
Western China	N/A	17.1	17.0	9.9	133.6	48.9

Sources: Compiled from China Census Bureau, *The 2004 China's Economic Census Data with GIS Maps* (Beijing: All China Market Research Co., LTD, 2004); China Data Institute, *China Geo-Explore*, 2012, retrieved from: https://www.chinageoexplorer.com/cge/; China Data Institute, *Atlas of Religions in China*, 2008, retrieved from: https://chinadatacenter.net/Data/ServiceContent.aspx?id=1573.

Figure 8.3 illustrates that the three regions exhibited parallel and consistent growth rates from 1911 to 1978. However, a significant shift occurred in 1978 when all regions experienced a sharp increase in Buddhist temple construction. Western China consistently held the lead in the number of temples until approximately 1995 when Eastern China surpassed the West and took the top position.

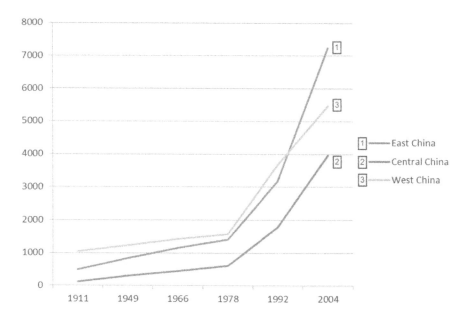

Figure 8.3 Evolution of Buddhist Temples in Eastern, Central, and Western China (1911–2004).

Sources: Compiled from China Census Bureau, *The 2004 China's Economic Census Data with GIS Maps* (Beijing: All China Market Research Co., LTD, 2004); China Data Institute, *China Geo-Explore*, 2012, retrieved from: https://www.chinageoexplorer.com/cge/; China Data Institute, *Atlas of Religions in China*, 2008, retrieved from: https://chinadatacenter.net/Data/ServiceContent.aspx?id=1573.

90 *The Evolution of Buddhist Temples*

Additionally, Figure 8.4 presents a range of noteworthy trends. Initially, 1949 marked the peak of Buddhist temple construction. The advent of the Communist government, however, triggered a sharp decline in temple growth by 1978. Subsequently, after 1992, the momentum for Buddhist temple construction began to wane across all three regions (Figure 8.4).

After examining the evolution of Buddhist temples in the four Buddhist Mountain areas and the three Chinese regions, it is essential to analyze national trends both spatially and statistically. The spatial analysis provides a visual representation of how Buddhist temples changed across the country from 1911 to 2004. It is evident that Buddhist temples gradually became more concentrated along the east coast. In contrast, the far western regions, particularly in Xinjiang, Gansu, and Qinghai provinces, have fewer temples due to the predominance of Islam as the primary religion in northwestern China.

In terms of statistical analysis, Table 8.5 provides insights into the national growth rate of Buddhist temples spanning the years 1911–2004. Notably, when comparing these growth rates with those of the three regions, it becomes evident

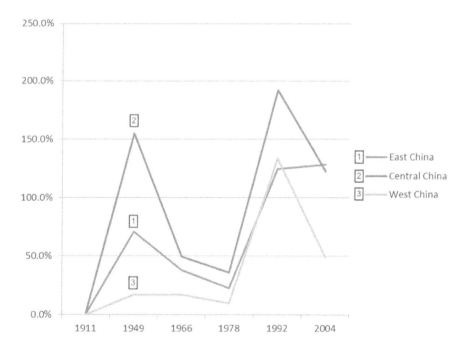

Figure 8.4 Varied Growth Rates of Buddhist Temples in Eastern, Central, and Western China (1911–2004).

Sources: Compiled from China Census Bureau, *The 2004 China's Economic Census Data with GIS Maps* (Beijing: All China Market Research Co., LTD, 2004); China Data Institute, *China Geo-Explore*, 2012, retrieved from: https://www.chinageoexplorer.com/cge/; China Data Institute, *Atlas of Religions in China*, 2008, retrieved from: https://chinadatacenter.net/Data/ServiceContent.aspx?id=1573.

Table 8.5 Number of Buddhist Temples in China (1911–2004).

Region / Year	1911	1949	1966	1978	1992	2004	Growth rate (1911–2004) (%)
China	1,650	2,357	3,032	3,595	8,624	16,676	911
Eastern China	489	835	1,153	1,413	3,171	7,243	1,381
Central China	118	301	450	611	1,783	3,969	3,264
Western China	1,043	1,221	1,429	1,571	3,670	5,464	424

Sources: Compiled from China Census Bureau, *The 2004 China's Economic Census Data with GIS Maps* (Beijing: All China Market Research Co., LTD, 2004); China Data Institute, *China Geo-Explore*, 2012, retrieved from: https://www.chinageoexplorer.com/cge/; China Data Institute, *Atlas of Religions in China*, 2008, retrieved from: https://chinadatacenter.net/Data/ServiceContent.aspx?id=1573.

that both Eastern China (1,381%) and Central China (3,264%) significantly exceeded the national average growth rate of 911%.

In an effort to assess the diverse growth rates of Buddhist temples across the four Mountain areas, the three regions, and the entire nation following Deng Xiaoping's reforms, this study has unveiled intriguing trends as illustrated in Table 8.6. To begin with, it is noteworthy that Western China witnessed a reduction in its growth rate post-1992, as compared to the periods from 1978 to 1992 and 1992 to 2004. This trend, however, does not hold for the Mount Emei area in Leshan, Sichuan, which experienced an exception to this decline. This anomaly prompts scholars to delve deeper into understanding why Leshan demonstrated exceptional growth between 1992 and 2004, underscoring the unpredictability and volatility inherent in projecting future Buddhist temple numbers solely based on past average growth rates.

Table 8.6 Comparative Growth Rates of Buddhist Temples across the Four Mountain Areas, Three Regions, and the Entire Nation (1978–2004).

Locations / Year	1978–1992 (%)	1992–2004 (%)
Zhoushan (Eastern China)	1,870	105
Xinzhou (Central China)	180	26
Chizhou (Central China)	36	32
Leshan (Western China)	27	171
Eastern China	124	128.4
Central China	192	122.6
Western China	134	48.9
China	140	93

Sources: Compiled from China Census Bureau, *The 2004 China's Economic Census Data with GIS Maps* (Beijing: All China Market Research Co., LTD, 2004); China Data Institute, *China Geo-Explore*, 2012, retrieved from: https://www.chinageoexplorer.com/cge/; China Data Institute, *Atlas of Religions in China*, 2008, retrieved from: https://chinadatacenter.net/Data/ServiceContent.aspx?id=1573.

Furthermore, Western China exhibited a growth rate of temples comparable to the national average from 1978 to 1992 (134% vs. 140%). However, this dynamic shifted between 1992 and 2004, as Western China's growth rate (49%) lagged behind the national growth rate (93%). This contrast suggests that the western region may have allocated more resources toward the construction of Islamic mosques, while other regions continued to witness a consistent supply of Buddhist temples.

8.5 Evolving correlations between Buddhist Temples, other religious sites, and economic factors

In addition to investigating the development of Buddhist temples across diverse locations and timeframes, introducing extra variables proves to be a valuable approach for gaining deeper insights into the Buddhist market and economy in China. For instance, comparing the varying growth rates of Buddhist temples with those of Protestant churches, Catholic churches, Islamic mosques, and Daoist abbeys can provide a hierarchy of Buddhist temple growth among these four major religious sites. As depicted in Table 8.7, the data reveals that the growth rate of Buddhist temples closely mirrored that of Islamic mosques from 1911 to 2004 (9.11 times vs. 8.07 times). However, Buddhist temple construction lagged significantly behind Protestant churches (124.08 times), Daoist temples (19.23 times), and Catholic churches (16.92 times).

Moreover, when examining the period of Deng Xiaoping's reform and Jiang Zemin's Era (1978–2004) in particular, Table 8.8 illustrates a consistent growth trend among Buddhist temples. During this timeframe, the Buddhist sites consistently held the fourth position among the five religious sites, both from 1978 to 1992 and from 1992 to 2004.

Nevertheless, as shown in Figure 8.5, the count of Buddhist temples consistently maintained its position in second place. Furthermore, the rankings of the number of religious sites among the five major religions have shown minimal variation over time, adhering to the following order (from highest to lowest)

Table 8.7 Comparative Growth Rates of Five Religious Sites in China (1911–2004).

Religious Sites	1911	1949	1966	1978	1992	2004	Growth rate (unit: time)
Buddhist Temple	1650	2,357	3,032	3,595	8,624	16,676	9.11
Protestant Church	116	369	635	889	5,718	14,509	124.08
Catholic Church	135	255	317	355	1,095	2,419	16.92
Islamic Mosque	3,781	9,014	11,318	14,286	29,651	34,305	8.07
Daoist Abbey	244	493	748	969	2,330	4,938	19.24

Sources: Compiled from China Census Bureau, *The 2004 China's Economic Census Data with GIS Maps* (Beijing: All China Market Research Co., LTD, 2004); China Data Institute, *China Geo-Explore*, 2012, retrieved from: https://www.chinageoexplorer.com/cge/; China Data Institute, *Atlas of Religions in China*, 2008, retrieved from: https://chinadatacenter.net/Data/ServiceContent.aspx?id=1573.

Table 8.8 Comparative Growth Rate of Religious Sites of Five Religions in China (1978–2004).

Year Locations	1978–1992 (%)	1992–2004 (%)
Protestant Church	543	154
Catholic Church	208	121
Daoist Abbey	141	112
Buddhist Temple	140	93
Islamic Mosque	108	16

Sources: Compiled from China Census Bureau, *The 2004 China's Economic Census Data with GIS Maps* (Beijing: All China Market Research Co., LTD, 2004); China Data Institute, *China Geo-Explore*, 2012, retrieved from: https://www.chinageoexplorer.com/cge/; China Data Institute, *Atlas of Religions in China*, 2008, retrieved from: https://chinadatacenter.net/Data/ServiceContent.aspx?id=1573.

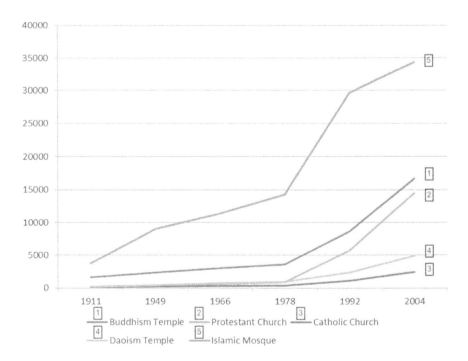

Figure 8.5 Patterns of Buddhist Temple Development in China (1911–2004).

Sources: Compiled from China Census Bureau, *The 2004 China's Economic Census Data with GIS Maps* (Beijing: All China Market Research Co., LTD, 2004); China Data Institute, *China Geo-Explore*, 2012, retrieved from: https://www.chinageoexplorer.com/cge/; China Data Institute, *Atlas of Religions in China*, 2008, retrieved from: https://chinadatacenter.net/Data/ServiceContent.aspx?id=1573.

94 *The Evolution of Buddhist Temples*

Table 8.9 Comparative Growth Rates between Buddhist Temples and Other Socioeconomic Factors (1966–2004).

Factor \ Year	1966	1978	1992	2004	Growth rates (1966–2004) (%)
Buddhist Temple	3,032	3,595	8,624	16,676	450
Total Population (100,000)	7,454	9,626	5,748	12,999	74
GDP Per Capita (RMB)	892.45	1,365.51	3,939.93	10,954.14	1,127
Higher Education School Number	434	598	1,053	1,731	299
Ratio of Urban Population (%)	17.9	17.9	27.5	41.8	134

Sources: Compiled from China Census Bureau, *The 2004 China's Economic Census Data with GIS Maps* (Beijing: All China Market Research Co., LTD, 2004); China Data Institute, *China Geo-Explore*, 2012, retrieved from: https://www.chinageoexplorer.com/cge/; China Data Institute, *Atlas of Religions in China*, 2008, retrieved from: https://chinadatacenter.net/Data/ServiceContent.aspx?id=1573.

since 1911: Islamic mosques, Buddhist temples, Protestant churches, Daoist abbeys, and the Catholic Church.

Furthermore, examining the growth rates of Buddhist temples in comparison to other social and economic factors may unveil correlations between religious and socioeconomic development. As data on certain socioeconomic subjects before 1966 is unavailable, Table 8.9 offers a comparison of growth rates between Buddhist temples, the total population, the number of universities, and GDP per capita from 1966 to 2004.

Table 8.9, presented above, conveys significant insights regarding the role of the economy and education in the development of Buddhist temples. First, it highlights the remarkable growth of Buddhist temples, which appears to be closely linked to positive trends in total population, individual income, higher education, and urbanization in China. This observation supports the theory that education and economic prosperity have a positive impact on religious development, in alignment with existing research (Street, 1992; Yazdani and Mamoon, 2012; Keister and Borelli, 2014). Second, the substantial increase in China's GDP per capita, which surged by more than 11 times from 1966 to 2004, emerges as a crucial factor driving the development of Chinese Buddhism, as well as the enthusiasm for other major religions. Evidently, economic prosperity and societal stability played vital roles in providing financial support for religious adherents and sustaining their religious activities (Chen, 2000; Lejon and Agnafors, 2011; Gill, 2013). Moreover, against the backdrop of the challenges of the Gilded Age in China, a growing number of people sought spiritual fulfillment and embraced religious pursuits (Greenfeld, 2009; Boettke, 2010). Figure 8.6 further illustrates the strikingly similar and parallel patterns of growth between Buddhist temples and GDP per capita since 1966.

Last, it's important to note that as a result of urbanization and the significant increase in the urban population from 17.9% to 41.8% between 1966 and 2004, farmers and migrant laborers faced the challenges of relocation and dislocation. Consequently, many of them sought to maintain or adapt their religious beliefs

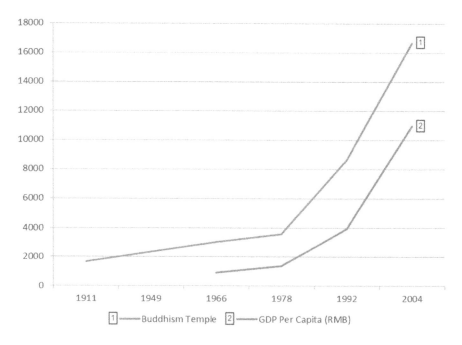

Figure 8.6 Comparative Growth of Buddhist Temples and GDP Per Capita (1966–2004).

Sources: Compiled from China Census Bureau, *The 2004 China's Economic Census Data with GIS Maps* (Beijing: All China Market Research Co., LTD, 2004); China Data Institute, *China Geo-Explore*, 2012, retrieved from: https://www.chinageoexplorer.com/cge/; China Data Institute, *Atlas of Religions in China*, 2008, retrieved from: https://chinadatacenter.net/Data/ServiceContent.aspx?id=1573.

while living in urban areas. These requests have acted as an additional driving force behind the construction of more Buddhist temples in urban regions to cater to the demand within the Buddhist market. In parallel with the growth pattern of GDP per capita, Figure 8.7 provides insight into the relationship between the growth rates of urbanization and Buddhist temples. In 1978, there was a substantial gap between the two growth rates, but this gap gradually narrowed over time, and by 2004, the growth rates of urbanization and Buddhist temples were closely aligned.

From a statistical perspective, Table 8.10 provides strong evidence of a remarkably high correlation between the growth of Buddhist temples and various social and economic factors. Notably, the most substantial correlation coefficient exists between Buddhist temples and Daoist abbeys (0.9993), suggesting a significant alignment in the supply and demand dynamics of "native religions" like Buddhism and Daoism in the religious market. As demonstrated in Table 8.8 earlier, both Buddhist and Daoist temples exhibited similar growth rates from 1978 to 1992 (140% vs. 141%) and from 1992 to 2004 (93% vs. 112%). This shared growth pattern might also account for the similarities in the regulations imposed by the Chinese government on both religions (Sherring and Longstaff, 1906; Jan, 1984; Leung, 2005).

96 *The Evolution of Buddhist Temples*

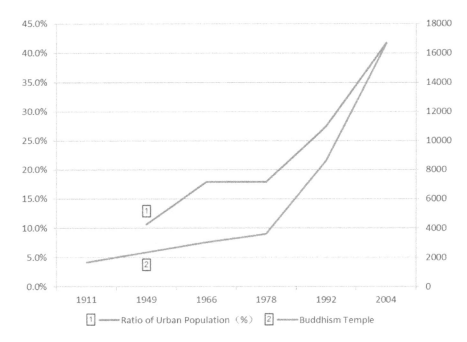

Figure 8.7 Comparative Growth of Buddhist Temples and Urbanization (1949–2004).

Sources: Compiled from China Census Bureau, *The 2004 China's Economic Census Data with GIS Maps* (Beijing: All China Market Research Co., LTD, 2004); China Data Institute, *China Geo-Explore*, 2012, retrieved from: https://www.chinageoexplorer.com/cge/; China Data Institute, *Atlas of Religions in China*, 2008, retrieved from: https://chinadatacenter.net/Data/ServiceContent.aspx?id=1573.

Table 8.10 Correlation Coefficient between Buddhist Temples and Other Religious Sites and Socioeconomic Factors.

Subjects	Number of Buddhist temples
Total Population (100,000)	0.7082
Islamic Mosque	0.9325
Ratio of Urban Population (%)	0.9817
Higher Education School Number	0.9845
GDP Per Capita (RMB)	0.9931
Protestant Church	0.9964
Catholic Church	0.9986
Taoism Temple	0.9993

Sources: Compiled from China Census Bureau, *The 2004 China's Economic Census Data with GIS Maps* (Beijing: All China Market Research Co., LTD, 2004); China Data Institute, *China Geo-Explore*, 2012, retrieved from: https://www.chinageoexplorer.com/cge/; China Data Institute, *Atlas of Religions in China*, 2008, retrieved from: https://chinadatacenter.net/Data/ServiceContent.aspx?id=1573.

8.6 Conclusion

The ebb and flow of Buddhist temples across various locations and years since 1911 have served as a crucial vantage point for gaining insights into the Chinese Buddhist market and political economy. These evolving patterns in the four Buddhist Mountain areas, China's diverse regions, and the nation as a whole warrant scholarly exploration of the intricate connections between Buddhist temples, other religious sites, and socioeconomic development.

It is undeniable that as we consider the growth of Buddhist temples from 1911 to 2004, we must also ponder whether Buddhist development encountered a bottleneck effect post-2004, potentially losing its forward momentum. In such a scenario, can external socioeconomic and political factors reignite the vitality of the Buddhist market? While commercialization and marketization have undoubtedly propelled Buddhist temple construction, can they inadvertently undermine the core principles and values of Buddhism, such as honesty, frugality, and generosity (Wright, 1957; Schumacher, 2003; Pradesh, 2012; Yu, 2013)? How should Buddhist leaders strike a balance between the quality and quantity of Buddhist affairs? How can Buddhism foster improved dialogue and collaboration with other major religions, promoting both social stability and religious freedom (Jones, 1995; Jnawali, 2009)? Clearly, these are vital areas warranting further scholarly investigation.

Note

1 With the publisher's permission, segments of this chapter are excerpted from the article authored by Zhaohui Hong and co-authored by his graduate student, Jiamin Yan, "Mapping the Development of Chinese Buddhist Temples since 1911: Statistical and Spatial Studies," *Asian Profile*, 43 (4) (2015b):369–388. Mr. Yan has granted permission and provided written consent to exclude his name as co-author of this book. The original work has been significantly revised and updated for this book.

References

Ashiwa, Y., and D.L. Wank. 2006. "The Politics of a Reviving Buddhist Temple: State, Association, and Religion in Southeast China," *The Journal of Asian Studies*, 65 (2):337–359.
Birnbaum, R. 2003. "Buddhist China at the Century's Turn," *The China Quarterly*, 174 (3):428–450.
Boettke, P.J. 2010. "Spiritual Capital and Economic Development: An Overview," *The Hidden Form of Capital: Spiritual Influences in Societal Progress*, L.B. Peter and R. Gordon, eds., pp. 29–40. New York: Anthem Press.
Chen, Y. 2000. "The Duel Effects of Religion on Social Stability," *Journal of Qinhai Ethnic College*, 26 (1):3–7.
China Census Bureau. 2004. *The 2004 China's Economic Census Data with GIS Maps*. Beijing: All China Market Research Co., LTD.
China Data Institute. 2008. *Atlas of Religions in China*. Retrieved from: https://chinadatacenter.net/Data/ServiceContent.aspx?id=1573
China Data Institute. 2012. *China Geo-Explore*. Retrieved from: https://www.chinageoexplorer.com/cge/
Daniels, P.L. 1998. "Economic Change, the Environment and Buddhism in Asia," *International Journal of Social Economics*, 25 (6/7/8):968–1004.

Darian, J.C. 1977. "Social and Economic Factors in the Rise of Buddhism," *Sociology of Religion*, 38 (3):226–238.
Fisher, G. 2008. "The Spiritual Land Rush: Merit and Morality in New Chinese Buddhist Temple Construction," *The Journal of Asian Studies*, 67 (1):143–170.
FitzGerald, C.P. 1967. "Religion and China's Cultural Revolution," *Pacific Affairs*, 40 (1/2):124–129.
Gill, A. 2013. "Religious Liberty & Economic Development: Exploring the Causal Connections," *The Review of Faith & International Affairs*, 11 (4):5–23.
Greenfeld, L. 2009. *The Spirit of Capitalism: Nationalism and Economic Growth*. Cambridge: Harvard University Press.
Harris, I., ed. 1999. *Buddhism and Politics in Twentieth-Century Asia*. London and New York: Continuum.
He, Z. 2007. "The Urban Buddhist Temple Economy and Its Expansion of Social Functions under the Institutional Transition – A Case Study in Shanghai, China," *Commercial Modernization*, 34 (2):25–28.
Jan, Y.H. 1984. "The Religious Situation and the Studies of Buddhism and Taoism in China: An Incomplete and Imbalanced Picture," *Journal of Chinese Religions*, 12 (1):37–64.
Jing, Y. 2006. *Buddhism and Economic Reform in Mainland China*. Santa Barbara, CA: Abc-Clio Press.
Jnawali, D. 2009. "Buddhism and Global Peace: Perspectives on Cultural Geography," *The Third Pole: Journal of Geography Education*, 5 (2):28–36.
Jones, K. 1995. *Buddhism and Social Action: An Exploration*. New York: Buddhist Publication Society.
Keister, L.A., and E.P. Borelli. 2014. "Religion and Wealth Mobility," *Religion and Inequality in America: Research and Theory on Religion's Role in Stratification*, L.A. Keister and D.E. Sherkat, eds., pp. 119–145. Cambridge: Cambridge University Press.
Kieschnick, J. 2003. *The Impact of Buddhism on Chinese Material Culture*. Princeton, NJ: Princeton University Press.
Kulessa, M. 1990. "Deng's Reforms 1976–1988," *From Technology Transfer to Technology Management in China*, T. Leuenberger, ed., pp. 3–13. New York: Springer.
Lancashire, D. 1977. "Buddhism in Modern China," *Religion, State and Society: The Keston Journal*, 5 (4):220–228.
Lejon, K., and M. Agnafors. 2011. "Less Religion, Better Society? On Religion, Secularity, and Prosperity in Scandinavia," *Dialog*, 50 (3):297–307.
Leung, B. 2005. "China's Religious Freedom Policy: The Art of Managing Religious Activity," *The China Quarterly*, 184 (4):894–913.
Obadia, L. 2011. "Is Buddhism Like a Hamburger? Buddhism and the Market Economy in a Globalized World," *Research in Economic Anthropology*, 31 (4):99–120.
Pradesh, U. 2012. "Buddhism and Economics: An Analysis and Reflection," *Quest International Multidisciplinary Research Journal*, 1 (2):2278–4497.
Schumacher, E.F. 2003. "Buddhist Economics," *Philosophy of Technology: The Technological Condition-An Anthology*, R. Scharff and V. Dusek, eds., pp. 510–540. New York: Wiley.
Sherring, C.A., and T.G. Longstaff. 1906. *Western Tibet and the British Borderland: The Sacred Country of Hindus and Buddhists, with an Account of the Government, Religion, and Customs of Its Peoples*. New York: E. Arnold.
Street, N.L. 1992. *In Search of Red Buddha: Higher Education in China after Mao Zedong, 1985-1990*. New York: Idea Press Books.
Uprety, P.R. 1996. "The Economics of Buddhism: An Alternative Model for Community Development," *Contributions to Nepalese Studies*, 23 (1):119–124.
Welch, H. 1969. "Buddhism since the Cultural Revolution," *The China Quarterly*, 40 (1):127–136.
Wright, A.F. 1957. "The Economic Role of Buddhism in China," *The Journal of Asian Studies*, 16 (3):408–414.

Yazdani, N., and D. Mamoon. 2012. "Economics, Education and Religion: Can Western Theories Be Generalized across Religions," *Munich Personal Repec Archive*, 2 (1):1–21.
Yu, D.S. 2013. *The Spread of Tibetan Buddhism in China: Charisma, Money, Enlightenment*. New York: Routledge.
Zhejiang Statistic Bureau. 2013. *Zhejiang tongji nianjian* (Zhejiang Statistical Yearbook, 2013). Beijing: Zhongguo tongji chubanshe.

9 Quantitative Analysis of Daoist Abbeys[1]

9.1 Introduction

Chinese Daoism, originating during the Eastern Han dynasty (AD 126–144), stands as China's sole native religion. Unlike Buddhism, which emerged in India, and Confucianism, which is an ideology rather than a religion, Daoism holds deep cultural and spiritual roots within China. Daoist abbeys, as sacred places for religious worship and cultural ceremonies led by Daoist priests, provide valuable insights into the development of Daoism in China. Therefore, this chapter endeavors to chart the evolution of Chinese Daoist abbeys from 1911 to 2004, shedding light on China's native religion, political evolution, and socioeconomic progress.

This study's focus on changing Daoist abbeys spans six pivotal years—1911, 1949, 1966, 1978, 1992, and 2004—each representing significant political and economic milestones in modern China. For example, 1911 marks the founding of the Republic of China, while 1949 marks the establishment of the People's Republic of China. In 1966, Mao's Cultural Revolution initiated extensive anti-religious campaigns, which continued until his death in 1976. Following Mao's death, China entered a political transition period, with Mao's influence persisting under President Hua Guofeng from 1976 to 1978. The critical year 1978 witnessed the launch of economic reforms and the open-door policy by Deng Xiaoping, leading to newfound religious freedom and expansive growth for Chinese religions, including Daoism. However, post-1992, with Deng Xiaoping's declining influence due to the Tiananmen incident in 1989 and his health, President Jiang Zemin took the reins of leadership, instigating the persecution of certain religious groups, such as Falun Gong in 1999, and discouraging the construction of religious sites. Although Jiang relinquished his position as President and head of the Communist Party, he remained as the Chinese military's commander-in-chief until 2004. Therefore, the study concludes with 2004 as the terminal point.

In essence, this research spans four distinct political eras in modern China: Republican China (1911–1949), Mao's China (1949–1976), Deng's China (1978–1992), and Jiang's China (1992–2004). Recognizing the relatively limited separation between church and state in Chinese society, this study emphasizes the significance of comprehending religious development within the context of political regimes and leadership dynamics.

DOI: 10.4324/9781003495451-9

9.2 Data and methodology

Our data collection heavily relied on official data published in the 2004 China Economic Census Data with GIS Maps (China Census Bureau, 2004). This data was meticulously validated and integrated into our research by our collaborative team at Purdue University and the University of Michigan. To enhance accessibility and understanding, we've visualized all data and made it accessible on the innovative *China Geo-Explore* (China Data Institute, 2012). Unless explicitly stated otherwise, all data referenced in this chapter originate from the aforementioned sources. According to official data, there were 4,938 Daoist abbeys in China in 2004. However, it's important to note that this dataset does not cover every individual city and county throughout the entire period spanning 1911–2004. Therefore, when conducting case studies, we had to select specific years for which data were available for particular cities. In addition to the primary data concerning Daoist abbeys, we also drew upon official sources such as the 2000 China Census (National Bureau of Statistics of China, 2010), data related to urbanization and urban population ratios (National Bureau of Statistics of China, 2004a), GDP per capita statistics (National Bureau of Statistics of China, 2005), and the number of Chinese universities and colleges (National Bureau of Statistics of China, 2004b).

Our research methodology predominantly employs statistical methods to calculate changing numbers, general growth rates, and average annual growth rates of Daoist abbeys, as evidenced by various tables and figures. Furthermore, we employ spatial methods to visualize the evolving locations of Daoist abbeys in different regions and periods, illustrated through a variety of maps. This comparative study is instrumental in unveiling the rankings of Daoist abbey construction in comparison to other religious sites, including Protestant churches, Buddhist abbeys, Islamic mosques, and Catholic churches.

To conduct further comparative analysis on the correlations between religious sites and socioeconomic factors, it's essential to examine relevant indicators such as population growth rates, higher education institutions, GDP per capita, and urbanization. Additionally, to comprehensively map the changing patterns of Daoist abbeys since 1911, a historical perspective was necessary. This allowed us to study the periodization of Daoist abbey development across six distinct periods. Likewise, discussions regarding the relationship between church and state and between religion and society necessitated a religious perspective to comprehend the intricate interactions between Chinese politics, society, economy, and religion over the past century. Therefore, this chapter employs interdisciplinary research methods, offering a multifaceted approach that encompasses quantitative, spatial, comparative, historical, and religious viewpoints in the study of Chinese Daoist abbeys.

9.3 Case studies on Daoist Abbeys

China boasts over a dozen renowned Daoist abbeys, each steeped in cultural and historical significance. To facilitate our case study on Daoist abbeys, we have thoughtfully selected three distinguished abbeys, each situated in a different region of China: (1) Xuanmiao Abbey, located in Suzhou City, Jiangsu province, in the eastern region (Xuanmiaoguan, 2014); (2) Wudang Abbey, situated in Shiyan City, Hubei province, in the central region (Zhu, 2006; China Wudang, 2014); and (3) Yuequan Abbey, found in Tianshui City, Gansu province, in the western region of China (Ting, 2006; Liu, 2011).

Given the absence of comprehensive data prior to 1992, our case studies for these specific areas, where famous Daoist abbeys are located, solely focus on the years 1992 and 2004. First of all, the evolving locations of Daoist abbeys in Suzhou City, home to the Xuanmiao Abbey, between 1992 and 2004, have remarkably increased from 3 to 11, with expansion in both west and northeast directions. Likewise, located in central China, Shiyan City changed the locations of Daoist abbeys surrounding the Wudang Abbey from 1992 to 2004, but it only added two more abbeys during the 12-year period. In the vicinity of the Yuquan Abbey in Tianshui City, Western China, there was a remarkable surge in Daoist abbey growth between 1992 and 2004. Positioned at the City's heart, the Yuquan Abbey played a vital role in fostering the proliferation of Daoist abbeys throughout the City, causing their numbers to double, increasing from 26 to 49 in just a span of 12 years.

Table 9.1 statistically shows the changing numbers of Daoist abbeys in the three cities in 1992 and 2004.

Although Tianshui City had the largest number of abbeys in 2004 (49), Suzhou City had the highest growth rate (267%) (see Table 9.2).

In particular, the average annual growth rate was notable in Suzhou City, where the number of Daoist abbeys increased by 11.4% on average in the years from 1992 to 2004 (see Table 9.3).

Analyzing the development of Daoist abbeys in the cities surrounding three renowned Daoist abbeys holds significant importance for gaining insights into regional and national trends in Daoist abbey expansion. The cases from these cities reveal that the growth of Daoist abbeys maintained impressive momentum, increasing in both numbers and extending in multiple directions. Notably, the prominent Daoist abbeys play a pivotal role in stimulating and facilitating the growth of

Table 9.1 Changing Number of Daoist Abbeys in the Three Cities (1992 and 2004).

Region	Year 1992	2004
Shiyan City	4	6
Suzhou City	3	11
Tianshui City	26	49

Sources: Compiled from China Census Bureau, *The 2004 China's Economic Census Data with GIS Maps* (Beijing: All China Market Research Co., LTD, 2004); China Data Institute, *China Geo-Explore*, 2012, retrieved from: https://www.chinageoexplorer.com/cge/.

Table 9.2 The Growth Rates of the Daoist Abbeys in the Three Cities from 1992 to 2004.

Region / Year	1992–2004 (%)
Shiyan City	50
Suzhou City	267
Tianshui City	88

Sources: Compiled from China Census Bureau, *The 2004 China's Economic Census Data with GIS Maps* (Beijing: All China Market Research Co., LTD, 2004); China Data Institute, *China Geo-Explore*, 2012, retrieved from: https://www.chinageoexplorer.com/cge/.

regional Daoist abbeys, acting as centers for Daoism and Daoist believers in their respective areas (Chan, 2005; Zhu, 2006; Piao and Wei, 2010).

9.4 The evolving regional and national landscape of Daoist Abbeys

Mainland China can be divided into three major regions: Eastern, Central, and Western China. There were the shifting locations of Daoist abbeys during six key historical periods (1911, 1949, 1966, 1978, 1992, and 2004). Evidently, Eastern China stands out as the region with the highest concentration of Daoist sites, boasting the largest number of abbeys and the most extensive abbeys coverage in 2004, marking it as a peak year for Daoist abbeys proliferation.

Table 9.4 provides statistical insights into the numbers and growth rates of Daoist abbeys in the three regions of China from 1911 to 2004. Eastern China consistently maintained the highest number of Daoist abbeys among the three regions in the six historical years since 1911. For instance, in 1911, Daoist abbeys in Eastern China accounted for 80% of the total national abbeys (198 out of 249). However, by 2004,

Table 9.3 The Average Annual Growth Rates in the Three Cities (1992–2004).

Region / Year	1992–2004 (%)
Shiyan City	3.4
Suzhou City	11.4
Tianshui City	5.4

Sources: Compiled from China Census Bureau, *The 2004 China's Economic Census Data with GIS Maps* (Beijing: All China Market Research Co., LTD, 2004); China Data Institute, *China Geo-Explore*, 2012, retrieved from: https://www.chinageoexplorer.com/cge/.

Table 9.4 Number of Daoist Abbeys in Eastern, Central, and Western China (1911–2004).

Region \ Year	1911	1949	1966	1978	1992	2004	Growth rate (1911–2004) (%)
Eastern China	198	369	567	704	1,369	3,143	1,487
Central China	22	62	93	131	389	875	3,877
Western China	29	62	88	134	572	920	3,072

Sources: Compiled from China Census Bureau, *The 2004 China's Economic Census Data with GIS Maps* (Beijing: All China Market Research Co., LTD, 2004); China Data Institute, *China Geo-Explore*, 2012, retrieved from: https://www.chinageoexplorer.com/cge/.

this percentage had decreased to 69% (3,143 out of 4,938), indicating a gradual expansion of Daoist abbey construction to other regions over the past century.

Meanwhile, Table 9.4 indicates that central China experienced the highest overall growth rate from 1911 to 2004, with an impressive 3,877% increase (22 abbeys in 1911 to 875 abbeys in 2004). However, as shown in Table 9.5, the growth rates varied during different historical periods. Central China exhibited the highest growth rate only during the years of Republican China (1911–1949), with a growth rate of 182%. In contrast, Eastern China had the highest abbey growth rates during the initial phase of Mao's China (1949–1966) at 54% and during Jiang's China (1992–2004) at 130%. Western China, on the other hand, saw the fastest abbey growth during the second phase of Mao's China (1966–1978) with a growth rate of 52% and during Deng's China (1978–1992) at a remarkable 327%.

Furthermore, Table 9.5 illustrates that the most rapid growth period for all three regions occurred during Deng Xiaoping's leadership (1978–1992). During this period, the eastern, central, and western regions of China experienced significant growth in Daoist abbeys, with growth rates of 94%, 197%, and 327%, respectively. Interestingly, even the tumultuous Cultural Revolution (1966–1976) did not halt the expansion of Daoist abbey construction. Instead, all three regions continued to witness significant abbey growth during this period, with growth rates of 24%, 41%, and 52%, respectively.

Another notable observation from Table 9.5 is the remarkable inconsistency in the growth of Daoist abbeys in Western China from 1978 to 2004. During the period

Table 9.5 Growth Rates of Daoist Abbeys in Eastern, Central, and Western China (1911–2004).

Region \ Year	1911	1949 (%)	1966 (%)	1978 (%)	1992 (%)	2004 (%)
Eastern China	N/A	86	54	24	94	130
Central China	N/A	182	50	41	197	125
Western China	N/A	114	42	52	327	61

Sources: Compiled from China Census Bureau, *The 2004 China's Economic Census Data with GIS Maps* (Beijing: All China Market Research Co., LTD, 2004); China Data Institute, *China Geo-Explore*, 2012, retrieved from: https://www.chinageoexplorer.com/cge/.

Quantitative Analysis of Daoist Abbeys 105

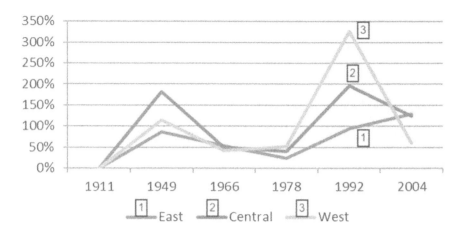

Figure 9.1 Differential Growth Rates of Daoist Abbeys in Eastern, Central, and Western China (1911–2004).

Sources: Compiled from China Census Bureau, *The 2004 China's Economic Census Data with GIS Maps* (Beijing: All China Market Research Co., LTD, 2004); China Data Institute, *China Geo-Explore*, 2012, retrieved from: https://www.chinageoexplorer.com/cge/.

from 1978 to 1992, Daoist abbeys in the western region experienced an exceptional surge, with a growth rate of 327%. However, this growth rate witnessed a significant decline, plummeting to 61% in the subsequent years from 1992 to 2004. This dramatic oscillation is vividly illustrated in Figure 9.1. To fully comprehend the underlying factors contributing to this unique trend, further qualitative and policy studies are warranted.

Furthermore, when examining the average annual growth rate, it becomes evident that Mao's China (1949–1978) experienced the lowest abbey growth across all three regions. Notably, the growth rate of abbeys during Mao's China was even lower than the average growth rate observed throughout the entire Modern China period (1911–2004), as indicated in Table 9.6. In stark contrast, both Deng's China (1978–1992) and Jiang's China (1992–2004) recorded the highest average annual growth rates.

Table 9.6 The Average Annual Growth Rate of Daoist Abbeys in the Three Regions of China (1911–2004).

Region	Year	1911–2004 (%)	1949–1978 (%)	1978–2004 (%)
East		3.02	2.25	5.92
Central		4.04	2.61	7.69
West		3.79	2.69	7.69

Sources: Compiled from China Census Bureau, *The 2004 China's Economic Census Data with GIS Maps* (Beijing: All China Market Research Co., LTD, 2004); China Data Institute, *China Geo-Explore*, 2012, retrieved from: https://www.chinageoexplorer.com/cge/.

106 *Quantitative Analysis of Daoist Abbeys*

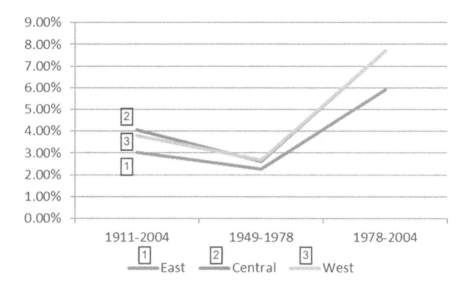

Figure 9.2 The Patterns of Average Annual Growth of Daoist Abbeys in the Three Regions of China (1911–2004).

Sources: Compiled from China Census Bureau, *The 2004 China's Economic Census Data with GIS Maps* (Beijing: All China Market Research Co., LTD, 2004); China Data Institute, *China Geo-Explore*, 2012, retrieved from: https://www.chinageoexplorer.com/cge/.

Figure 9.2 illustrates much clearer developing patterns for the growth of abbeys in the three regions, which shared similar directions of abbey construction during the same time periods.

Drawing insights from the case studies of the three cities and the three regions in China, we can derive general characteristics of Daoist abbey development across the nation from 1911 to 2004. The statistical data indicates that the overall growth rate of Daoist abbeys in the nation (1,924%) was lower than that observed in Central and Western China (3,877% and 3,072%) but higher than the growth rate in Eastern China from 1911 to 2004 (1,487%) (refer to Table 9.7).

Table 9.7 Daoist Abbey Counts in China (1911–2004).

Year Region	1911	1949	1966	1978	1992	2004	Growth rate (1911–2004) (%)
China	244	493	748	969	2,330	4,938	1,924
Eastern China	198	369	567	704	1,369	3,143	1,487
Central China	22	62	93	131	389	875	3,877
Western China	29	62	88	134	572	920	3,072

Sources: Compiled from China Census Bureau, *The 2004 China's Economic Census Data with GIS Maps* (Beijing: All China Market Research Co., LTD, 2004); China Data Institute, *China Geo-Explore*, 2012, retrieved from: https://www.chinageoexplorer.com/cge/.

Table 9.8 Comparative Growth Rates of Daoist Abbeys among the Three Cities, Three Regions, and the Entire Nation from 1978 to 2004.

Locations / Year	1978–1992 (%)	1992–2004 (%)
Eastern China	94	130
Central China	197	125
Western China	327	61
China	140	112

Sources: Compiled from China Census Bureau, *The 2004 China's Economic Census Data with GIS Maps* (Beijing: All China Market Research Co., LTD, 2004); China Data Institute, *China Geo-Explore*, 2012, retrieved from: https://www.chinageoexplorer.com/cge/.

When we examine the periods of Deng's China (1978–1992) and Jiang's China (1992–2004), except for Eastern China, all other regions and the nation as a whole showed reduced growth rates compared to Deng's China era (see Table 9.8). This suggests that the remarkable growth in Daoist abbey construction gradually lost momentum after 1992.

9.5 Evolving relationships between Daoist Abbeys, religious sites of other faiths, and socioeconomic factors

Examining the religious sites of other Chinese religions can offer valuable insights into the distinctive trends observed in Daoist abbey development. Consequently, we have analyzed the changing numbers of Protestant churches, Buddhist temples, Islamic mosques, Catholic churches, and Daoist abbeys in China from 1911 to 2004, as detailed in Table 9.9.

Table 9.9 highlights that the growth rate of Daoist sites (19.23 times) remained in the second position when compared with other religious sites from the four main religions in China during the period from 1911 to 2004. However, concerning the

Table 9.9 Comparative Growth Rates of Religious Sites for the Five Major Religions in China (1911–2004).

Religious site / Year	1911	1949	1966	1978	1992	2004	Growth rate (1911–2004) (unit: time)
Daoist Abbey	244	493	748	969	2,330	4,938	19.24
Buddhist Temple	1,650	2,357	3,032	3,595	8,624	16,676	9.11
Protestant Church	116	369	635	889	5,718	14,509	124.08
Catholic Church	135	255	317	355	1,095	2,419	16.92
Islamic Mosque	3,781	9,014	11,318	14,286	29,651	34,305	8.07

Sources: Compiled from China Census Bureau, *The 2004 China's Economic Census Data with GIS Maps* (Beijing: All China Market Research Co., LTD, 2004); China Data Institute, *China Geo-Explore*, 2012, retrieved from: https://www.chinageoexplorer.com/cge/.

108 *Quantitative Analysis of Daoist Abbeys*

Table 9.10 Comparative Growth Rate of Religious Sites for the Five Major Religions in China (1978–2004).

Locations / Year	1978–1992 (%)	1992–2004 (%)
Daoist Abbey	141	112
Protestant Church	543	154
Catholic Church	208	121
Buddhist Temple	140	93
Islamic Mosque	108	16

Sources: Compiled from China Census Bureau, *The 2004 China's Economic Census Data with GIS Maps* (Beijing: All China Market Research Co., LTD, 2004); China Data Institute, *China Geo-Explore*, 2012, retrieved from: https://www.chinageoexplorer.com/cge/.

number of religious sites, Daoist abbeys were ranked fourth (4,938) during the same period, surpassing only the count of Catholic churches (2,419).

During the periods of Deng's China and Jiang's China from 1978 to 2004, the growth of Daoist abbeys shifted from the second to the third rank in both Deng's and Jiang's China. This shift occurred because the Catholic Church curtailed the growth rate of Daoist abbeys construction after 1978. Nonetheless, both Daoist abbeys and Buddhist temples exhibited similar growth patterns, with Daoism slightly trailing behind (141% vs. 140% during Deng's China and 112% vs. 93% during Jiang's China) (refer to Table 9.10). This may suggest that as Chinese or Asian native religions, both Daoism and Buddhism experienced parallel government regulations, religious demand and supply dynamics, and financial support.

When examining the average annual growth rates of religious sites for all five major Chinese religions since 1911, Table 9.11 provides significant insights. First, regarding the average annual growth rates from 1911 to 2004, Daoist abbeys ranked second (3.29%), with a rate lower than that of Protestant churches (5.33%) and

Table 9.11 Average Annual Growth Rates of Religious Sites for the Five Religions.

Religious Sites	1911–2004 (%)	1911–1949 (%)	1949–1966 (%)	1966–1978 (%)	1978–1992 (%)	1992–2004 (%)
Daoist Abbey	3.29	1.87	2.48	2.18	6.47	6.46
Islamic Mosque	2.40	2.31	1.35	1.96	5.35	1.22
Catholic Church	3.15	1.69	1.29	0.95	8.38	6.83
Protestant Church	5.33	3.09	3.24	2.84	14.22	8.07
Buddhist Temple	2.49	0.94	1.49	1.43	6.45	5.42

Sources: Compiled from China Census Bureau, *The 2004 China's Economic Census Data with GIS Maps* (Beijing: All China Market Research Co., LTD, 2004); China Data Institute, *China Geo-Explore*, 2012, retrieved from: https://www.chinageoexplorer.com/cge/.

higher than that of Catholic churches (3.15%). Second, while the religious sites for the other four religions all experienced a decrease in their annual growth rates during Jiang's China, Daoist abbeys maintained similar growth rates between Deng's China (6.47%) and Jiang's China (6.46%). This suggests that the momentum of Daoist abbey growth remained impressive in the 21st century. Finally, when comparing the periods of Republican China (1911–1949) and the Cultural Revolution (1966–1978), some noteworthy trends emerge. On one hand, Protestant churches, Catholic churches, and Islamic mosques faced their most challenging growth periods during the Cultural Revolution. On the other hand, both Daoist abbeys and Buddhist temples experienced significantly faster growth rates during the Cultural Revolution (2.18% and 1.43%) compared to the statistics from the Republican China era (1.87% and 0.94%). This observation may spark scholarly interest in investigating whether Mao's government regulations and the religious market during the national cultural upheaval from 1966 to 1978 were more conducive to the development of these two native religions than the conditions during Republican China.

In addition to comparing the differences among religious sites for five religions, it can provide added value to explore the correlations between Daoist abbey development and other socioeconomic factors, such as population growth rates, urbanization, GDP per capita, and the presence of higher education institutions. As certain socioeconomic data are unavailable before 1966, our comparative study is focused on the period from 1966 to 2004. Table 9.12 illustrates that, from 1966 to 2004, the growth rates of Daoist abbeys exceeded those of the total population, higher education institutions, and urbanization.

Interestingly, when analyzing the average annual growth rates, Daoist abbey development closely paralleled the growth of the other four socioeconomic factors from 1966 to 2004, with one exception being the population growth (−3.62%) from 1978 to 1992, attributed to Deng Xiaoping's one-child policy initiated in 1979 (Short and Zhai, 1998; Fong, 2004; Wang, 2005) (see Table 9.12).

Table 9.12 Comparative Average Annual Growth Rates between the Religious Sites of Five Main Religions and Other Socioeconomic Factors.

Factor \ Year	1966–1978 (%)	1978–1992 (%)	1992–2004 (%)
Daoist Abbeys	2.18	6.47	6.46
Total Population (100,000)	2.15	−3.62	7.04
GDP Per Capita (RMB)	3.61	7.86	8.89
Higher Education School Number	2.71	4.12	4.23
Ratio of Urban Population	0.00	3.11	3.55

Sources: Compiled from China Census Bureau, *The 2004 China's Economic Census Data with GIS Maps* (Beijing: All China Market Research Co., LTD, 2004); China Data Institute, *China Geo-Explore*, 2012, retrieved from: https://www.chinageoexplorer.com/cge/; National Bureau of Statistics of China, 2010 *Population Census* (Beijing: National Statistic Press, 2010); National Bureau of Statistics, *The Chinese Population Statistical Yearbook (2004)* (Beijing: National Statistic Press, 2004); National Bureau of Statistic, *Education and Culture, 2004* (Beijing: All China Marketing Research Co., Ltd., 2004).

Table 9.13 The Coefficient between Daoist Abbeys and Other Religious Sites and Socioeconomic Factors.

	Number of Daoist abbeys
Total Population (100,000)	0.6646
Islamic Mosques	0.9274
Higher Education School Number	0.9940
Protestant Church	0.9955
GDP Per Capita (RMB)	0.9969
Ratio of Urban Population (%)	0.9980
Catholic Church	0.9983
Buddhist Temple	0.9990

Sources: Compiled from China Census Bureau, *The 2004 China's Economic Census Data with GIS Maps* (Beijing: All China Market Research Co., LTD, 2004); China Data Institute, *China Geo-Explore*, 2012, retrieved from: https://www.chinageoexplorer.com/cge/; National Bureau of Statistics of China, *2010 Population Census* (Beijing: National Statistic Press, 2010); National Bureau of Statistics, *The Chinese Population Statistical Yearbook (2004)* (Beijing: National Statistic Press, 2004); National Bureau of Statistic, *Education and Culture, 2004* (Beijing: All China Marketing Research Co., Ltd., 2004).

In terms of the coefficient, Table 9.13 affirms that Daoist abbey development exhibited the strongest correlation with Buddhist temple growth (0.9990) and relatively weaker connections with population growth (0.6646).

9.6 Conclusion

Mapping the evolution of Chinese Daoist abbeys since 1911 has unveiled distinctive patterns across cities surrounding famous Daoist abbeys, the three major regions encompassing 31 provinces, and the entire nation. The ebbs and flows in Daoist abbey construction since 1911 serve as markers for the political and socioeconomic milestones in Republican China, Mao's China, Deng's China, and Jiang's China. Four influential political figures, Jiang Jieshi, Mao Zedong, Deng Xiaoping, and Jiang Zemin, played pivotal roles in shaping Chinese religious policies in general, and Daoist sites in particular (Sautman, 1992; Stewart, 2001; Cabestan and Guill, 2012; Lampton, 2014). Our quantitative study indicates that while Protestant, Catholic, and Islamic sites faced substantial challenges during Mao's China, both Daoist abbeys and Buddhist temples experienced comparatively smoother growth, with higher growth rates than those during the Jiang Jieshi-led Republican China.

Recognizing the study's quantitative nature, we acknowledge the necessity of conducting qualitative inquiries to delve into the underlying factors driving the evolving trends of Daoist abbeys in modern China, as well as the roles of political leaders in shaping religious development. This research should inspire scholars to delve into empirical and theory-driven facets pertaining to the impact of Daoist abbey development on Daoism itself, religious regulations, the religious market, urbanization, economic progress, and social stability. It is clear that further efforts, encompassing both qualitative and quantitative dimensions, are warranted in the comprehensive examination of the development of the Daoist abbey in China.

Note

1 With the publisher's permission, segments of this chapter are excerpted from the article authored by Zhaohui Hong and co-authored by his graduate student, Jiamin Yan, "Quantitative Studies on the Historical Development of Chinese Daoist Abbeys since 1911," *Journal of Asia Pacific Studies*, 4 (1) (2015):33–57. Mr. Yan has granted permission and provided written consent to exclude his name as co-author of this book. The original work has been significantly revised and updated for this book.

References

Cabestan, J.P., and E. Guill. 2012. "Is Xi Jinping the Reformist Leader China Needs?" *China Perspectives*, 3 (1):69–76.
Chan, S.C. 2005. "Temple-Building and Heritage in China," *Ethnology*, 44 (1):65–79.
China Census Bureau. 2004. *The 2004 China's Economic Census Data with GIS Maps*. Beijing: All China Market Research Co., LTD.
China Data Institute. 2012. *China Geo-Explore*. Retrieved from: https://www.chinageoexplorer.com/cge/
China Wudang. 2014. *Introduction of Wudang Temple*. Retrieved from: http://www.chinawudang.com/wdjhb/wdjz.asp
Fong, V.L. 2004. *Only Hope: Coming of Age under China's One-Child Policy*. Stanford, CA: Stanford University Press.
Lampton, D.M. 2014. *Following the Leaders: Ruling China, from Deng Xiaoping to Xi Jinping*. Berkley, CA: University of California Press.
Liu, Y.X. 2011. "Origin of Historical Changes of the Fu Xi Temple and the Fu Xi City," *China Ancient City*, 6:1–8.
National Bureau of Statistics of China. 2004a. *The Chinese Population Statistical Yearbook (2004)*. Beijing: National Statistic Press.
National Bureau of Statistics of China. 2004b. *Education and Culture*. Beijing: All China Marketing Research Co., Ltd.
National Bureau of Statistics of China. 2005. Gross Domestic Product in China (2004). Beijing: National Statistic Press.
National Bureau of Statistics of China. 2010. *2010 Population Census*. Beijing: National Statistic Press.
Piao, Y.J., and P. Wei. 2010. "Study on Landscape in Taoist Temple," *Modern Landscape Architecture*, 19 (1):1–23.
Sautman, B. 1992. "Sirens of the Strongman: Neo-Authoritarianism in Recent Chinese Political Theory," *The China Quarterly*, 129 (2):72–102.
Short, S.E., and F.Y. Zhai. 1998. "Looking Locally at China's One-Child Policy," *Studies in Family Planning*, 29 (4):373–387.
Stewart, W. 2001. *Deng Xiaoping: Leader in a Changing China*. Minneapolis, MN: Twenty-First Century Books.
Ting, W.S.B.D. 2006. "The Witchcraft Idea Reflected in the Moxibustion Custom of Fuxi Sacrifices in the Tianshui Fuxi Temple," *Nationalities Research in Qinghai*, 2:1–29.
Wang, F. 2005. "Can China Afford to Continue Its One-Child Policy?" *Honolulu: East-West Center*, 77 (2):1–12.
Xuanmiaoguan. 2014. "Introduction about Xuanmiao Temple," 15 March 2014, http://www.szxmg.com (assessed on 17 July 2014).
Zhu, D.Q. 2006. "A Commemoration to the Establishing of Wudang Imperial Temples," *Journal of Yunyang Teachers College*, 4:3–14.

10 A Spatial Exploration of the Catholic Market[1]

10.1 Introduction

The Catholic market, at its core, hinges on the delicate interplay between the Catholic population's demand and the supply of Catholic churches (Iannaccone, 1991; Stark and Finke, 2000; Finke and Stark, 2005; Yang, 2006). Prevailing qualitative and conventional research leads to a resounding consensus among scholars: today's Chinese Catholic market is marked by an overwhelming demand that surpasses the available supply. Consequently, Catholic churches are facing issues of overcrowding and overpopulation (Yang, 2006, 2010). However, the scholarly discourse largely lacks virtualized, digital, and quantifiable depictions of the Catholic church shortage in China.

Enter geographic information system (GIS), an invaluable tool that equips scholars with the capability to employ geospatial and digital methods to chart the ebb and flow of the Catholic market in China. Past studies have paved the way by examining the shortage of Protestant churches in China, employing spatial, digital, statistical, and comparative lenses (Hong and Zeng, 2012; Hong, Yan and Cao, 2014; Hong and Yan, 2015a). In the spirit of continuity, this chapter extends the research paradigm to shine a spotlight on the Catholic church deficit in China. Our canvas consists of nine emblematic cities that span China's diverse regions.

This chapter dissects Catholic density by delving into the headcount of the Catholic population and the number of Catholic churches, culminating in the calculation of the average number of Catholics served by each church. Furthermore, to gauge church availability and accessibility within the selected nine cities, it is important to deploy two spatial methodologies that visualize and quantify the distances and travel times between Catholic residential areas and their nearest place of worship. Following the establishment of reasonable statistical criteria for assessing church deficits, this chapter identifies specific cities grappling with a shortage of Catholic churches in China. Our spatial research methodologies and unique perspectives are useful to illuminate new facets of understanding the religious market and religious economy.

10.2 Methodology

This chapter employs a formidable arsenal of statistical and spatial techniques to delve into the density, availability, and accessibility of Catholic churches in China's Eastern, Central, and western regions during the year 2004. Leveraging conventional

DOI: 10.4324/9781003495451-10

statistical methods, we embark on a journey to calculate the average number of Catholics per church, a pivotal metric that unveils the density of churches in each of our selected cities. Complementing this statistical approach, our spatial methodology steps onto the stage, offering visual insights into the precise locations of Catholic churches. The resulting quantitative tableau unveils the statistical data that underscores the equilibrium, or lack thereof, between church supply and Catholic demand. It's a stark reality: the fewer Catholics each church accommodates, the more pronounced the church shortage becomes. Armed with standardized measurements, we unveil the regions grappling with a scarcity of Catholic churches.

But our analysis doesn't stop at density. We venture into the domains of church availability and accessibility by estimating the distances and travel times between Catholic residential areas and their nearest parish. The longer the journey or the minutes ticking away on this pilgrimage, the more acute the church shortage looms. Enter ArcGIS 10.1, our trusty spatial tool, which empowers us to scrutinize the accessibility and availability of Catholic churches in our designated areas.

Our first spatial methodology, the Two-Step Floating Catchment Area (2SFCA), takes center stage. Its mission is to estimate driving times from Catholic residential zones to the nearest church within our nine cities. Through this method, we statistically reveal the average number of Catholic faithful who cannot reach their nearest church within the stipulated timeframe—a sobering revelation. Furthermore, to fortify and validate our findings, we introduce a second spatial technique, the Network Analysis Method (NAM), which measures both driving time and distance. The divergence between the 2SFCA and the NAM warrants attention. The former relies on a simplified approach, using straight-line distance to calculate travel time due to limited street map data in the selected nine cities. This method assumes a uniform distribution of the Catholic population across the region. While it's not without its shortcomings, it represents the second-best option given the incomplete data from the Chinese government.

In contrast, the NAM transcends these limitations by leveraging district maps instead of street maps as the primary reference. It seamlessly integrates network data, maps, and spatial information using GIS and other spatial statistical methods to provide estimates of both travel time and distance. The NAM also taps into Google Maps, considering average driving speeds and calculating starting and ending locations for randomly selected cities around the epicenter of the representative city. The outcome will demonstrate a dynamic visualization of diverse travel times (in minutes) and distances within the specified location.

In sum, the methodological arsenal pierces the heart of the Catholic church conundrum in China, shedding light on its intricacies. Equipped with these innovative spatial research tools, we illuminate hidden truths, forging new paths in the understanding of religious markets and economic development.

10.3 Data

Unearthing accurate and comprehensive data on the total Catholic population in China is a formidable challenge due to the labyrinth of disparate data sources and the conspicuous absence of religious information in China's official census records. Consequently, scholars must navigate this intricate terrain, drawing from reputable institutions and Chinese government references. For instance, the Pew Foundation's 2011 estimate posited that there were approximately 9,180,000 Catholics in China in 2010, constituting 0.7% of the overall population (Pew Research Center, 2011: 97). In contrast, the official Blue Book on Chinese religions, issued by the Chinese Academy of Social Sciences (CASS) (Wang, 2010: 98), adopted the Xinde Institute for Cultural Studies' estimate of around 5.7 million Catholics in 2009 (Xinde Institute for Cultural Studies, 2009). The Pew Research Center, in its wisdom, appended an additional 3.3 million Catholics exclusively affiliated with unregistered Catholic congregations (Pew Research Center, 2011: 98). For the purposes of this chapter, the author has opted for the conservative estimate of 5.7 million as the benchmark figure for China's Catholic population.

The complexity deepens when we delve into calculating and estimating Catholics at the city level. Surprisingly, very few institutions have conducted systematic surveys on the local Catholic populations. The exceptions to this rule are found in city yearbooks, the work of individual scholars, and scattered online information sources. In our quest to maintain regional equilibrium when selecting Catholic churches in China, this study has pinpointed three major cities in each of China's three geographical regions. In the Eastern region, we zeroed in on Shanghai, China's largest city; Fuzhou, the provincial capital of Fujian; and Wenzhou, often referred to as the "Chinese Jerusalem" in Zhejiang province. Additionally, we selected three provincial capital cities in the Central region, including Shijiazhuang in Hebei Province, Wuhan in Hubei Province, and Zhengzhou in Henan Province. In the western region, we turned our attention to three more provincial capital cities: Xi'an in Shaanxi Province, Chongqing, and Guiyang in Guizhou province. Map 10.1 offers a visual representation of the locations of these nine cities within the broader Chinese landscape.

Due to the scarcity of comprehensive data, it is unfeasible to obtain data for Catholics across all cities in the same year. Therefore, this chapter opts for years that are in proximity to the early 21st century. Table 10.1 showcases the number of Catholics in both the nation and the nine selected cities, drawing from a variety of references listed in column 4.

When it comes to tallying the number of Catholic churches in China, precision is elusive. The China Census Bureau reported 2,419 registered Catholic churches in 2004 (China Census Bureau, 2004). However, in 2010, the Blue Book on Chinese Religion suggested a count of 5,967 Catholic churches and places of worship (Wang, 2010: 98). It's crucial to note that this figure encompasses a significant number of independent and unregistered Catholic churches, lacking legal recognition and disassociated from the official Patriotic Catholic Association (Pew Research Center, 2011). Furthermore, the count of 5,967 churches is based on the year 2009, whereas the figure of 2,419 harks back to 2004 records. Consequently, this chapter adheres to the 2,419 Catholic church figures published by the China Census Bureau.

A Spatial Exploration of the Catholic Market 115

Map 10.1 Location of the Nine Cities in the Three Regions of China.
Source: Redesigned by the author.

Table 10.1 Catholic Population in China and Its Nine Cities, 2000–2010.

Location	Catholic population	Percentage of Catholic	Reference
China	5,700,000	0.44	Wang (2010: 98)
Fuzhou	63,989	3.01	Yao (2000)
Wenzhou	18,450	1.35	Wen (2002: 42–43)
Shanghai	68,704	1.11	Shanghai Statistical Bureau (2004)
Shijiazhuang	19,845	1.07	Office of Shijiazhuang Government (2002)
Chongqing	53,775	0.86	Xie (2012: 25)
Xi'an	42,728	0.83	Office of Xi'an Government (2005)
Guiyang	5,000	0.26	Guizhou Database (2000)
Wuhan	6,406	0.15	Wuhan Statistical Bureau (2000, 2005)
Zhengzhou	1,684	0.05	Zhengzhou Government (2010)

Source: See column 4 of Table 10.1.

116 *A Spatial Exploration of the Catholic Market*

Table 10.2 The Number of Catholic Churches in the United States, China, and the Nine Cities (2004).

Location	Number of Catholic churches
United States	22,095
China	2,419
Wenzhou	33
Shanghai	17
Xi'an	15
Guiyang	8
Fuzhou	7
Chongqing	7
Wuhan	6
Shijiazhuang	2
Zhengzhou	1

Sources: China Census Bureau, *The 2004 China's Economic Census Data with GIS Maps* (Beijing: All China Market Research Co., LTD., 2004).

Moreover, the China Census Bureau (2004) furnishes data on the number of Catholic congregations at the city level. Table 10.2 presents an overview of Catholic church data for both the nation and the nine selected cities in 2004. For comparative context, the table also includes information on Catholic churches in the United States.

10.4 Results and findings

To gauge the density of Catholics in our selected nine cities, it's imperative to consider both the Catholic population and the number of Catholic churches. While the size of these churches does play a role in determining the average number of Catholics they serve, accurately estimating the size of each church necessitates intensive empirical investigations—a task beyond the scope of this project. Additionally, although it may be feasible to gather information on the number of available seats in each church, accurately measuring the actual participation rate of Catholics during weekend religious services remains a challenging endeavor. Consequently, this project chooses to calculate the average density based solely on the number of Catholics and Catholic churches, without factoring in the size, seating capacity, or attendance rates of individual churches.

Table 10.3 illuminates five critical pieces of data regarding the density of Catholics in the selected nine cities, the entire nation, and the United States. As previously discussed in Table 10.1, given the constraints of available data from the same year, we've selected data from the early 21st century instead of exact same-year data. Among the nine cities, Shanghai boasts the largest Catholic population (68,700), unsurprising given its status as China's largest city. However, when we consider the percentage of Catholics in relation to the total population, Fuzhou, the capital city of Fujian province, stands out with the highest proportion of Catholics

Table 10.3 The Density of Catholics in China and Its Nine Cities, 2004.

City/nation	Number of Catholics	Percentage of Catholics	Number of Catholic churches	Average number of Catholics per church	Rankings of density
Shijiazhuang	19,800	1.07	2	9,900	11
Fuzhou	64,000	3.01	7	9,143	10
Chongqing	53,800	0.86	7	7,686	9
Shanghai	68,700	1.11	17	4,041	8
United States	64,800,000 (2005)	23.90	22,095	2,933	7
Xi'an	42,700	0.83	15	2,847	6
China	5,700,000	0.44	2,419	2,356	5
Zhengzhou	1,700	0.05	1	1,700	4
Wuhan	6,400	0.15	6	1,067	3
Guiyang	5,000	0.26	8	625	2
Wenzhou	18,500	1.35	33	561	1

Source: See column 4 of Table 10.1.

(3.01%), a figure seven times greater than the national average (0.44%). In terms of the number of Catholic churches, Wenzhou, the only non-provincial capital city among our selected nine, boasts 33 Catholic churches, nearly double the number in Shanghai (17). This can be attributed to historical legacies, its east coast location, and, notably, fewer government regulations during the Deng Xiaoping era in China (1978–1997) (Cao, 2010; Chan, 2011).

After presenting data on the Catholic population and Catholic churches, we can now ascertain the average number of Catholics per church in each location. As indicated by Table 10.3, Shijiazhuang city grapples with overcrowding, with an average of 9,900 Catholics sharing a single church. Conversely, Wenzhou city enjoys the most favorable church density rate, with 561 Catholics per church on average. This figure is more than five times better than the church density rate in the United States (2,933) and four times better than the national average in China (2,356). Last, Table 10.3 provides insights into the rankings of Catholic church density, showcasing that both China (#5) and the United States (#7) occupy middle positions among the nine Chinese cities. Remarkably, China's ranking for Catholic density surpasses that of the United States. This discrepancy may stem from the availability of different-sized churches (with larger churches in the United States) and potential underestimations of the Chinese Catholic population due to political sensitivities (Hadaway, Marler and Chaves, 1993; Potter, 2003; Morris, 2011; Hanson, 2014).

For a more illuminating comparison of Catholic densities, Figure 10.1 presents rankings of average Catholics served by each church in the nine cities, China, and the United States. Regardless of the potential incompleteness or inaccuracies in church size data, the staggering figure of approximately 5,000 Catholics per church is not just astonishing but also untenable.

Having briefly explained in the section on methodology, in an effort to address the accessibility of Catholic churches in the specific area, the 2SFCA is an effective spatial method used to measure driving time between the Catholic

118 *A Spatial Exploration of the Catholic Market*

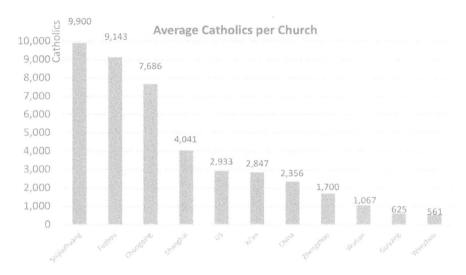

Figure 10.1 The Density of Catholics in China and the United States, 2004.
Source: See column 4 of Table 10.1.

residential areas and the closest church. The faster time represents better accessibility in which Catholic individuals are able to participate in their church services as quickly as possible.

Benefitting from GIS, spatial maps of Catholic accessibility in the selected nine cities can be visualized by the 2SFCA. The area covered by the main area in Map 10.1 shows that Catholic individuals can reach their nearest church within 30 minutes of one-way driving. In addition, the 2SFCA is setting r>1/10,000 or 0.0001 as the basic measurement of church accessibility—demonstrated by the black area—while or white area means 1/10,000>r>1/15,000 and 1/15,000>r>=0. In other words, the larger black area the better accessibility the Catholic population has. Therefore, both Shanghai and Wenzhou cities should have their best accessibility score, as they have been covered by all black area. To save the space, we selected Wenzhou as the sample (see Map 10.2).

In the meantime, Shijiazhuang and Wuhan could be considered to have relatively favorable accessibility rankings, as most of their areas exhibit a mix of both black area and white area, as demonstrated in Map 10.3. To conserve space, we've designated Shijiazhuang city with reference to Map 10.3.

Furthermore, considering that Xi'an and Chongqing cities in the western region of China are predominantly marked with white areas rather than the black area (as depicted in Map 10.4), they could be categorized as having a third-tier level of Catholic church accessibility score.

Last, the areas with the least favorable church accessibility encompass Fuzhou, Guiyang, and Zhengzhou, as a significant portion of their territories is enveloped in the white area illustrated in Map 10.5 for Guiyang city as a sample.

A Spatial Exploration of the Catholic Market   119

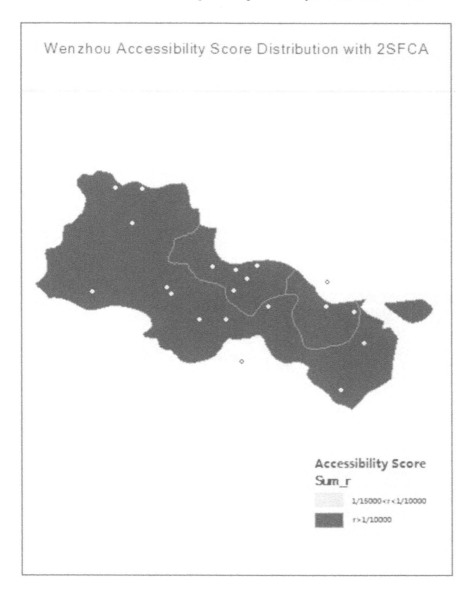

Map 10.2 The Best Areas of the Catholic Church Accessibility Scores by the 2SFCA (Wenzhou).

Sources: China Census Bureau, *The 2004 China's Economic Census Data with GIS Maps* (Beijing: All China Market Research Co., LTD., 2004).

120 *A Spatial Exploration of the Catholic Market*

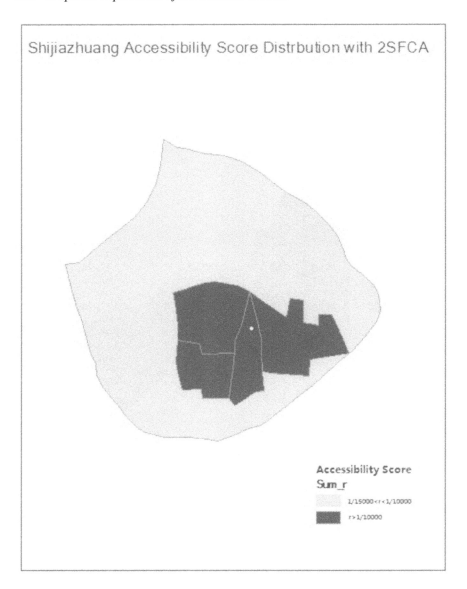

Map 10.3 The Second Best Areas of the Catholic Church Accessibility Scores by the 2SFCA (Shijiazhuang).

Sources: China Census Bureau, *The 2004 China's Economic Census Data with GIS Maps* (Beijing: All China Market Research Co., LTD., 2004).

A Spatial Exploration of the Catholic Market 121

Map 10.4 The Third Best Areas of the Catholic Church Accessibility Scores by the 2SFCA (Xi'an).

Sources: China Census Bureau, *The 2004 China's Economic Census Data with GIS Maps* (Beijing: All China Market Research Co., LTD., 2004).

122 *A Spatial Exploration of the Catholic Market*

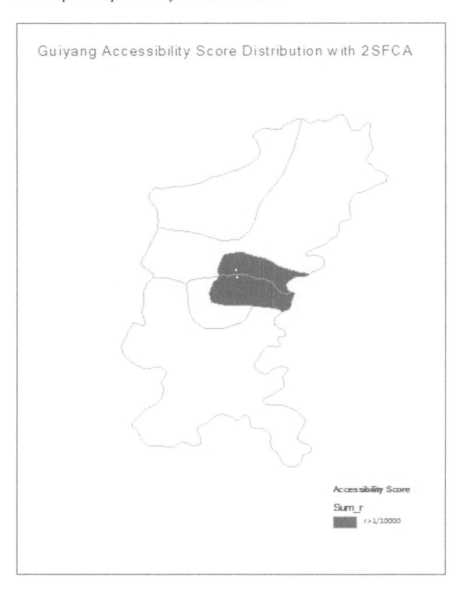

Map 10.5 The Worst Areas of the Catholic Church Accessibility Scores by the 2SFCA (Guiyang).

Sources: China Census Bureau, *The 2004 China's Economic Census Data with GIS Maps* (Beijing: All China Market Research Co., LTD., 2004).

Table 10.4 Catholic Church Accessibility in China by the 2SFCA.

Cities	Percentage of the Catholic population taking more than 30 minutes to the nearest church	Ranking
Guiyang	92	9
Zhengzhou	77	8
Fuzhou	76	7
Xi'an	55	6
Chongqing	49	5
Shijiazhuang	46	4
Wuhan	25	3
Shanghai	0.00	1
Wenzhou	0.00	1

Sources: Compiled from Xinde Institute for Cultural Studies, *Zhongguo Tianzhujiao Ziliao Tongji, 2009 Nian Yu 1948 Nian* (Statistics on Chinese Catholic Documents, 2009 and 1948), *Xinde Daily;* Pew Research Center, "Report 1: Religious Affiliation," *Pew Research Center's Religion & Public Life Project, 2010,* retrieved from https://www.pewresearch.org/topic/religion/; Research Project Team, *The Survey Report on China's Christians, Annual Report on China's Religions (2010),* edited by Jin Ze and Qiu Yonghui, Beijing: Shehui kexue wenxian chubanshe, pp. 190–212; China Census Bureau, *The 2004 China's Economic Census Data with GIS Maps* (Beijing: All China Market Research Co., LTD, 2004); China Data Institute, *China Geo-Explore,* 2012, retrieved from: https://www.chinageoexplorer.com/cge/.

Converting the aforementioned spatial insights into statistical data, Table 10.4 illustrates the varying percentages of Catholics in the nine cities who require more than 30 minutes of one-way driving to reach their nearest churches. Consequently, six cities exhibit a scenario where over 45% of Catholics cannot access their nearest church within a 30-minute drive. Conversely, both Shanghai and Wenzhou boast greater church accessibility for their Catholic communities. Wenzhou's exceptional accessibility can be attributed to the fact that only 561 Catholics, on average, share a single church—a remarkably high density of Catholic churches compared to the other eight cities in China (refer to Table 10.3). In the case of Shanghai, while its Catholic density is not particularly favorable (with 4,041 Catholics, on average, sharing one church), the presence of a modern public transportation system and well-developed facilities likely assists the densely populated Catholic community in reaching their churches swiftly.

Clearly, the statistical rankings of Catholic church accessibility align seamlessly with the spatial discoveries visualized through Maps 10.1–10.4. Wenzhou and Shanghai stand out with the top rankings and the most favorable accessibility scores, while Guiyang, Zhengzhou, and Fuzhou find themselves at the bottom of the performance list, as substantiated by the spatial maps. Combining innovative spatial methods with conventional statistical techniques adds significant value to the study of the Catholic market.

In our pursuit of validating the 2SFCA results, it becomes imperative to employ another spatial method, the NAM, to address driving distances and travel times between Catholic residential areas and the nearest church. To maintain consistency, this project establishes fixed criteria of 12 km and 30 minutes of one-way driving to gauge the average distance and driving time between these two specified points.

124 *A Spatial Exploration of the Catholic Market*

Maps 10.6–10.8 offer visual representations of driving routes to Catholic churches in the three representative cities. Here, the inner circle denotes a 15-minute driving radius, the middle circle with white color signifies a 30-minute drive, and the largest outer circle represents a 45-minute drive. Regions outside of outer circle indicate that Catholic individuals are unable to reach their nearest church within a 45-minute timeframe. Specific spots on the map mark the locations of Catholic churches (Hong and Yan, 2015a: 3). Evidently, the presence of more inner and middle circle areas within a city signifies better church accessibility and availability. Thus, as illustrated in Map 10.8, Shanghai, Fuzhou, and Wenzhou, all situated in the eastern region of China, emerge as the most favorable areas for Catholic individuals seeking quick and convenient access to their churches.

Map 10.6 The Best Areas of the Catholic Church Availability and Accessibility by the NAM (Fuzhou).

Sources: China Census Bureau, *The 2004 China's Economic Census Data with GIS Maps* (Beijing: All China Market Research Co., LTD., 2004).

A Spatial Exploration of the Catholic Market   125

Map 10.7 The Second Best Areas of the Catholic Church Availability and Accessibility by the NAM (Wuhan).

Sources: China Census Bureau, *The 2004 China's Economic Census Data with GIS Maps* (Beijing: All China Market Research Co., LTD., 2004).

As the areas with the second-best church availability and accessibility, Wuhan, Xi'an, and Shijiazhuang cities have more inner and middle areas covered (see Map 10.7 for Wuhan city as a sample).

Finally, Map 10.8 shows there are few inner and middle areas over the cities of Chongqing, Guiyang, and Zhengzhou. Chongqing city may show an example.

Table 10.5 provides the NAM statistical data regarding the accessibility and availability of Catholic churches in the nine cities. Especially, Wenzhou consistently secures the highest ranking for church accessibility in both 2SFCA and NAM, as well as church density according to the statistical method. On the other end of the spectrum, Chongqing and Shijiazhuang demonstrate persistently poor church accessibility, with 66% of Catholics in Chongqing (ranked 9 out of 9) and 54% in Shijiazhuang (ranked 6 out of 9) unable to reach their

126 *A Spatial Exploration of the Catholic Market*

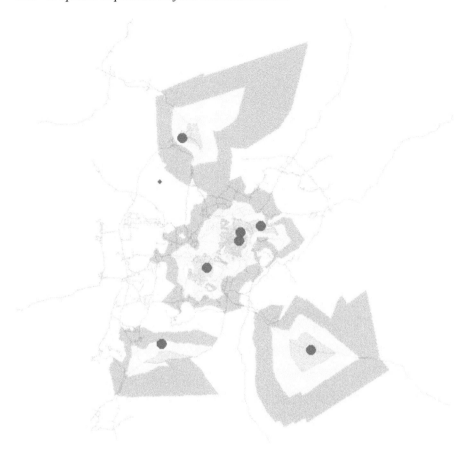

Map 10.8 The Worst Areas of the Catholic Church Availability and Accessibility by the NAM (Chongqing).

Sources: China Census Bureau, *The 2004 China's Economic Census Data with GIS Maps* (Beijing: All China Market Research Co., LTD., 2004).

nearest church. This aligns with their rankings for church density as indicated in Tables 10.3 and 10.4.

Crucially, the visualized maps presented in Maps 10.6–10.8 align seamlessly with the spatial statistics elucidated in Table 10.5. For instance, Wenzhou, Fuzhou, and Shanghai, which rank in the top three for church availability and accessibility based on statistical data, are also underscored as the most accessible areas in Map 10.8. Similarly, both the statistical data and spatial maps unanimously identify Chongqing, Zhengzhou, and Guiyang as the cities with the most pronounced deficits in terms of Catholic church availability and accessibility. The convergence of findings from spatial and statistical methods underlines the significance of integrating diverse research approaches when exploring the intricacies of the religious market in China.

Table 10.5 Catholic Church Accessibility in the Nine Cities by the NAM (30 Minutes).

12 km (30 minute)	Accumulated area (km²)	Catholic and area coverage (%)	Percentage of Catholics who can't reach the nearest church	Number of Catholics who can't reach	Ranking
Chongqing	1,280.66	34	66	35,376	9
Zhengzhou	390.67	41	59	990	8
Guiyang	490.42	44	56	2,781	7
Shijiazhuang	504.02	46	54	10,663	6
Xi'an	1,408.60	47	53	22,605	5
Wuhan	566.56	50	50	3,210	4
Shanghai	787.58	54	46	31,805	3
Fuzhou	413.32	60	40	25,615	2
Wenzhou	1,298.44	64	36	6,576	1

Sources: Compiled from Xinde Institute for Cultural Studies, *Zhongguo Tianzhujiao Ziliao Tongji, 2009 Nian Yu 1948 Nian* (Statistics on Chinese Catholic Documents, 2009 and 1948), *Xinde Daily*; Pew Research Center, "Report 1: Religious Affiliation," *Pew Research Center's Religion & Public Life Project, 2010*, retrieved from https://www.pewresearch.org/topic/religion/; Research Project Team, *The Survey Report on China's Christians, Annual Report on China's Religions (2010)*, edited by Jin Ze and Qiu Yonghui, Beijing: Shehui kexue wenxian chubanshe, pp. 190–212; China Census Bureau, *The 2004 China's Economic Census Data with GIS Maps* (Beijing: All China Market Research Co., LTD, 2004); China Data Institute, *China Geo-Explore*, 2012, retrieved from: https://www.chinageoexplorer.com/cge/.

10.5 Discussions

The examination of Catholic density, Catholic church availability, and church accessibility in the selected nine cities leads to the proposal of three viable criteria for identifying areas with shortages of Catholic churches. First, considering the average density of Catholics in China (2,356 Catholics per church) and the United States (2,933 Catholics per church), it is reasonable to designate areas where more than 5,000 Catholics, on average, share a single church as suffering from a Catholic church shortage in China. By this criterion, Shijiazhuang (Central China), Fuzhou (Eastern China), and Chongqing (Western China) would all be classified as facing church shortages. This criterion aligns with the standard used to identify Protestant church shortages in China as defined (Hong and Yan, 2015a).

Moreover, the data presented in Table 10.4 can be used to establish a second criterion for evaluating Catholic church shortages, emphasizing church accessibility via the 2SFCA method. Areas in a specific city where over 45% of Catholics are required to spend more than 30 minutes on a one-way journey or 60 minutes for a round trip to reach their nearest church should be categorized as locations experiencing church shortages. According to this second standard, in addition to Guiyang (92%), Zhengzhou (77%), and Xi'an (55%), three other cities, Fuzhou (76%), Chongqing (49%), and Shijiazhuang (46%), should be identified as areas with Catholic church shortages, mirroring the findings of the first criterion based on Catholic density. Consequently, six cities can be categorized as facing shortages of Catholic churches based on the second standard.

128 A Spatial Exploration of the Catholic Market

Table 10.6 Combined Rankings of Catholic Church Shortage in the Nine Cities.

Cities	Density rankings	Rankings by NAM	Rankings by 2SFCA	Combined rankings	Final rankings
Chongqing	7	9	5	7.0	9
Zhengzhou	4	8	8	6.7	8
Shijiazhuang	9	6	4	6.3	7
Guiyang	2	7	9	6.0	6
Fuzhou	8	2	7	5.7	5
Xi'an	5	5	6	5.3	4
Shanghai	6	3	2	3.7	3
Wuhan	3	4	3	3.3	2
Wenzhou	1	1	1	1.0	1

Sources: Compiled from Xinde Institute for Cultural Studies, *Zhongguo Tianzhujiao Ziliao Tongji, 2009 Nian Yu 1948 Nian* (Statistics on Chinese Catholic Documents, 2009 and 1948), *Xinde Daily;* Pew Research Center, "Report 1: Religious Affiliation," *Pew Research Center's Religion & Public Life Project, 2010,* retrieved from https://www.pewresearch.org/topic/religion/; Research Project Team, *The Survey Report on China's Christians, Annual Report on China's Religions (2010),* edited by Jin Ze and Qiu Yonghui, Beijing: Shehui kexue wenxian chubanshe, pp. 190–212; China Census Bureau, *The 2004 China's Economic Census Data with GIS Maps.* (Beijing: All China Market Research Co., LTD, 2004); China Data Institute, *China Geo-Explore,* 2012, retrieved from: https://www.chinageoexplorer.com/cge/.

Last, drawing from the NAM results in Table 10.5, a third criterion can be incorporated. If over 45% of Catholics in a city must travel more than 12 km and 30 minutes to reach their nearest church, that city should be categorized as an area with a church shortage. Consequently, the NAM suggests that seven cities fall into this category. Evidently, the NAM provides a more precise calculation and a stricter standard compared to the 2SFCA, given its utilization of street map data as opposed to district maps (Hong and Yan, 2015a: 14).

In summary, by averaging the rankings from the three methods assessing Catholic church density, availability, and accessibility, information about the church shortage situation can be ascertained. Table 10.6 presents the combined rankings of Catholic church shortages in the nine cities across China's three regions. Based on the three criteria used to evaluate Catholic church shortages and the combined rankings of the nine selected cities, it is pertinent to designate the top five worst cities as areas facing Catholic church shortages in China. These cities are Chongqing (west), Zhengzhou (central), Shijiazhuang (central), Guiyang (west), and Fuzhou (east). Consequently, these five cities should focus on constructing additional Catholic churches to enhance church density and accessibility, thus restoring equilibrium in the supply and demand dynamics of the Catholic market and economy.

10.6 Conclusion

This chapter has harnessed the power of three statistical and spatial methodologies to dissect Catholic church density, accessibility, and availability within the nine major cities, spanning China's three primary regions. By introducing three tangible criteria for pinpointing Catholic church shortages, this study has singled out five cities characterized by high Catholic demand but limited church supply, thereby highlighting the existence of church shortages. These criteria may serve as valuable tools for comprehending the Catholic market in other Chinese urban centers.

Undoubtedly, this spatial exploration of the religious market and church deficiencies represents a dynamic approach capable of complementing and enhancing traditional research methods, such as qualitative and empirical studies. Despite the inherent limitations of data provided by the Chinese government in terms of completeness and adequacy, the application of spatial methodologies supported by GIS stands to contribute significant value through its innovative approach and remarkable findings in the realm of religious studies, especially regarding Catholic church accessibility.

With optimism, it is anticipated that this spatial exploration of Chinese religion and society will not only inspire but also influence the national census to incorporate more detailed information on the numbers of Catholics and Catholic churches at the national, regional, and city levels. Additionally, it may catalyze efforts to create more accurate spatial street maps and district maps, a pivotal development for ensuring reliable and reputable studies that map and visualize the Catholic market and economy with precision.

Note

1 With the publishers' permission, segments of this chapter are excerpted from the articles authored by Zhaohui Hong and co-authored by his graduate student, Jianfeng Jin, "The Spatial Study of Catholic Market in China," *Asian Journal of Social Sciences and Management Studies*, 2 (3) (2015): 142–151; "The Digital and Spatial Study of Catholic Market in Urban China," *Urbanization and Party Survival in China: People vs. Power*, ed., X. Li and X. Tian, pp. 119–131. New York: Lexington Books. Mr. Jin has granted permission and provided written consent to exclude his name as co-author of this book. The original papers have been significantly revised and updated for this book.

References

Cao, N. 2010. *Constructing China's Jerusalem: Christians, Power, and Place in Contemporary Wenzhou*. Redwood City, CA: Stanford University Press.
Chan, S. H. 2011. "Rethinking the Role of the Catholic Church in Building Civil Society in Contemporary China: The Case of Wenzhou Diocese," *Annual Review of the Sociology of Religion: Religion and Politics*, 2 (2):177–193.
China Census Bureau. 2004. *The 2004 China's Economic Census Data with GIS Maps*. Beijing: All China Market Research Co., LTD.
Guizhou Database. 2000. "Records of Guiyang," Guizhou Database. Retrieve from: http://dfz.gznu.edu.cn/tpi/WebSearch/Search_DataInit.aspx?dbid=132&dbcode=Empty12
Hadaway, C. K, P. L. Marler, and M. Chaves. 1993. "What the Polls Don't Show: A Closer Look at U.S. Church Attendance," *American Sociological Review*, 58 (6):741–752.
Hanson, E. O. 2014. *The Catholic Church in World Politics*. Oxford: Princeton University Press.
Hong, Z., and J. Yan. 2015a. "Mapping Accessibility and Shortage of the Protestant Church in China: Applying Two Spatial Research Methods," *Asian Journal of Social Science and Management Studies*, 2 (1):8–22.
Hong, Z., J. Yan, and L. Cao. 2014. "Spatial and Statistical Perspectives on the Protestant Church Shortage in China: Case Studies in Hangzhou, Zhengzhou, Hefei and Fuzhou," *Journal of Third World Studies*, XXIII (Spring):30–39.

Hong, Z., and L. Zeng. 2012. "Spatial Identification of the Christian Church Shortage: A Case Study in Hangzhou City," *American Review of China Studies*, 13 (1): 17–36.

Iannaccone, L. R. 1991. "The Consequences of Religious Market Structure: Adam Smith and the Economics of Religion," *Rationality and Society*, 3 (2):156–177.

Finke, R., and R. Stark. 2005. *The Churching of America, 1776-2005. Winners and Losers in Our Religious Economy.* New Brunswick, NJ: Rutgers University Press.

Morris, C. 2011. *American Catholic: The Saints and Sinners Who Built America's Most Powerful Church.* New York: Vintage.

Shanghai Statistical Bureau. 2004. *2004 nian Shanghai tongji nianjian* (Yearbook of Shanghai 2004). Retrieve from: https://tjj.sh.gov.cn/tjnj/20170629/0014-1000190.html

Office of Shijiazhuang Government. 2002. *Shijiazhuang zongjiao gankuan* (Religion in Shijiazhuang). Retrieved from http://www.sjzdag.cn/col/1597972592569/2022/11/04/1667546496861.html

Office of Xi'an Government. 2005. *Xian nianjian* (Yearbook of Xian). Xian: Xian Publishing House.

Pew Research Center. 2011. "Global Christianity–A Report on the Size and Distribution of the World's Christian Population" (Regional Distribution of Christians: Appendix C: Methodology for China-Overview of Findings and Method). *Pew Research Center.* Retrieve from: https://www.pewresearch.org/religion/2011/12/19/global-christianity-regions/

Potter, P. B. 2003. "Belief in Control: Regulation of Religion in China," *The China Quarterly*, 174 (2):317–337.

Stark, R., and R. Finke. 2000. *Acts of Faith: Explaining the Human Side of Religion.* Berkeley, CA: University of California Press.

Wen, C. J. 2002. "The Present Catholic Diocese of Wenzhou," *Catholic Church in China*, 6 (1):42–43.

Wang, F. 2010. "Weishime Renwenxue Yu Shehui Kexue Jixu GIS" (Why Do Humanities and Social Sciences Need GIS)," *Kongjian Zonghe Renwenxue Yu Shehui Kexue Yanjiu* (Spatially Integrated Humanities and Social Science), Lin Hui, Lai Jingui and Zhou Chenghu, eds., pp. 3–16. Beijing: Kexue chubanshe.

Wuhan Statistical Bureau. 2000. "Shehui, renmin he shijian" (Social, People and Events). *Wuhan Shizhi 1980-2000.* Retrieve from: https://dfz.wuhan.gov.cn/sqgk/whsq/

Wuhan Statistical Bureau. 2005. "Wuhan zongti qingkuan" (General Information of Wuhan). *Yearbook of Wuhan 2005.* Retrieve from: https://www.cnstats.org/tjgb/201001/hbwhs-2005-lsp.html

Xie, B. Y. 2012. "Gospel Sharing in Catholic Diocese of Chongqing," *Catholic Church in China*, 16 (2):23–25.

Xinde Institute for Cultural Studies. 2009. *Zhongguo Tianzhujiao Ziliao Tongji, 2009 Nian Yu 1948 Nian* (Statistics on Chinese Catholic Documents, 2009 and 1948), *Xinde Daily*.

Yang, F. 2006. "The Red, Black, and Gray Markets of Religion in China," *The Sociological Quarterly*, 47 (1):93–122.

Yang, F. 2010. "Religion in China Under Communism: A Shortage Economy Explanation," *Journal of Church and State*, 52 (1):3–33.

Yao, W. S. 2000. *Fuzhou zongjiao jilu* (Religion Record of Fuzhou). Fujian: Fujian People's Publishing House.

Zhengzhou Government. 2010. "Zhengzhou jieshao" (Introduction of Zhengzhou). Retrieve from: https://www.zhengzhou.gov.cn/

11 Quantitative Studies on Islamic Mosques[1]

11.1 Introduction

Islam, as one of the five major religions recognized by the Chinese government, has witnessed remarkable growth, evident in the surge of mosque constructions since 1911. The Islamic mosque serves as a multifaceted institution, serving as a community hub, an educational center, and a place of worship, where Muslims rejuvenate their spirituality, strengthen their connection with their Creator, foster bonds with fellow Muslims, and reaffirm their sense of belonging (Hillenbrand, 2004; Raeisian, 2013). Therefore, comprehending the growth of Islamic mosques offers valuable insights into the development of Chinese Islam and the broader religious and societal landscape in China.

This chapter examines six vital years spanning the past century as key reference points for understanding the evolution of Islamic mosques. These years—1911, 1949, 1966, 1978, 1992, and 2004—signify crucial turning points in Chinese political history and religious development. For example, 1911 marked the establishment of the Republic of China following the abolition of the empire and dynasty. The year 1949 saw the rise of atheistic Communism with the establishment of the People's Republic of China. The Cultural Revolution, or the "Cultural Catastrophe," emerged prominently in 1966 (La Dany, 1967; Cheek, 1997). In 1978, Deng Xiaoping initiated revolutionary reforms and the open-door policy, a period during which Islamic expansion was tolerated and even encouraged. Deng's era provided a fertile ground for religious fervor in China from 1978 to 1992 (Goldman, 1986; Yahuda, 1993). However, after the Tiananmen incident of 1989, religious freedom was negatively impacted. Muslims, in particular, gradually came to be associated with violence, separatism, and disruption according to Chinese government propaganda (Hao, 1997; Zuo and Benford, 1995). Consequently, the growth rate of Islamic mosques declined in the post-Deng China era, spanning from 1992 to 2004. Since the latest official data on Islamic mosques was released in 2004, this study focuses on that year as its endpoint (Israeli, 2002; Gladney, 2003). Given the intertwined nature of state and religion in modern China, selecting significant political milestones is essential for comprehending the changing dynamics of Islamic mosque establishment since 1911.

This chapter also conducts a case study focusing on four representative cities in Xinjiang province to chart the growth of Islamic mosques since 1911. By examining

DOI: 10.4324/9781003495451-11

132 *Quantitative Studies on Islamic Mosques*

three different regions (East, Central, and West) of China, it expands its geographical scope from cities to regions and ultimately analyzes the national landscape of Islamic mosques. To comprehend the evolving patterns of mosque development, the chapter explores the correlations between Islamic mosque growth, other major religions, and various socioeconomic factors. Employing historical, comparative, religious, statistical, and spatial perspectives, this chapter pioneers interdisciplinary research on Islamic mosques in contemporary China.

11.2   Data and methodology

The primary data source for this study is the Chinese government's data on Islamic mosques. The comprehensive dataset, edited and published by the China Census Bureau (China Census Bureau, 2004), allows tracking of mosque numbers, locations, and construction years in China from 1854 to 2004. Furthermore, the *Spatial Explorer of Religion* (now *China Geo-Explore*) (China Data Institute, 2012) offers a spatial information platform that provides data on Islamic mosques at the county, city, province, and national levels. This platform integrates religious site data with other socioeconomic metrics such as population figures, GDP, urbanization rates, and educational attainment.

Supplementary data sources include (1) population data from the 2000 China census (National Bureau of Statistics of China, 2001); (2) official government data on urbanization and the urban population ratio (National Bureau of Statistics of China, 2014); (3) official GDP figures and GDP per capita data (National Bureau of Statistics of China, 2004b); and (4) official data regarding the number of Chinese universities and colleges (National Bureau of Statistics of China, 2004a).

Employing a range of research methods, this chapter utilizes spatial analysis to visualize and map the locations of Islamic mosques in different periods and regions. Statistical techniques are employed to present specific mosque counts, total growth rates, average annual growth rates, and correlation coefficients through tables and figures. The chapter adopts a bottom-up research approach (Jarvis, 1993) to explore Islamic mosques initially from the perspective of four cities and one county before transitioning to patterns observed in the three regions and the nation as a whole, spanning from 1911 to 2004. In an effort to decipher the unique growth patterns of Islamic mosques, this chapter contrasts them with the religious sites of other major religions and other socioeconomic factors. Lastly, it adopts a religious studies perspective to analyze the relationship between state and religion and briefly discusses the qualitative factors influencing fluctuations in Islamic mosque development in China. In summary, by embracing multiple spatial, statistical, historical, comparative, and religious perspectives, this chapter endeavors to map the trajectory of Islamic mosque development in China from 1911 to 2004.

11.3   Case studies on Islamic Mosques in Xinjiang

To chart the overarching pattern of Islamic mosque construction in China, it is crucial to delve into Xinjiang, the most prominent Islamic region, as a case study. Situated in northwestern China, Xinjiang stands as the country's largest province

Table 11.1 Percentage of Xinjiang Mosques in China (1911–2004).

	1911	1949	1966	1978	1992	2004
Xinjiang	3,471	8,083	9,828	11,998	21,533	23,679
China	3,781	9,014	11,318	14,286	29,651	34,305
Percentage of Xinjiang (%)	92	90	87	84	73	69

Sources: China Census Bureau, *The 2004 China's Economic Census Data with GIS Maps* (Beijing: All China Market Research Co., LTD., 2004); China Data Institute, *China Geo-Explore*, 2012, retrieved from: https://www.chinageoexplorer.com/cge/.

and historically served as an essential gateway to Central Asia and Europe due to its proximity to the Silk Road. In 2004, Xinjiang hosted more than 69% of all Chinese mosques, totaling 23,679 (refer to Table 11.1).

Taking into account factors like city size, population, and regional significance, our selection comprises the following areas: (1) Urumqi city, the provincial capital and the largest city in Xinjiang province; (2) Kashgar city, the most prominent city in southern Xinjiang; (3) Korla city, representative of the central Xinjiang region; and (4) Aketao, a county located in southern Xinjiang. These selections aim to illustrate the diverse mosque development patterns observed across cities and counties (China Top Tours, 2014; Warrior Tours, 2014; Baike 2014).

Given the evolving mosque landscape in Urumqi from 1911 to 2004, the number of mosques in Urumqi city grew more than elevenfold, surging from 22 mosques to a total of 265. Intriguingly, the growth rate of mosques during Mao's era (1949–1978) exceeded that of Deng and the post-Deng period (1978–2004). Despite a similar timeframe (29 years from 1949 to 1978 compared to 26 years from 1978 to 2004), mosque growth during Mao's era registered a 172% increase (from 43 to 117), whereas the growth rate during Deng and post-Deng's tenure amounted to only 127% (from 117 to 265) (refer to Table 11.2). Furthermore, the average annual growth rate was 3.51% during Mao's regime, slightly higher than the 3.19% observed during Deng and post-Deng's leadership.

Table 11.2 Evolution of Islamic Mosque Numbers in the Four Xinjiang Cities (1911–2004).

City / Year	1911	1949	1966	1978	1992	2004
Aketao	271	410	490	533	610	638
Kashgar	232	375	399	473	590	622
Korla	11	15	17	44	141	165
Urumqi	22	43	89	117	224	265

Sources: China Census Bureau, *The 2004 China's Economic Census Data with GIS Maps* (Beijing: All China Market Research Co., LTD., 2004); China Data Institute, *China Geo-Explore*, 2012, retrieved from: https://www.chinageoexplorer.com/cge/.

To comprehend these analogous mosque development patterns under different political regimes, we can consider several factors. First, it's possible that Mao's regime did not engage in significant destruction of mosques in Urumqi from 1949 to 1978 (Forbes, 1976; Israeli, 1981; Dreyer, 1982). Second, Urumqi, being a major city, may have had ample space and robust demand for accelerated mosque construction prior to 1978 (Dillon, 1996; DeAngelis, 1997; Israeli, 1997). Third, taking into account the social stability in the capital city, religious regulations in Urumqi during Deng and post-Deng's China were stringent, opposing further mosque construction (Xin, 2005; Brown, 2010; Gladney, 2004).

Aketao County exhibited similar trends to those observed in Urumqi (Table 11.2). To begin with, the number of mosques in Aketao experienced a notable 135% increase between 1911 and 2004. Markedly, the rate of mosque construction during Mao's era surpassed that during Deng's and the post-Deng era. Specifically, Mao's China witnessed a 30% growth in mosques (from 410 to 533), whereas Deng and post-Deng's China demonstrated a 20% growth (from 533 to 648) (as shown in Table 11.3).

In terms of the average annual growth rate, Mao's China also outpaced Deng and post-Deng's China, recording a rate of 0.91% compared to 0.69% (refer to Table 11.4). However, while examining two other prominent cities in Xinjiang, Kashgar and Korla, there were distinct trends in their growth rates and average annual growth rates during the two eras (refer to Table 11.2). Nonetheless, the statistical data paints a clear picture of the evolving mosque construction rates in both Kashgar and Korla cities from 1911 to 2004 (refer to Table 11.2). When we delve into the contrast between Mao's era and the Deng and post-Deng eras, Kashgar city saw a 26% increase in mosques during Mao's regime (from 375 to 473), while the period of Deng and post-Deng witnessed a 32% growth rate (see Table 11.3). Regarding the average annual growth rate, Mao's era exhibited a lower figure compared to Deng and post-Deng's era (0.8% vs. 1.06%) (refer to Table 11.4).

Similarly, in Korla city, mosques increased by 193% during Mao's era (from 15 to 44), while Deng and post-Deng's era experienced a substantial 275% growth (from 44 to 165) (see Table 11.3). The patterns also extend to their average annual

Table 11.3 The Growth Rates of the Islamic Mosques in Four Cities (1949–2004).

City	1949–1978 (%)	1978–2004 (%)	Differences (%)
Aketao	30	20	−10
Kashgar	26	32	+6
Korla	193	275	+82
Urumqi	172	127	−45

Sources: China Census Bureau, *The 2004 China's Economic Census Data with GIS Maps* (Beijing: All China Market Research Co., LTD., 2004); China Data Institute, *China Geo-Explore*, 2012, retrieved from: https://www.chinageoexplorer.com/cge/.

Table 11.4 The Average Annual Growth Rate of Islamic Mosques in the Four Cities (1911–2004).

City	Year 1911–2004 (%)	1949–1978 (%)	1978–2004 (%)
Aketao	0.92	0.91	0.69
Kashgar	1.07	0.80	1.06
Korla	2.95	3.78	5.22
Urumqi	2.71	3.51	3.19

Sources: China Census Bureau, *The 2004 China's Economic Census Data with GIS Maps* (Beijing: All China Market Research Co., LTD., 2004); China Data Institute, *China Geo-Explore*, 2012, retrieved from: https://www.chinageoexplorer.com/cge/.

growth rates, with Mao's period recording a lower rate than Deng's period (3.78% vs. 5.72%) (refer to Table 11.4).

While the growth rates varied among the four cities, their evolving patterns exhibited striking similarities, as evident in Figure 11.1. Figure 11.1 illustrates that the trajectory of mosque construction in Xinjiang has consistently trended upward since 1911, despite the region enduring numerous civil conflicts, religious upheavals, and international influences (Shichor, 1994; Bovingdon, 2001; Becquelin, 2004). This visualization further underscores a parallel development pattern in the

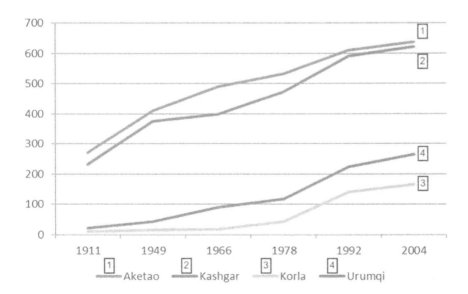

Figure 11.1 Evolution of Islamic Mosque Numbers in the Four Xinjiang Cities (1911–2004).

Sources: China Census Bureau, *The 2004 China's Economic Census Data with GIS Maps* (Beijing: All China Market Research Co., LTD., 2004); China Data Institute, *China Geo-Explore*, 2012, retrieved from: https://www.chinageoexplorer.com/cge/.

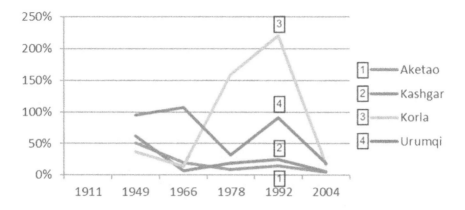

Figure 11.2 Growth Rates of Islamic Mosques in the Four Xinjiang Cities.

Sources: China Census Bureau, *The 2004 China's Economic Census Data with GIS Maps* (Beijing: All China Market Research Co., LTD., 2004); China Data Institute, *China Geo-Explore*, 2012, retrieved from: https://www.chinageoexplorer.com/cge/.

four cities, reflecting the robust and stable growth of their Islamic mosques over the past century.

In contrast to the consistent trend in changing mosque numbers, the growth rate of mosques exhibited notable variability across different years. As depicted in Figure 11.2, Urumqi experienced growth from 1949 to 1966, while the other three regions witnessed declines during the same period. However, during the subsequent period from 1966 to 1978, Urumqi and Aketao both exhibited lower growth rates, while the other two cities experienced growth, with Korla demonstrating an astonishingly high growth rate. The sole common trend emerged during the years from 1978 to 1992, marked by universal mosque growth in all four areas. Similarly, all four regions shared comparable declining rates from 1992 to 2004, albeit with variations in the extent of the decline.

Additionally, for a more comprehensive overview of Xinjiang, it is crucial to examine the evolving mosque numbers and growth rates for the entire province. As presented in Table 11.5, mosques in Xinjiang increased by a significant factor of 5.82 from 1911 to 2004. Focusing on the periods of Mao, Deng, and post-Deng, spanning from 1949 to 2004, we observe that the number of mosques rose by 48% during Mao's era, whereas Deng's and post-Deng's era witnessed a more

Table 11.5 The Changing Islamic Mosques in Xinjiang (1911–2004).

Year	1911	1949	1966	1978	1992	2004
Mosque Number	3,471	8,083	9,828	11,998	21,533	23,679

Sources: China Census Bureau, *The 2004 China's Economic Census Data with GIS Maps* (Beijing: All China Market Research Co., LTD., 2004); China Data Institute, *China Geo-Explore*, 2012, retrieved from: https://www.chinageoexplorer.com/cge/.

substantial increase of 97%. Similarly, concerning the average annual growth rate, Deng and post-Deng's China surpassed Mao's China in Xinjiang, recording rates of 2.65% and 1.37%, respectively.

Notably, it is worth highlighting that Urumqi and Aketao cities exhibited an exceptional trend during Mao's era, where their mosque growth rates surpassed those of Deng and post-Deng's era. In contrast, Kashgar and Korla cities exemplified the typical mosque construction patterns in Xinjiang, with Deng's and post-Deng's China demonstrating higher growth rates compared to Mao's regime.

11.4 The changing regional and national patterns of Islamic Mosques

Additionally, for a more comprehensive overview of Xinjiang, it is vital to examine the evolving mosque numbers and growth rates for the entire province. As presented in Table 11.5, mosques in Xinjiang increased by a significant factor of 5.82 from 1911 to 2004. Focusing on the periods of Mao, Deng, and post-Deng, spanning from 1949 to 2004, we observe that the number of mosques rose by 48% during Mao's era, whereas Deng's and post-Deng's eras witnessed a more substantial increase of 97%. Similarly, concerning the average annual growth rate, Deng and post-Deng's China surpassed Mao's China in Xinjiang, recording rates of 2.65% and 1.37%, respectively.

Outstandingly, it is worth highlighting that Urumqi and Aketao cities exhibited an exceptional trend during Mao's era, where their mosque growth rates surpassed those of Deng and post-Deng's eras. In contrast, Kashgar and Korla cities exemplified the typical mosque construction patterns in Xinjiang, with Deng's and post-Deng's China demonstrating higher growth rates compared to Mao's regime.

Case studies on the four representative cities in the most popular region for Islam have provided meaningful background and patterns of Islamic mosques for further study on the different regions of China and the whole nation. Currently, China is divided into three major regions, including Eastern China (11 provinces), Central China (8 provinces), and Western China (12 provinces). Chinese Muslims and Islamic mosques dominate Western China due to ethnic, regional, and historical reasons (Lipman, 1998; Dillon, 2003; Fischer, 2005).

There were the changing locations of Islamic mosques in both Eastern and Central China from 1911 to 2004. They demonstrate two common patterns. First of all, both regions kept their consistent growth patterns since 1911. While the Eastern region increased its number of mosques by 9.56 times (54 vs. 570) from 1911 to 2004, the Central region rose by 10.92 times (64 vs. 763) in the same period (see Table 11.6). In addition, with respect to the different growth rates of mosques between Mao's China, Deng, and post-Deng's China, both regions also shared analogous characteristics. For instance, the Eastern region increased its number of mosques by 50% (145 vs. 217) during Mao's China and amplified by 163% (217 vs. 570) under Deng and post-Deng's leadership. Similarly, Central China showed a growth rate of 107% (135 vs. 279) in Mao's era and increased by 173% (279 vs. 763) in Deng's and post-Deng's era (see Table 11.6).

Table 11.6 Number of Islamic Mosques in Eastern, Central, and Western China (1911–2004).

Region \ Year	1911	1949	1966	1978	1992	2004
East	54	145	191	217	436	570
Central	64	135	231	279	536	763
West	3,663	8,734	10,896	13,790	28,679	32,972

Sources: China Census Bureau, *The 2004 China's Economic Census Data with GIS Maps* (Beijing: All China Market Research Co., LTD., 2004); China Data Institute, *China Geo-Explore*, 2012, retrieved from: https://www.chinageoexplorer.com/cge/.

Remarkably, when we turn our attention to Western China, the landscape of Islamic mosques presents striking disparities. As illustrated in Table 11.6, Western China's mosques constitute a staggering 96% of the total mosques in China. This highly skewed distribution underscores the significant influence wielded by Western Muslims in shaping the trajectory of Chinese Islam. Moreover, the growth of mosques in this region exhibited remarkable dynamics, increasing eightfold from 1911 to 2004. During this period, it saw a 58% surge in Mao's era and an impressive 139% boost during Deng's and the post-Deng era. Clearly, the years spanning from 1978 to 2004, encompassing Deng's leadership and its aftermath, marked a pivotal period that offered newfound opportunities for the rapid expansion of Islamic mosque infrastructure.

When we assess the most prolific period of mosque growth in China since 1911, Table 11.7 reveals that the Republic of China era (1911–1949) stands out as the peak growth period across all three regions. During this time, the number of mosques surged by 169%, 111%, and 138%, respectively, in the eastern, central, and western parts of China. Conversely, the Cultural Revolution years (1966–1978) marked the least favorable period for growth, yet even during this challenging phase, the numbers still increased by 14%, 21%, and 27% in the respective regions. However, it's noteworthy that mosque growth lost its momentum post-1992, as growth rates significantly decelerated by 31%, 42%, and 15%, respectively, in the three regions.

Table 11.7 The Growth Rates of Islamic Mosques in Eastern, Central, and Western China (1911–2004).

Region \ Year	1911	1949 (%)	1966 (%)	1978 (%)	1992 (%)	2004 (%)
East	N/A	169	32	14	101	31
Central	N/A	111	71	21	92	42
West	N/A	138	25	27	108	15

Sources: China Census Bureau, *The 2004 China's Economic Census Data with GIS Maps* (Beijing: All China Market Research Co., LTD., 2004); China Data Institute, *China Geo-Explore*, 2012, retrieved from: https://www.chinageoexplorer.com/cge/.

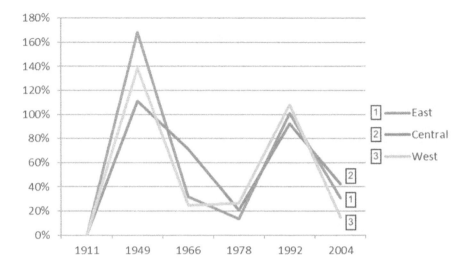

Figure 11.3 The Different Growth Rates of Islamic Mosques in Eastern, Central, and Western China (1911–2004).

Sources: China Census Bureau, *The 2004 China's Economic Census Data with GIS Maps* (Beijing: All China Market Research Co., LTD., 2004); China Data Institute, *China Geo-Explore*, 2012, retrieved from: https://www.chinageoexplorer.com/cge/.

Figure 11.3 exhibits parallel historical trends of fluctuations since 1911. Remarkably, the years 1949 and 1992 marked two historical peaks in Islamic mosque expansion, while the years 1966, 1978, and 2004 symbolized declines in new mosque constructions. A significant takeaway from the year 1992 was that after 14 years of "religious fervor" during Deng's reform era (from 1978 to 1992), the previously explosive growth of Islamic mosques had either decelerated or lost its momentum. This underscores the caution required when making predictions and estimates regarding future mosque growth, as relying solely on previous average annual growth rates might prove unreliable due to the inconsistent, irregular, and unstable nature of long-term growth rates (as seen in Table 11.8).

Table 11.8 The Average Annual Growth Rate of Islamic Mosques in the Three Regions of China (1911–2004).

Region	Year 1911–2004 (%)	1949–1978 (%)	1978–2004 (%)
East	2.57	1.40	3.78
Central	2.70	2.53	3.41
West	2.39	1.59	3.41

Sources: China Census Bureau, *The 2004 China's Economic Census Data with GIS Maps* (Beijing: All China Market Research Co., LTD., 2004); China Data Institute, *China Geo-Explore*, 2012, retrieved from: https://www.chinageoexplorer.com/cge/.

Table 11.9 Number of Islamic Mosques in China (1911–2004).

Region \ Year	1911	1949	1966	1978	1992	2004	Growth rate (1911–2004) (%)
China	3,781	9,014	11,318	14,286	29,651	34,305	807
Eastern China	54	145	191	217	436	570	956
Central China	64	135	231	279	536	763	1,092
Western China	3,663	8,734	10,896	13,790	28,679	32,972	800

Sources: Compiled from China Census Bureau, *The 2004 China's Economic Census Data with GIS Maps* (Beijing: All China Market Research Co., LTD., 2004); China Data Institute, *China Geo-Explore*, 2012, retrieved from: https://www.chinageoexplorer.com/cge/.

From a statistical standpoint, Table 11.9 reveals an interesting insight. Despite the fact that a staggering 96% of mosques were concentrated in Western China, its growth rate, registering at 800%, was the lowest compared to the national average of 807%, as well as the growth rates in Eastern China (956%) and Central China (1,092%) from 1911 to 2004. This phenomenon can be attributed to the already substantial baseline of mosques in Western China.

When we divide China into two distinct periods, namely Deng's China (1978–1992) and post-Deng's China (1992–2004), we can glean meaningful insights that shed light on the development of Islamic mosques (refer to Table 11.10). First, it is evident that most Chinese regions experienced mosque growth rates in triple digits during these periods, with the exception of Central China. Furthermore, during the period of 1992–2004, a significant deceleration in growth rates was observed across all four cities in Xinjiang, the three regions of China, and the entire nation, without any exceptions. To understand the political factors contributing to this abrupt decline in growth rates, we can consider the adverse impacts stemming

Table 11.10 Comparative Growth Rates of Islamic Mosques between the Four Cities of Xinjiang, the Three Regions and the Whole Nation (1978–2004).

Locations \ Year	1978–1992 (%)	1992–2004 (%)
Aketao	14	5
Kashgar	25	5
Korla	220	17
Urumqi	91	18
Eastern China	101	31
Central China	92	42
Western China	108	15
China	108	16

Sources: China Census Bureau, *The 2004 China's Economic Census Data with GIS Maps* (Beijing: All China Market Research Co., LTD., 2004); China Data Institute, *China Geo-Explore*, 2012, retrieved from: https://www.chinageoexplorer.com/cge/.

from the Tiananmen Incident of 1989 and the terrorist attacks in Xinjiang and other regions (Zuo and Benford, 1995; Yeoh, 2014). Consequently, the Chinese government shifted from a supportive policy to more stringent regulations, particularly opposing the construction of additional mosques in Northwestern China (Israeli, 2002; Potter, 2003; Carlson, 2005; Leung, 2005).

11.5 Evolving relationships between Islamic Mosques and Chinese society

In order to gain a comprehensive understanding of the development of Islamic mosques since 1911, it is crucial to employ comparative, historical, and qualitative methods. To facilitate this, we have chosen to include Buddhist temples, Catholic churches, Daoist abbeys, and Protestant churches as four additional reference points for comparing growth rates over the past century.

Table 11.11 outlines the comparative growth rates of religious sites for these five religions in China from 1911 to 2004. This comparative analysis of religious sites reveals several key insights. Firstly, it highlights that Islamic mosques accounted for over 47% of the total religious sites in China by 2004. This underscores the preference among Chinese Muslims for organized mosques, which have played a pivotal role in facilitating Islamic group activities (Jaschok and Shui, 2013; Chisti, 1979; Gaubatz, 1998).

Additionally, the growth rate of Islamic mosques ranked the lowest among the five religions, while Protestant churches experienced the highest growth rate. Although benchmarks have differed since 1911, these findings suggest that Islamic mosques may have comparatively limited potential for further growth when compared to Protestant churches (Bagader, 1981; Donohue and Esposito, 1982; Israeli, 1997; Gardozo, 2007).

Turning our attention to post-1978 China, the rankings of growth rates for religious sites among the five religions exhibit remarkable similarities to the period

Table 11.11 Comparative Growth Rates of Religious Sites across Five Religions in China (1911–2004).

Religious Sites \ Year	1911	1949	1966	1978	1992	2004	Growth rate (1911–2004) (unit: times)	Percentage of total religious sites
Islamic Mosque	3,781	9,014	11,318	14,286	29,651	34,305	8.07	47
Buddhist Temple	1,650	2,357	3,032	3,595	8,624	16,248	8.85	22
Catholic Church	135	255	317	355	1,095	2,419	16.92	3
Daoist Abbey	244	493	748	969	2,330	4,938	19.24	7
Protestant Church	116	369	635	889	5,718	14,509	124.08	20

Sources: Compiled from China Census Bureau, *The 2004 China's Economic Census Data with GIS Maps* (Beijing: All China Market Research Co., LTD., 2004); China Data Institute, *China Geo-Explore*, 2012, retrieved from: https://www.chinageoexplorer.com/cge/.

Table 11.12 The Comparative Growth Rates of Religious Sites for the Five Religions in China (1978–2004).

Religious sites / Year	1978–1992 (%)	1992–2004 (%)
Islamic Mosques	108	16
Buddhist Temple	140	88
Daoist Abbey	141	112
Catholic Churches	208	121
Protestant Churches	543	154

Sources: Compiled from China Census Bureau, *The 2004 China's Economic Census Data with GIS Maps* (Beijing: All China Market Research Co., LTD., 2004); China Data Institute, *China Geo-Explore*, 2012, retrieved from: https://www.chinageoexplorer.com/cge/.

from 1911 to 2004 (refer to Table 11.12). Islamic mosques, once again, occupy the lowest position in terms of growth rates during the periods of 1978–1992 (108%) and 1992–2004 (16%). This observation underscores the fact that the expansion of religious sites for all five major religions experienced a sluggish phase during Deng's and post-Deng's China, particularly from 1992 to 2004. This presents a sobering perspective on the development of Chinese Islam and the Muslim community, especially in contrast to the optimism expressed by many scholars regarding the religious resurgence in China (Madsen, 2010; Madsen, 2011; Meng, 2011).

It is essential to emphasize that this chapter primarily focuses on statistical and quantitative studies, thus our primary objective is not to delve into the qualitative reasons behind the fluctuations in Islamic mosques. Nevertheless, the significant disparity in growth rates between the pre-1992 and post-1992 periods may hint at potential future challenges and limitations for Islam in China.

Furthermore, examining the average annual growth rates of religious sites for the five primary religions offers additional insights. As illustrated in Table 11.13, it becomes evident that the period crossing from 1992 to 2004 represented the most challenging era in terms of the average annual growth rate for Islamic mosques, which stood at a mere 1.22%. This rate was even lower than that observed during the Cultural Revolution period (1966–1978), which registered an average annual growth rate of 1.35%. Conversely, when considering the average annual growth rate from 1911 to 2004, Islamic mosques exhibited the slowest annual growth rate at 2.4%. In stark contrast, the Protestant church consistently maintained the highest annual growth rate throughout all the time periods from 1911 to 2004 (refer to Table 11.13).

In addition to comparing the varying growth rates among the religious sites of the five major religions, it is imperative to explore the correlations between the expansion of Islamic mosques and various socioeconomic factors. For this purpose, Table 11.14 compiles comparable growth rates encompassing Islamic mosques, total population, GDP per capita, the number of colleges, and the urban population-to-rural population ratio, focusing specifically on the period from 1966 to 2004.

Table 11.13 The Average Annual Growth Rates of the Religious Sites of Five Main Religions.

Religions	1911–2004 (%)	1911–1949 (%)	1949–1966 (%)	1966–1978 (%)	1978–1992 (%)	1992–2004 (%)
Islamic Mosque	2.40	2.31	1.35	1.96	5.35	1.22
Catholic Church	3.15	1.69	1.29	0.95	8.38	6.83
Protestant Church	5.33	3.09	3.24	2.84	14.22	8.07
Buddhist Temple	2.49	0.94	1.49	1.43	6.45	5.42
Daoist Abbey	3.29	1.87	2.48	2.18	6.47	6.46

Sources: Compiled from China Census Bureau, *The 2004 China's Economic Census Data with GIS Maps* (Beijing: All China Market Research Co., LTD., 2004); China Data Institute, *China Geo-Explore*, 2012, retrieved from: https://www.chinageoexplorer.com/cge/.

This timeframe was selected due to a lack of data concerning GDP per capita and college numbers before 1966. Upon analyzing this data, we observe that the growth rate of Islamic mosques (203%) surpasses that of the total population (74%) and the urban-rural population ratio (134%), yet it lags behind the growth rates of colleges (299%) and GDP per capita (1,127%).

The significant correlations between mosque growth and urbanization carry profound implications. The rate of urbanization consistently outpaced the growth rate of Islamic mosques until around 1980. However, from 1980 to 2000, mosque construction witnessed a more rapid expansion compared to urbanization, marking a shift in the developmental trajectories of the two factors. The intersection points in 1980 and 2000 serve as critical junctures, signifying distinct paces of

Table 11.14 The Comparative Growth Rates between the Islamic Mosques and Other Social Economic Factors (1966–2004).

Subjects	1966	1978	1992	2004	Growth rates (1966–2004) (%)
Total Population (100,000)	7,454	9,626	5,748	12,999	74
Ratio of Urban Population (%)	18	18	28	42	133
Islamic Mosques	11,318	14,286	29,651	34,305	203
Higher Education School Number	434	598	1,053	1,731	299
GDP Per Capita (RMB)	893	1,366	3,940	10,954	1,127

Sources: Compiled from National Bureau of Statistics of China, *2010 Population Census* (Beijing: National Statistic Press, 2010); National Bureau of Statistics of China, *Jiaoyu yu Wenhua* (Education and Culture) (Beijing: All China Marketing Research Co., Ltd., 2004); National Bureau of Statistics of China, *Zhongguo guomin shengchan zongzhi, 2004* (Gross Domestic Product in China, 2004) (Beijing: National Statistic Press, 2004); China Census Bureau, *The 2004 China's Economic Census Data with GIS Maps* (Beijing: All China Market Research Co., LTD., 2004); China Data Institute, *China Geo-Explore*, 2012, retrieved from: https://www.chinageoexplorer.com/cge/.

Table 11.15 The Coefficient between the Islamic Mosques and Other Religious Sites and Socio-Economic Factors.

Subjects	Number of Islamic mosques
Total Population (100,000)	0.3404
GDP Per Capita (RMB)	0.8783
Protestant Church	0.9010
Catholic Church	0.9144
Ratio of Urban Population(%)	0.9258
Daoist Abbey	0.9274
Buddhist Temple	0.9370
Higher Education School Number	0.9464

Sources: Compiled from National Bureau of Statistics of China, *2010 Population Census* (Beijing: National Statistic Press, 2010); National Bureau of Statistics of China, *Jiaoyu yu Wenhua* (Education and Culture) (Beijing: All China Marketing Research Co., Ltd., 2004); National Bureau of Statistics of China, *Zhongguo guomin shengchan zongzhi, 2004* (Gross Domestic Product in China, 2004) (Beijing: National Statistic Press, 2004); China Census Bureau, *The 2004 China's Economic Census Data with GIS Maps* (Beijing: All China Market Research Co., LTD., 2004); China Data Institute, *China Geo-Explore*, 2012, retrieved from: https://www.chinageoexplorer.com/cge/.

evolution between mosques and urbanization. Notably, after the year 2000, the growth of Islamic mosques could not keep up with the accelerated pace of urbanization (Bagader, 1981; Pillsbury, 1981; Gladney, 1996).

It is evident that urbanization has stimulated the demand for Islamic mosques, underlining the importance of achieving a harmonious balance between the needs of urban Muslims and the availability of urban mosques to sustain a healthy and viable religious market (Ho, 2013). When the supply of mosques fails to meet the demands of urban Muslim populations, the shortage becomes apparent, inevitably leading to social instability and religious turmoil (Yang, 2006; Yang, 2010; Wang and Yang, 2011).

Furthermore, correlation coefficients provide valuable insights into the connections between Islamic mosques, religious sites of other faiths, and various socioeconomic factors. Table 11.15 underscores that the weakest correlation exists between mosques and the total population, while the number of colleges exhibits the strongest correlation with the number of mosques.

11.6 Conclusion

The multifaceted analysis of Islamic mosques in China since 1911, encompassing spatial, statistical, historical, comparative, and religious perspectives, holds significant implications for the study of Chinese Islam and Modern China as a whole. To begin with, the uneven distribution of Islamic mosques, comprising 47% of all Chinese religious sites, raises noteworthy concerns. Despite the gradual expansion of mosque distribution from Xinjiang to other regions since 1911, wherein 92% of mosques were concentrated in Xinjiang, the province still accommodates 69% of the nation's total mosques in 2004 (refer to Table 11.1).

Furthermore, when juxtaposed with religious sites from the four other major religions, the overall growth and average annual growth of Islamic mosques consistently ranked the lowest, particularly during the period from 1992 to 2004. This potentially serves as a cautionary sign of stagnation in mosque and Islamic development in the future.

It is necessary to acknowledge that this chapter primarily centers on quantitative and spatial investigations, leaving a comprehensive exploration of the qualitative factors influencing mosque development beyond the scope of our research. Nevertheless, the quantitative findings are poised to inspire scholars to delve into the potential issues surrounding the historical and religious evolution of Chinese Islam.

Notes

1 With the publisher's permission, segments of this chapter are excerpted from the article authored by Zhaohui Hong and co-authored by his graduate student, Jiamin Yan, "The Quantitative Studies on the Chinese Islamic Mosques since 1911," *Islamic Quarterly*, 59 (1) (2015):1–39. Mr. Yan has granted permission and provided written consent to exclude his name as co-author of this book. The original work has been significantly revised and updated for this book.

References

Bagader, A.A. 1981. "Muslims in China: Some Popular Middle Eastern Perceptions," *Journal Institute of Muslim Minority Affairs*, 3 (2):59–65.
Baike. 2014. *Aketao xian jieshao* (Akto County Introduction). Baike, Baidu. Retrieved from: http://baike.baidu.com/view/261355.htm
Becquelin, N. 2004. "Staged Development in Xinjiang," *The China Quarterly*, 178 (2):358–378.
Bovingdon, G. 2001. "The History of Xinjiang," *Twentieth-Century China*, 26 (2):95–139.
Brown, M. 2010. "Xinjiang on Fire Again," *Stanford Journal of East Asian Affairs*, 2 (4):10–14.
Carlson, E.R. 2005. "China's New Regulations on Religion: A Small Step, Not a Great Leap, Forward," *Brigham Young University Law Review*, 2005 (3):747–1625.
Cheek, T. 1997. *Propaganda and Culture in Mao's China: Deng Tuo and the Intelligentsia*. Oxford: OUP Catalogue.
China Census Bureau. 2004. *The 2004 China's Economic Census Data with GIS Maps*. Beijing: All China Market Research Co., LTD.
China Data Institute. 2012. *China Geo-Explore*. Retrieved from: https://www.chinageoexplorer.com/cge/
China Top Tours. 2014. *Wulumuqi jieshao* (Urumqi Introduction). China Top Tours. Retrieve from: https://www.britannica.com/place/Urumqi
Chisti, S.K. 1979. "Muslim Population of Mainland China: An Estimate," *Journal Institute of Muslim Minority Affairs*, 1 (2):75–85.
DeAngelis, R.C. 1997. "Muslims and Chinese Political Culture," *The Muslim World*, 87 (2):151–168.
Dillon, M. 1996. "Muslims in Post-Mao China," *Journal of Muslim Minority Affairs*, 16 (1):41–47.
Dillon, M. 2003. *Xinjiang: China's Muslim Far Northwest*. London: Routledge.
Donohue, J.J., and J.L. Esposito, eds. 1982. *Islam in Transition: Muslim Perspectives*. New York: Oxford University Press.
Dreyer, J.T. 1982. "The Islamic Community of China," *Central Asian Survey*, 1 (2–3):31–60.

Fischer, A.M. 2005. "Close Encounters of an Inner Asian Kind: Tibetan-Muslim Co-Existence and Conflict in Tibet Past and Present," *Crisis States Research Centre Working Papers Series*, 1 (68):1–27.
Forbes, A.D. 1976. "The Muslim National Minorities of China," *Religion*, 6 (1):67–87.
Gardozo, M. 2007. "The Future of Islam in China," *The Muslim World*, 30 (1):76–84.
Gaubatz, P. 1998. "Mosques and Markets: Traditional Urban Form on China's Northwestern Frontiers," *Traditional Dwellings and Settlements Review*, 4 (2):7–21.
Gladney, D.C. 1996. *Muslim Chinese: Ethnic Nationalism in the People's Republic (No. 149)*. Cambridge,MA: Harvard University Asia Center.
Gladney, D.C. 2003. "Islam in China: Accommodation or Separatism?" *The China Quarterly*, 174 (1):451–467.
Gladney, D.C. 2004. "Islam in China," *Islam in World Cultures: Comparative Perspectives*, R. Michael Feener, ed., pp. 161–182. Santa Barbara, CA: Bloomsbury.
Goldman, M. 1986. "Religion in Post Mao China," *The Annals of the American Academy of Political and Social Science*, 483 (1):146–156.
Hao, Z. 1997. "May 4th and June 4th Compared: A Sociological Study of Chinese Social Movements," *Journal of Contemporary China*, 6 (14):79–99.
Hillenbrand, R. 2004. *Islamic Architecture: Form, Function, and Meaning*. New York: Columbia University Press.
Ho, W.Y. 2013. "Mobilizing the Muslim Minority for China's Development: Hui Muslims, Ethnic Relations and Sino-Arab Connections," *Journal of Comparative Asian Development*, 12 (1):84–112.
Israeli, R. 1981. "The Muslim Minority in the People's Republic of China," *Asian Survey*, 21 (8):901–919.
Israeli, R. 1997. "A New Wave of Muslim Revivalism in China," *Journal of Muslim Minority Affairs*, 17 (2):269–282.
Israeli, R. 2002. *Islam in China: Religion, Ethnicity, Culture, and Politics*. Boston, MA: Lexington Books.
Jarvis, P.G. 1993. "Prospects for Bottom-Up Models," *Scaling Physiological Processes: Leaf to Globe*, 15 (1):115–126.
Jaschok, M., and S.J. Shui. 2013. *The History of Women's Mosques in Chinese Islam*. Surrey: Routledge.
La Dany, L. 1967. "Mao's China: The Decline of a Dynasty," *Foreign Affairs*, 45 (4):610–623.
Leung, B. 2005. "China's Religious Freedom Policy: The Art of Managing Religious Activity," *The China Quarterly*, 184 (2):894–913.
Lipman, J.N. 1998. *Familiar Strangers: A History of Muslims in Northwest China*. New York: The University of Washington Press.
Madsen, R. 2010. "The Upsurge of Religion in China," *Journal of Democracy*, 21 (4):58–71.
Madsen, R. 2011. "Religious Renaissance in China Today," *Journal of Current Chinese Affairs*, 40 (2):17–42.
Meng, X. 2011. "Study on Current 'Religious Fever' Phenomenon of China," *Canadian Social Science*, 7 (2):147–152.
National Bureau of Statistics of China. 2001. *2010 Population Census*. Beijing: National Statistic Press.
National Bureau of Statistics of China. 2004a. *Jiaoyu yu Wenhua* (Education and Culture). Beijing: All China Marketing Research Co., Ltd.
National Bureau of Statistics of China. 2004b. *Zhongguo guomin shengchan zongzhi, 2004* (Gross Domestic Product in China, 2004). Beijing: National Statistic Press.
National Bureau of Statistics of China. 2014. *Statistical Communiqué of the People's Republic of China on the 2013 National Economic and Social Development*. Beijing: National Statistic Press.
Pillsbury, B.L. 1981. "The Muslim Population of China: Clarifying the Questions of Size and Ethnicity," *Journal Institute of Muslim Minority Affairs*, 3 (2):35–58.

Potter, P.B. 2003. "Belief in Control: Regulation of Religion in China," *The China Quarterly*, 174 (1):317–337.
Raeisian, G. 2013. "The Role of Mosques in Urban Development," *Journal of Civil Engineering and Urbanism*, 3 (3):101–103.
Shichor, Y. 1994. "Separatism: Sino-Muslim Conflict in Xinjiang," *Global Change, Peace & Security*, 6 (2):71–82.
Wang, Y., and F. Yang. 2011. "Muslim Attitudes Toward Business in the Emerging Market Economy of China," *Social Compass*, 58 (4):554–573.
Warrior Tours. 2014. *Korla Introduction*. Warrior Tours. Retrieve from: https://www.travelchinaguide.com/cityguides/korla.htm
Xin, W. 2005. "A Study on 'The Rules and Regulations of Southern Xinjiang'," *China's Borderland History and Geography Studies*, 3 (3):4–21.
Yahuda, M. 1993. "Deng Xiaoping: The Statesman," *The China Quarterly*, 135:551–572.
Yang, F. 2006. "The Red, Black, and Gray Markets of Religion in China," *The Sociological Quarterly*, 47 (1):93–122.
Yang, F. 2010. "Religion in China under Communism: A Shortage Economy Explanation," *Journal of Church and State*, 52 (1):3–33.
Yeoh, E.K.K. 2014. "The Quarter-Century Legacy of June Fourth: Prospects and Challenges in the Struggle of Post-1989 Dissent and Nonviolent Action in the People's Republic of China," *International Journal of China Studies*, 5 (2):453–553.
Zuo, J., and R.D. Benford. 1995. "Mobilization Processes and the 1989 Chinese Democracy Movement," *The Sociological Quarterly*, 36 (1):131–156.

12 Spatial Analysis of Mosques

Case Studies in Xinjiang and Ningxia[1]

12.1 Introduction

While Chapter 11 delves into digital and quantitative studies of Chinese mosques, this chapter will shift its focus to spatial studies of mosques, specifically honing in on two distinct regions predominantly inhabited by Chinese Muslims. Noticeably, religious institutions and their locations play a vital role in understanding the religious market. Examining factors like density, availability, and accessibility of religious sites, including Islamic mosques, is essential to understanding the supply-side dynamics of this market. In fact, spatial methods, which encompass statistical, digital, and geographical aspects, offer effective tools for studying these aspects.

Spatial studies leverage geographic information systems (GISs) to explore spatial and temporal dimensions, trends, mapping, visualization, integration, and geo-temporal analysis. These methods have been increasingly applied in religious studies to provide both chronological and spatial perspectives, quantitatively measure the supply (religious sites) and demand (religious believers) in a religious market, and create religious atlases and historical trends.

With the support of the Henry Luce Foundation and efforts from scholars at the University of Michigan and Purdue University, the *Spatial Explorer of Religion* was established in 2012 (now *China Geo-Explore*) (China Data Institute, 2012). This platform provides validated and revised data related to Chinese religions, including Islamic mosques. It offers a range of tools and features for visualizing and analyzing religious data, including mosque locations, religious development trends, and historical collections.

Traditional methods alone cannot address certain complex issues, such as those related to Islamic mosques. Qualitative and humanities studies provide only partial answers. To conduct broader comparative research, it's crucial to first quantitatively determine, for example, the percentage of Muslims who cannot access their nearest mosque within a reasonable distance and driving time. This spatial approach provides quantifiable criteria to measure mosque availability in specific regions, offering a new perspective on these issues.

This study focuses on Islamic mosques in Xinjiang and Ningxia, two provinces with the highest Muslim populations in China. By assessing the demand for Muslims and the supply of mosques in the Islamic market, the study calculates the

DOI: 10.4324/9781003495451-12

average number of Muslims per mosque, the average distance between Muslim residential areas and the nearest mosque, and the percentage of Muslims who can reach the nearest mosque within a designated driving time. Comparing rankings of density, availability, and accessibility of mosques in eight selected cities and prefectures, the study proposes criteria for understanding mosque accessibility in Xinjiang and Ningxia. Spatial methods illuminate our understanding of Muslims, mosques, and Islam, as well as religious studies, humanities, and social sciences more broadly.

12.2 Methodology

To assess the density, availability, and accessibility of Islamic mosques in the two provinces in China with significant Muslim populations, this study employs several spatial and statistical methods to measure and map the demand among Muslims and the supply of mosques in the year 2004. To gauge the density of mosques in each designated area, we estimate the average number of Muslims served by a single mosque, drawing from the data on the number of Muslims and mosques in eight selected cities and prefectures in China. Spatial maps and quantitative tables displaying the locations and counts of all mosques in these locations provide statistical evidence regarding whether the current supply of mosques meets the demand of the Muslim population. A higher average number of Muslims per mosque may suggest greater challenges in terms of mosque accessibility and availability.

In addressing mosque availability, this study employs the Location Analysis Method (LAM) to calculate the average distance between Muslim residential areas and the nearest mosque. The LAM is a crucial tool for measuring the distance between these two points and can depict the average percentage of Muslims who need to travel varying distances to attend their regular religious services. The distance that local Muslims must travel from their residences to the nearest mosque serves as an indicator of mosque availability; a longer distance may indicate that the demand for mosques exceeds the supply. Moreover, the LAM enables us to calculate the percentage of areas within a specific location where the supply either meets or falls short of the demand for mosques. Overall, the LAM effectively visualizes mosque availability both spatially and statistically.

To evaluate mosque accessibility, this study employs two spatial methods: The Network Analysis Method (NAM) and the Two-Step Floating Catchment Area (2SFCA), supported by ArcGIS. Both methods focus on measuring travel times from Muslim residential areas to the nearest mosques in the selected regions and estimating the percentage of Muslims who cannot reach their nearest mosque within a given timeframe. By using these two complementary methods, we can compare and contrast their results, enhancing the reliability of our research findings. It is worth noting that while the 2SFCA relies on a street map for travel time calculations, the NAM utilizes a district map. Due to limited street map data in the selected cities, the 2SFCA in this study uses straight-line distance to estimate travel time, assuming an even distribution of the Islamic population throughout the area.

On the other hand, the NAM integrates network data, maps, and spatial information through GIS and other spatial statistical methods to measure both driving time and distance. Notably, the NAM, supported by Google Maps, is capable of estimating average driving speeds in designated areas, which is crucial for calculating travel times and distances in a given location.

12.3 Data

Selecting appropriate Islamic institutions, sites, and locations for a case study of Islamic mosques and Muslims in China is relatively straightforward in the case of Xinjiang and Ningxia. As of 2004, Xinjiang was home to 52.64% (11,405,800/21,667,000) of the total Muslim population in China (Li, 2007: 20) and 68.93% (23,647/34,305) of Islamic mosques (China Census Bureau, 2004). In contrast, Ningxia accounted for 9.71% (2,102,986/21,667,000) of the total Muslim population in China (Ningxia Bureau of Statistics, 2005: 47) and 9.96% (3,416/34,305) of the country's mosques in 2004 (China Census Bureau, 2004). In essence, these two provinces accommodated over 62% of Chinese Muslims and nearly 80% of the country's mosques.

However, the lack of complete data on Muslims at the county and city levels posed a challenge in selecting specific cities or prefectures. After considering various factors such as city size, population, and geographical location, this study has chosen eight cities and prefectures, with four in each of the two provinces, to facilitate geographic comparisons. In each province, we have selected one provincial capital city and three prefectures.

For example, in Xinjiang, the project focuses on the provincial capital city of Urumqi and three prefectures: Yining, Hetian, and Kashgar. Historically and geographically, Xinjiang is divided into two regions based on Mount Tian. Northern Xinjiang is an economically developed area, while southern Xinjiang boasts rich economic resources. To ensure a balanced geographic representation, we selected Yining and Urumqi to represent northern Xinjiang and Hetian and Kashgar for the southern region.

Similarly, in Ningxia, aside from the capital city of Yinchuan, we have chosen the northern prefectures of Shizuishan and Wuzhong, as well as the southern prefecture of Guyuan as case studies. Capital cities typically benefit from enhanced access to cultural, social, economic, and political resources, which facilitates mosque development, membership conversion, religious gatherings, and organization of religious services. These eight selected areas in the two provinces provide valuable insights into their religious, economic, and geographical patterns. Please refer to Map 12.1 for a visual representation of these chosen cities and prefectures in Xinjiang and Ningxia.

This study draws upon five essential datasets to support its research objectives.

1 Number of Total Chinese Islamic Mosques: Official data from the 2004 China Economic Census Data, accompanied by GIS maps, forms the bedrock of this study's mosque-related statistics. The 2004 dataset, released by the China Census Bureau in 2004, reported a total of 34,305 mosques nationwide (China

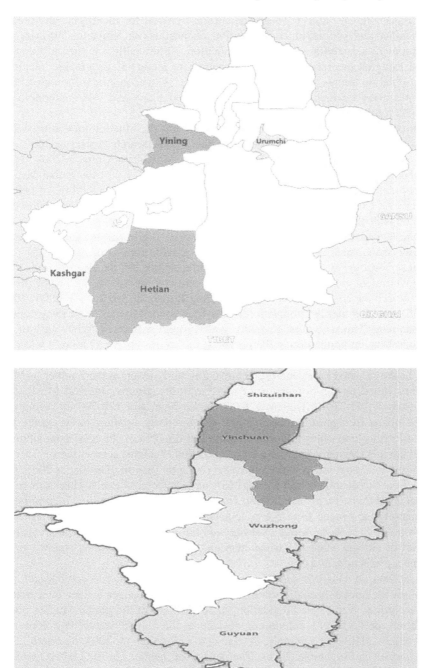

Map 12.1 The Selected Eight Cities and Prefectures in Xinjiang (top) and Ningxia (bottom).
Source: Redesigned by the author.

152 Spatial Analysis of Mosques

Census Bureau, 2004). These statistics are crucial for identifying the precise number and geographical distribution of mosques in Xinjiang, Ningxia, and the eight selected areas under examination. Additionally, the Spatial Explorer of Religion incorporates Islamic mosque data, alongside geographic locations, population figures, non-Islamic religious sites, and economic information. This integration enables the application of spatial maps and GIS methodologies within this research.

2 Number of Total Chinese Muslims: To establish the Muslim population within China, this study relies on data from the Pew Research Project in 2009. According to this source, there were 21,667,000 Muslims in China in 2009, representing 1.6% of the country's total population and 1.4% of the global Muslim population (Pew Research Center, 2010). Due to the unavailability of precise data on Chinese Muslims in 2004, this study employs the 2004 mosque data alongside the 2009 Muslim population figures.

3 Number of Chinese Muslims at Local Levels: While current Chinese central government data and global surveys do not provide population numbers for Chinese Muslims at local levels, valuable information can be gleaned from local government gazettes, prefecture, county, and city records, as well as empirical research papers. For instance, the Xinjiang Bureau of Statistics in 2005 (2005: 39) reported that the population of the four major Muslim minority groups in Xinjiang (Hui, Uyghurs, Kazakhs, and Kyrgyz) accounted for 99.46% of the total Muslim population in the province. Given this approximation, it was estimated that there were 11,405,800 Muslims in Xinjiang in 2004 (Li, 2007: 20). For the selected cities and prefectures, this study assumes the number of Muslims based on the population of these minority groups: 446,600 Muslims in Urumqi, 171,330 in Hetian, 326,260 in Kashgar, and 139,080 in Yining city (Xinjiang Bureau of Statistics, 2005: 41). Similarly, in Ningxia, where the Hui nationality and other minorities comprised 35.78% of the total population in 2004, it is estimated that there were 2,065,000 Muslims, accounting for 35.78% of the total population in the same year (Ningxia Bureau of Statistics 2005: 47).

4 Spatial Street and District Maps at City and Prefecture Levels: This study relies on a combination of resources to calculate mosque accessibility, incorporating spatial street maps from the "CloudMade" website, district map information from the "Bo Ya Di Ming" website, and the comprehensive mapping capabilities of Google Maps at various administrative levels, including country, province, prefecture, and city.

5 US Data on Muslims and Mosques: To provide context and comparison, this study includes data on the number of Muslims and mosques in the United States. According to the Pew Foundation, in 2007, 0.6% of the global Muslim population, or 1,852,473 individuals, resided in the United States (Pew Research Center, 2010). Additionally, A. Jamal's estimation in 2005 reported 1,209 mosques in the United States. The density of mosques in the United States is notably higher, with an average of 1,532 Muslims per mosque. In contrast, in reference to China's 2,166,700 Muslims and 34,305 mosques between 2004 and 2009, the density was 632 Muslims per mosque.

Table 12.1 Muslims in Xinjiang, China (2004).

City	Muslim population (10,000)	Percentage of total population (national average: 1.67% of total population in China)	Percentage of Muslims in China
Kashgar	326.26	88	15
Hetian	171.33	93	8
Yining	139.08	56	6
Urumqi	44.66	24	2

Source: Xinjiang Bureau of Statistics, *Xingjiang nianjian, 2005* (Yearbook of Xinjiang 2005) (Beijing: China Statistics Press, 2005).

These five key datasets form the foundation of our research, enabling a comprehensive analysis of mosque density, accessibility, and availability in China, while also allowing for valuable comparisons with the United States.

Leveraging official data released by China's National Bureau of Statistics in 2004, the Spatial Explorer of Religion provides a comprehensive visualization of the geographical distribution of Islamic mosques in Xinjiang and its four selected cities and prefectures. Statistically, Xinjiang boasted 23,647 mosques, with 2,042 in Kashgar, 1,142 in Hetian, 581 in Yining, and 344 in Urumqi. To assess the density of Muslims in Xinjiang, it is essential to acquire data regarding the Muslim population, enabling the calculation of both the average number of Muslims per mosque and the percentage of Muslims within the total population. Table 12.1 outlines the Muslim population in Xinjiang as of 2004.

Remarkably, in the year 2004, both Hetian and Kashgar exhibited a striking feature: Muslim residents constituted roughly 90% of their respective populations. Moreover, these two regions were home to over 23% of China's entire Muslim community. This unique demographic landscape, where one religion prevails overwhelmingly, beckons scholars of religious studies to delve into a range of intriguing topics. These include the historical factors that contributed to such religious dominance, the regulatory framework governing religious practices, and the complexities of social diversity within these areas.

When comparing the number of Muslims to the count of mosques, it becomes relatively straightforward to calculate the average number of Muslims served by a single mosque in Xinjiang. Nevertheless, due to the lack of empirical data regarding the size and seating capacity of each mosque, this study regrettably cannot delve into these dimensions, which would be valuable for a comprehensive understanding of Muslim population density (refer to Table 12.2 for additional details).

Clearly, there exists a substantial disparity in the average number of Muslims per mosque between Xinjiang and China as a whole, with figures standing at 485 and 632, respectively. Notably, within the selected four areas in Xinjiang, this discrepancy becomes even more pronounced, with a range of 1,298–2,394 Muslims per mosque observed in 2004. This situation raises pertinent questions regarding overcrowded mosques and the high population density of Muslims at the city and prefecture levels within Xinjiang, issues that merit scholarly investigation.

154 Spatial Analysis of Mosques

Table 12.2 The Density of Muslims in Xinjiang, 2004.

	Number of Muslims (10,000)	Percentage of Muslims	Number of mosques	Average number of Muslims per mosques	Rankings of density
Yining	139.08	0.11	581	2,394	6
Kashgar	326.26	0.25	2,042	1,598	5
Hetian	171.33	0.13	1,142	1,500	4
Urumqi	44.66	0.03	344	1,298	3
China	2,166.70	1.67	34,305	632	2
Xinjiang	1,146.82	0.87	23,647	485	1

Source: Xinjiang Bureau of Statistics, *Xingjiang nianjian, 2005* (Yearbook of Xinjiang 2005) (Beijing: China Statistics Press, 2005).

In parallel, Ningxia presents a comparable pattern with regard to the density of its Muslim population. The region hosts 416 mosques in Yinchuan, 1,203 in Guyuan, 164 in Shizuishan, and 752 in Wuzhong, respectively. Furthermore, Table 12.3 presents the Muslim population data for Ningxia. Evidently, the percentage of Muslims within the total population in Ningxia is notably lower than that in Xinjiang, as all four selected areas in Ningxia have less than 50% of Muslims within their populations. Nevertheless, both provincial capital cities, Urumqi and Yinchuan, share similar percentages of Muslims: 24% in Urumqi (Xinjiang Bureau of Statistics, 2005: 41) versus 26.16% in Yinchuan (Ningxia Bureau of Statistics, 2005: 47). This phenomenon underscores the propensity for capital cities to exhibit religious pluralism and social diversity (Gladney, 1996; Abdulla, 2006; Banchoff, 2008; Brown and Brown, 2011).

Likewise, to gauge the density of the Muslim population in Ningxia, we can estimate the average number of Muslims per mosque by examining the respective counts of Muslims and mosques. Table 12.4, reveals a scenario akin to that observed in Xinjiang: in the selected four areas of Ningxia, a larger number of Muslims attended religious services at each mosque compared to the average figures for the entire province of Ningxia and the entire nation. Each of the selected cities boasted over 700 Muslims per mosque, whereas Ningxia as a province had an average of 604, and the national average stood at 632 in 2004.

Table 12.3 Number of Muslims in Ningxia, China (2004).

City	Muslim population (10,000)	Percentage of Muslims in the total population (national average: 1.67% of total population in China)	Percentage of Muslims in China
Guyuan	64.54	42.67	2.98
Wuzhong	59.76	48.26	2.76
Yinchuan	38.25	27.76	1.77
Shizuishan	15.15	20.86	0.70

Source: Ningxia Bureau of Statistics, *Yearbook of Ningxia 2005* (Beijing: China Statistics Press, 2005).

Table 12.4 The Density of Muslims in Ningxia, 2004.

	Number of Muslims (10,000)	Percentage of Muslims	Number of mosques	Average number of Muslims per mosques	Rankings of density
Shizuishan	15.15	0.01	164	924	6
Yinchuan	38.25	0.03	416	920	5
Wuzhong	59.76	0.05	752	795	4
China	2,166.70	1.67	34,305	632	3
Ningxia	210.3	0.16	3,416	616	2
Guyuan	64.54	0.05	1203	537	1

Source: Compiled from Ningxia Bureau of Statistics, *Yearbook of Ningxia 2005* (Beijing: China Statistics Press, 2005).

In presenting data on the density of Muslims and mosques in both provinces, the selected eight areas, as well as a comparative analysis of the United States and China, this study offers a comprehensive perspective on their respective rankings in terms of Muslim population density. As depicted in Table 12.5, Xinjiang Province, Guyuan City, and Ningxia Province emerge as the top three regions in this ranking, surpassing even the national average, which is placed fourth. Intriguingly, the United States exhibits a notably high density of the Muslim population, ranking tenth when compared to the cases in China.

Focusing on the selected eight areas in two provinces, Table 12.6 illustrates the rankings of these areas only.

Table 12.5 The Density of the Muslims in China and the United States, 2004.

	Number of Muslims (10,000)	Number of mosques	Average number of Muslims per mosque	Rankings
Yining	139.08	581	2,394	12
Kashgar	326.26	2042	1,598	11
United States	185.23	1,209	1,532	10
Hetian	171.33	1142	1,500	9
Urumqi	44.66	344	1,298	8
Shizuishan	15.15	164	924	7
Yinchuan	38.25	416	920	6
Wuzhong	59.76	752	795	5
China	2,166.70	34,305	632	4
Ningxia	210.3	3416	616	3
Guyuan	64.54	1203	537	2
Xinjiang	1,146.82	23,647	485	1

Sources: Compiled from Pew Research Center, "Report 1: Religious Affiliation," *Pew Research Center's Religion & Public Life Project, 2010*, retrieved from https://www.pewresearch.org/topic/religion/; Research Project Team, *The Survey Report on China's Christians, Annual Report on China's Religions (2010)*, edited by Jin Ze and Qiu Yonghui, Beijing: Shehui kexue wenxian chubanshe, pp. 190–212; China Census Bureau, *The 2004 China's Economic Census Data with GIS Maps* (Beijing: All China Market Research Co., LTD, 2004); China Data Institute, *China Geo-Explore*, 2012, retrieved from: https://www.chinageoexplorer.com/cge/; The Boya Diming Website, 2005, retrieved from http://www.tcmap.com.cn/.

156 *Spatial Analysis of Mosques*

Table 12.6 The Density of the Muslims in the Eight Areas, 2004.

	Average number of Muslims per mosques	Rankings
Yining	2,394	8
Kashgar	1,598	7
Hetian	1,500	6
Urumqi	1,298	5
Shizuishan	924	4
Yinchuan	920	3
Wuzhong	795	2
Guyuan	537	1

Sources: Compiled from Pew Research Center, "Report 1: Religious Affiliation," *Pew Research Center's Religion & Public Life Project, 2010*, retrieved from https://www.pewresearch.org/topic/religion/; Research Project Team, *The Survey Report on China's Christians, Annual Report on China's Religions (2010)*, edited by Jin Ze and Qiu Yonghui, Beijing: Shehui kexue wenxian chubanshe, pp. 190–212; China Census Bureau, *The 2004 China's Economic Census Data with GIS Maps* (Beijing: All China Market Research Co., LTD, 2004); China Data Institute, *China Geo-Explore*, 2012, retrieved from: https://www.chinageoexplorer.com/cge/; The Boya Diming Website, 2005, retrieved from http://www.tcmap.com.cn/.

Considering that the national average for Muslim demographic density stood at 632 Muslims per mosque, Xinjiang province recorded 485 Muslims per mosque, and Ningxia had 616 Muslims per mosque, it is reasonable to classify areas where the average exceeds 1,000 Muslims per mosque as experiencing a relative scarcity of mosque availability. Based on this criterion, all four areas within Xinjiang—Urumqi, Hetian, Kashgar, and Yining—should be categorized as locales with limited religious infrastructure supply.

12.4 Mosque availability: Applying the Location Analysis Method (LAM)

To substantiate or validate the metric of mosque supply determined by statistical Muslim population density, it is crucial to employ the LAM to investigate mosque availability. LAM is specifically designed to assess mosque accessibility by measuring the average distance between a Muslim residential area and the nearest mosque. It's important to acknowledge that there exist various dissimilarities between Chinese Muslims in Xinjiang and those in Ningxia, encompassing aspects of Islamic culture, lifestyle, communication, road infrastructure, and transportation methods, all of which can potentially influence the time it takes for individuals to commute from their residences to the nearest mosques. Nevertheless, due to the limitations in available data, this study necessitates a generalized approach across both provinces, assuming an average speed limit for private cars and public transportation. Moreover, considering the spatial constraints in measuring distance through the Spatial Explorer of Religion, this study adopts a

Map 12.2 Spatial Maps of Mosque Availability in Urumqi (LAM).

Sources: Compiled from Pew Research Center, "Report 1: Religious Affiliation," *Pew Research Center's Religion & Public Life Project, 2010,* retrieved from https://www.pewresearch.org/topic/religion/; Research Project Team, *The Survey Report on China's Christians, Annual Report on China's Religions (2010),* edited by Jin Ze and Qiu Yonghui, Beijing: Shehui kexue wenxian chubanshe, pp. 190–212; China Census Bureau, *The 2004 China's Economic Census Data with GIS Maps* (Beijing: All China Market Research Co., LTD, 2004); China Data Institute, *China Geo-Explore*, 2012, retrieved from: https://www.chinageoexplorer.com/cge/; The Boya Diming Website, 2005, retrieved from http://www.tcmap.com.cn/.

12-km benchmark for one-way distance measurement between Muslim residential locations and mosque sites.

Map 12.2 illustrates one of the four areas of Xinjiang, Urumqi. The circular region signifies the area within which Muslims can access their nearest mosque within a 12-km radius. Conversely, the areas beyond the circle indicate that Muslims residing there are located more than 12 km away from the nearest mosque. Essentially, those situated within the circle have quicker and more convenient access to their respective mosques.

Similarly, Map 12.3 shows the spatial pictures of mosque availability in one of the four areas in Ningxia, Yinchuan.

158 *Spatial Analysis of Mosques*

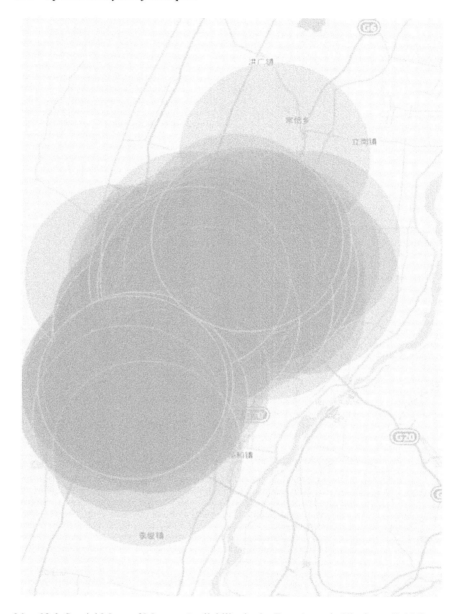

Map 12.3 Spatial Maps of Mosque Availability in the Four Areas in Yinchuan (LAM).

Sources: Compiled from Pew Research Center, "Report 1: Religious Affiliation," *Pew Research Center's Religion & Public Life Project, 2010,* retrieved from https://www.pewresearch.org/topic/religion/; Research Project Team, *The Survey Report on China's Christians, Annual Report on China's Religions (2010)*, edited by Jin Ze and Qiu Yonghui, Beijing: Shehui kexue wenxian chubanshe, pp. 190–212; China Census Bureau, *The 2004 China's Economic Census Data with GIS Maps* (Beijing: All China Market Research Co., LTD, 2004); China Data Institute, *China Geo-Explore*, 2012, retrieved from: https://www.chinageoexplorer.com/cge/; The Boya Diming Website, 2005, retrieved from http://www.tcmap.com.cn/.

Table 12.7 Comparative Mosque Availability in China, 2004 (LAM).

12 km	Number of Muslims who can't arrive at the nearest mosque (10,000)	Percentage of the total number of Muslims	Rankings of mosque availability
Kashgar	273.66	83.88	8
Hetian	117.3	68.47	7
Yining	86.28	62.03	6
Guyuan	30.26	34.89	5
Shizuishan	10.33	17.97	4
Wuzhong	0.19	0.30	3
Yinchuan	0	0	2
Urumqi	0	0	1

Sources: Compiled from Pew Research Center, "Report 1: Religious Affiliation," *Pew Research Center's Religion & Public Life Project, 2010*, retrieved from https://www.pewresearch.org/topic/religion/; Research Project Team, *The Survey Report on China's Christians, Annual Report on China's Religions (2010)*, edited by Jin Ze and Qiu Yonghui, Beijing: Shehui kexue wenxian chubanshe, pp. 190–212; China Census Bureau, *The 2004 China's Economic Census Data with GIS Maps* (Beijing: All China Market Research Co., LTD, 2004); China Data Institute, *China Geo-Explore*, 2012, retrieved from: https://www.chinageoexplorer.com/cge/; The Boya Diming Website, 2005, retrieved from http://www.tcmap.com.cn/.

To gain insights into the supply-side dynamics within the Islamic market across these eight areas, it becomes imperative to translate the spatial representation into a statistical table. Table 12.7 provides a comprehensive overview of key information regarding mosque availability. Notably, both provincial capital cities, Urumqi and Yinchuan, exhibit a favorable ratio between the number of mosques and the Muslim population. In these cities, no Muslim residents need to travel more than 12 km to reach their nearest mosque, implying that in larger urban centers characterized by higher Muslim population density, residents enjoy closer proximity to mosques. Conversely, in Kashgar, Hetian, and Yining within Xinjiang province, more than 50% of Muslims live 12 km or more away from their nearest mosque. This finding aligns with the statistical observations regarding Muslim population density presented in Table 12.6.

Drawing from the insights gleaned from the mosque availability case studies, a secondary criterion can be established for evaluating the supply-side dynamics within the Islamic market. Specifically, any area where more than 50% of Muslims are required to travel over 12 km to reach their nearest mosque should be categorized as having a relative dearth of mosque availability and supply. Accordingly, Kashgar, Hetian, and Yining in Xinjiang province meet this definition. It is worth noting that the 12-km threshold may be seen as arbitrary in indicating a relative lack of mosque supply. Nevertheless, the spatial methodologies employed in this study serve as a demonstration of innovative research techniques rather than the establishment of a precise threshold. Given the current spatial and digital platform provided by the Spatial Explorer of Religion, scholars have the flexibility to integrate updated data and develop alternative criteria for comprehending the supply-side dynamics within the Islamic market.

12.5 Mosque accessibility: The Two-Step Floating Catchment Area (2SFCA) method and the Network Analysis Method (NAM)

In addition to the statistical analysis assessing Muslim population density and the spatial LAM evaluating mosque availability, it is crucial to scrutinize mosque accessibility through the utilization of two spatial methodologies: the Two-Step Floating Catchment Area (2SFCA) and the Network Analysis Method (NAM).

By employing the 2SFCA method, Map 12.4 offers an illustration of mosque accessibility across one of the selected eight areas, Yining of Xinjiang. This method establishes a one-way driving time of 30 minutes from Muslim residential areas to their nearest mosque. The gray-shaded area signifies locations where Muslims can access their nearest mosque within this 30-minute timeframe. Conversely, areas without color indicate reduced accessibility to mosques, as residents in these regions must undertake journeys lasting more than 30 minutes one-way, whether by private or public transportation (Hong and Yan, 2015a: 8–9).

Table 12.8 explains the mosque accessibility in the eight areas statistically.

Considering the data presented in Table 12.8, it becomes justifiable to introduce a third criterion for gauging the relative inadequacy of mosque supply. Specifically, an area where over 50% of Muslims are required to spend more than 30 minutes in transit to reach the nearest mosque should be classified as one facing a relative dearth of mosque accessibility and supply.

The selection of a 30-minute one-way driving criterion for assessing the relative insufficiency of mosque supply draws inspiration from the criteria used to evaluate health professional shortage areas (HPSA) in the healthcare sector, as defined by the US National Institute for Health (NIH). HPSA designates an area as one with a healthcare clinic shortage if its residents cannot reach their nearest healthcare clinic within a 30-minute driving radius (U.S. Department of Health and Human Services, 2013). While a shortage of healthcare clinics can significantly impact human health and overall well-being, a relative scarcity of mosque supply may influence various aspects of Muslims' spiritual life and existence, even though measuring these intangibles statistically remains a challenging endeavor.

To validate the findings related to mosque accessibility obtained through the 2SFCA method, the application of the Network Analysis Method (NAM) offers supplementary insights. To maintain consistency with the spatial methodologies employed in the LAM and 2SFCA, it is essential to maintain a consistent 12-km distance and 30-minute driving time threshold. As a result, Map 12.5 delineates mosque accessibility across one of the selected eight locations, Wuzhong of Ningxia. The black markers represent the spatial locations of mosques, the inner gray area signifies the 6-km and 15-minute travel zone, the middle white area corresponds to the 12-km and 30-minute travel zone, and the outer gray area indicates the 18-km and 45-minute travel zone.

To provide a transparent representation of the mosque accessibility data derived from the Network Analysis Method (NAM), Table 12.9 presents the aggregated area and the corresponding percentage of Muslims based on a 12-km distance and a 30-minute one-way driving time. Crucially, Table 12.9 also

Spatial Analysis of Mosques 161

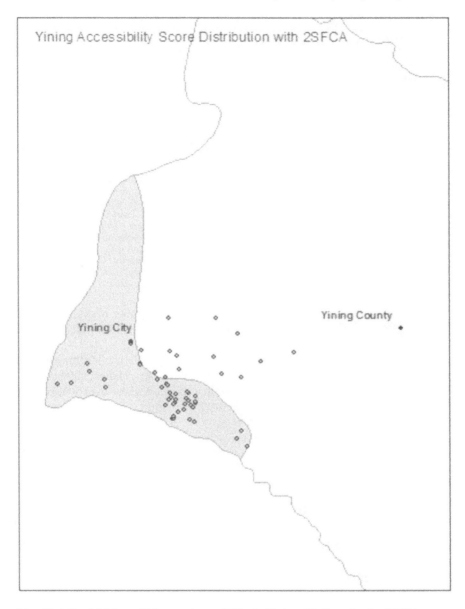

Map 12.4 Spatial Maps of Mosque Accessibility in Yining, Xinjiang, by the 2SFCA.

Sources: Compiled from Pew Research Center, "Report 1: Religious Affiliation," *Pew Research Center's Religion & Public Life Project, 2010,* retrieved from.

162 *Spatial Analysis of Mosques*

Table 12.8 Mosque Accessibility in China by the 2SFCA.

Cities	Percentage of Muslins taking more than 30 minutes to the nearest mosque	Ranking
Wuzhong	86.00	8
Guyuan	83.31	7
Hetian	75.12	6
Urumqi	75.01	5
Shizuishan	66.68	4
Yinchuan	59.99	3
Yining	50.15	2
Kashgar	49.92	1

Sources: Compiled from Pew Research Center, "Report 1: Religious Affiliation," *Pew Research Center's Religion & Public Life Project, 2010,* retrieved from https://www.pewresearch.org/topic/religion/; Research Project Team, *The Survey Report on China's Christians, Annual Report on China's Religions (2010)*, edited by Jin Ze and Qiu Yonghui, Beijing: Shehui kexue wenxian chubanshe, pp. 190–212; China Census Bureau, *The 2004 China's Economic Census Data with GIS Maps* (Beijing: All China Market Research Co., LTD, 2004); China Data Institute, *China Geo-Explore*, 2012, retrieved from: https://www.chinageoexplorer.com/cge/; The Boya Diming Website, 2005, retrieved from http://www.tcmap.com.cn/.

delineates the percentage of Muslims and the actual number of Muslims who are unable to reach their nearest mosque within the specified 12-km distance and 30-minute travel time.

In accordance with the third criterion indicating a relative insufficiency of mosque supply, attention should be directed toward Kashgar, Hetian, Guyuan, Shizuishan, and Yinchuan. These five areas exhibit a situation where over 50% of their Muslim populations must travel a distance of 12 km within a 30-minute timeframe to access their nearest mosques.

In an endeavor to address the disparities in mosque supply across the regions, as assessed by the three spatial methods, one possible approach is to calculate the average percentage of Muslims who cannot reach their nearest mosque within 12 km and 30 minutes. Table 12.10 presents the average rankings of mosque supply across the eight locations, amalgamating the findings obtained through the three spatial methods.

As depicted in Table 12.10, both capital cities, Yinchuan and Urumqi, exhibit a greater number of mosques relative to their Muslim populations, as more than 60% of Muslims in these cities can conveniently access their nearest mosque within a 12-km, 30-minute travel radius. Similarly, in two other prefectures within Ningxia Province, Shizuishan and Wuzhong, over 50% of Muslims can reach their nearest mosque within the specified distance and timeframe. However, the remaining four areas encompassing Kashgar, Hetian, Guyuan, and Yining occupy the top four positions for having a relative dearth of mosque supply, given that more than 50% of their Muslim populations are required to travel more than 12 km within a 30-minute timeframe to reach their nearest mosque.

Furthermore, in addition to the average rankings generated through the three spatial methods, it becomes essential to incorporate rankings based on Muslim

Spatial Analysis of Mosques 163

Map 12.5 Spatial Driving Maps in Wuzhong, Ningxia by the NAM.

Sources: Compiled from Pew Research Center, "Report 1: Religious Affiliation," *Pew Research Center's Religion & Public Life Project, 2010*, retrieved from https://www.pewresearch.org/topic/religion/; Research Project Team, *The Survey Report on China's Christians, Annual Report on China's Religions (2010)*, edited by Jin Ze and Qiu Yonghui, Beijing: Shehui kexue wenxian chubanshe, pp. 190–212; China Census Bureau, *The 2004 China's Economic Census Data with GIS Maps* (Beijing: All China Market Research Co., LTD, 2004); China Data Institute, *China Geo-Explore*, 2012, retrieved from: https://www.chinageoexplorer.com/cge/; The Boya Diming Website, 2005, retrieved from http://www.tcmap.com.cn/.

population density as an additional reference point signifying the supply-side dynamics within the Islamic market. Table 12.11 amalgamates the rankings for mosque accessibility, availability, and Muslim population density to present a comprehensive average ranking of mosque supply.

164 *Spatial Analysis of Mosques*

Table 12.9 Mosque Accessibility in the Eight Cities by the NAM (30 Minutes)

12 km (30 minute)	Accumulated area (km²)	Muslims and area coverage (%)	Percentage of Muslims who can't reach the nearest Mosque	Number of Muslims who can't reach
Urumqi	6,334.77	65.16	34.84	643,110
Yining	2,403.32	51.86	48.14	669,570
Wuzhong	3,122.82	51.80	48.20	286,285
Yinchuan	2,691.55	43.80	56.20	202,570
Shizuishan	3,095.02	43.79	56.21	80,989
Guyuan	385.88	40.00	60.00	386,902
Hetian	6,385.98	39.83	60.17	1,030,859
Kashgar	1,757.07	29.30	70.70	2,306,804

Sources: Compiled from Pew Research Center, "Report 1: Religious Affiliation," *Pew Research Center's Religion & Public Life Project, 2010*, retrieved from https://www.pewresearch.org/topic/religion/; Research Project Team, *The Survey Report on China's Christians, Annual Report on China's Religions (2010)*, edited by Jin Ze and Qiu Yonghui, Beijing: Shehui kexue wenxian chubanshe, pp. 190–212; China Census Bureau, *The 2004 China's Economic Census Data with GIS Maps* (Beijing: All China Market Research Co., LTD, 2004); China Data Institute, *China Geo-Explore*, 2012, retrieved from: https://www.chinageoexplorer.com/cge/; The Boya Diming Website, 2005, retrieved from http://www.tcmap.com.cn/.

As demonstrated by Table 12.11, the resultant rankings for the top four locations with a relative lack of mosque supply include the areas of Hetian, Kashgar, Yining, and Guyuan. These are the same four areas demonstrated by Table 12.10, although the orders of their rankings are slightly different. Therefore, tested by the four methods (the statistical, LAM, NAM, and 2SFCA) covering the subjects of Islamic density, availability, and accessibility, the three sensible criteria of the

Table 12.10 Average Rankings of the Mosque Supply in the Eight Areas by the LAM, NAM, and 2SFCA.

	Availability (LAM) (%)	Accessibility (NAM) (%)	Accessibility (2SFCA) (%)	Average by LAM, NAM, 2SFCA (%)	Average rankings
Kashgar	83.88	70.70	49.92	68.17	8
Hetian	68.47	60.17	75.12	67.92	7
Guyuan	34.89	60.00	83.31	59.40	6
Yining	62.03	48.14	50.15	53.44	5
Shizuishan	17.97	56.21	66.68	46.95	4
Wuzhong	0.30	48.20	86.00	44.83	3
Yinchuan	0.00	56.20	59.99	38.73	2
Urumqi	0.00	34.84	75.01	36.62	1

Sources: Compiled from Pew Research Center, "Report 1: Religious Affiliation," *Pew Research Center's Religion & Public Life Project, 2010*, retrieved from https://www.pewresearch.org/topic/religion/; Research Project Team, *The Survey Report on China's Christians, Annual Report on China's Religions (2010)*, edited by Jin Ze and Qiu Yonghui, Beijing: Shehui kexue wenxian chubanshe, pp. 190–212; China Census Bureau, *The 2004 China's Economic Census Data with GIS Maps* (Beijing: All China Market Research Co., LTD, 2004); China Data Institute, *China Geo-Explore*, 2012, retrieved from: https://www.chinageoexplorer.com/cge/; The Boya Diming Website, 2005, retrieved from http://www.tcmap.com.cn/.

Table 12.11 Combined Rankings of Mosque Supply in the Eight Cities.

	Density rankings	Rankings by LAM	Rankings by NAM	Rankings by 2SFCA	Combined rankings	Final rankings
Hetian	6	7	7	6	6.50	8
Kashgar	7	8	8	1	6.00	7
Yining	8	6	5	2	5.25	6
Guyuan	1	5	6	7	4.75	5
Wuzhong	2	3	3	8	4.0	4
Shizuishan	4	4	4	4	4.0	4
Yinchuan	3	7	2	3	3.75	2
Urumqi	5	3	1	5	3.5	1

Sources: Compiled from Pew Research Center, "Report 1: Religious Affiliation," *Pew Research Center's Religion & Public Life Project, 2010,* retrieved from https://www.pewresearch.org/topic/religion/; Research Project Team, *The Survey Report on China's Christians, Annual Report on China's Religions (2010),* edited by Jin Ze and Qiu Yonghui, Beijing: Shehui kexue wenxian chubanshe, pp. 190–212; China Census Bureau, *The 2004 China's Economic Census Data with GIS Maps* (Beijing: All China Market Research Co., LTD, 2004); China Data Institute, *China Geo-Explore,* 2012, retrieved from: https://www.chinageoexplorer.com/cge/; The Boya Diming Website, 2005, retrieved from http://www.tcmap.com.cn/.

mosque supply situation may determine that Hetian, Kashgar, and Yining in Xinjiang province and Guyuan in Ningxia province should be defined as the areas with the relative lack of mosque supply in China.

12.6 Conclusion

Applying the spatial methods to measure the supply side of Islamic market has explored and developed the research fields of Muslim population density as well as the availability and accessibility of mosques that are critical in studying the religious market of Islam. In dealing with complicated subjects, the multi-method research design contributes an added value to the reliability of research findings by comparing and contrasting the different research conclusions. In particular, the different spatial methods, such as the LAM, NAM, and 2SFCA, have generated complementary effects to improve the understanding of mosque supply in China.

Admittedly, it is quite possible that some Muslim residents in the selected areas choose to drive longer distances in order to attend a larger or better mosque or a particular one due to personal preference, but we won't know until more empirical studies are done. Certainly, there can be other additional reasons for Muslim individuals to attend a specific mosque due to sectarian differences, and ethnic affiliations, or simply because of their preferences for a particular Imam. In these scenarios, one would study the difference between areas that prefer a few large mosques to those with many small mosques—a matter for qualitative analysis that is out of the scope of this spatial and quantitative research. Therefore, this preliminary study is awaiting future findings through intensive surveys, interviews, and participant observation in these selected areas.

In addition, given the centralization or even manipulation of religious affairs in today's China, few, if any, can expect the accuracy and completion of religious data, including the number, location, and size of mosques. Also, a purely statistical definition of the supply side of the Islamic market may be inappropriate in a religious studies context. However, this study makes an effort to use multiple spatial methods to address the issue of mosque availability and accessibility. At the very least, it displays a methodology for establishing measurable criteria for mosque accessibility and availability from spatial, digital, and statistical perspectives. It is hoped that scholars will apply the spatial research design to more research subjects, such as the supply of all churches, temples, and mosques in the world, the balance between the supply and demand in the religious market, and the comparative study of religious institutions, sites, and locations. Such studies will lend themselves to a more comprehensive understanding of the social, cultural, and geopolitical implications of the religious market.

Note

1 With the publisher's permission, segments of this chapter are excerpted from the article authored by Zhaohui Hong and co-authored by his graduate student, Jianfeng Jin, "Spatial Study of Mosques—Xinjiang and Ningxia as Case Studies," *Review of Religion and Chinese Society*, 3 (2016): 223–260. Mr. Jin has granted permission and provided written consent to exclude his name as co-author of this book. The original work has been significantly revised and updated for this book.

References

Abdulla, R. 2006. "Islamic View on Pluralism," *European Judaism*, 39 (1):116–122.
Banchoff, T., ed., 2008. *Religious Pluralism, Globalization, and World Politics*. New York: Oxford University Press.
Brown, R. K., and R. E Brown. 2011. "The Challenge of Religious Pluralism: The Association between Interfaith Contact and Religious Pluralism," *Review of Religious Research*, 53 (3):323–340.
China Census Bureau. 2004. *The 2004 China's Economic Census Data with GIS Maps*. Beijing: All China Market Research Co., LTD.
China Data Institute. 2012. *China Geo-Explore*. Retrieved from: https://www.chinageoexplorer.com/cge/
Gladney, D. C. 1996. *Muslim Chinese: Ethnic Nationalism in the People's Republic*. Cambridge, MA: Harvard University Asia Center.
Hong, Z., and J. Jin. 2016. "Spatial Study of Mosques—Xinjiang and Ningxia as Case Studies," *Review of Religion and Chinese Society*, 3 (2):223–260.
Hong, Z., and J. Yan. 2015a. "Mapping Accessibility and Shortage of the Protestant Church in China: Applying Two Spatial Research Methods," *Asian Journal of Social Science and Management Studies*, 2 (1):8–22.
Li, J. 2007. "Muslim Population and New Model of Family Reproductive Health in Xinjiang, China," *Journal of Northwest Minorities Research*, 1 (3):19–32.
Ningxia Bureau of Statistics. 2005. *Yearbook of Ningxia 2005*. Beijing: China Statistics Press.
Pew Research Center. 2010. "Report 1: Religious Affiliation," *Pew Research Center's Religion & Public Life Project*. http://religions.pewforum.org/reports
U.S. Department of Health and Human Services. 2013. *Primary Medical Care HPSA Designation Criteria*. https://data.hrsa.gov/tools/shortage-area
Xinjiang Bureau of Statistics. 2005. *Xingjiang nianjian, 2005* (Yearbook of Xinjiang 2005). Beijing: China Statistics Press.

13 Religious Sites of Five Religions during the Cultural Revolution[1]

13.1 Introduction

The Chinese Cultural Revolution (1966–1976), led by Mao Zedong, is widely regarded as a catastrophic period in Chinese history (FitzGerald, 1967; Zuo, 1991; Barnouin and Yu, 1993; Clark, 2008; Schoenhals, 2015). Scholars largely concur that the religious persecutions instigated by Mao and executed by the Red Guards resulted in a human tragedy that claimed the lives of countless religious leaders and led to the destruction of numerous religious sites (Walder, 2002, 2004; Welch, 1969; Lee, 1980; Shen, 2006). It is essential to clarify that, within the context of this period, a "religious site" in China refers to a location, space, or institution where religious activities, such as worship and other services, took place. It may not necessarily involve the construction of a new building but often comprises a room within a building or even an individual house.

However, data from the 2004 China Economic Census, coupled with GIS maps published by the China Census Bureau (National Bureau of Statistics of China, 2010), presents a starkly contrasting narrative. According to this data source, mainland China established 2,554 new religious sites associated with the five major religions—Protestant churches, Catholic churches, Buddhist temples, Islamic mosques, and Daoist abbey—between 1966 and 1976. These data have undergone validation and rigorous analysis by scholars from the University of Michigan and Purdue University, and they are accessible through the Spatial Explorer of Religion (now *China Geo-Explore*), a dynamic spatial website (China Data Institute, 2012).

Questions and doubts regarding the reliability and accuracy of official data persist. Obviously, it is necessary to acknowledge limitations in providing more precise data to counter what is published by the current Chinese government. Nonetheless, scholars can contribute by presenting the data transparently and subjecting it to scrutiny from various angles, including comparative, religious, historical, digital, and spatial perspectives, while offering an objective assessment.

This study aims to unveil intriguing insights into the growth patterns of religious sites representing the five major religions during the Cultural Revolution. Employing a comparative approach, this chapter delves into the varying growth rates of religious sites across four distinct periods spanning from 1949 to 2004, thereby examining the relative pace of growth during the Cultural Revolution.

168 *Religious Sites of Five Religions during the Cultural Revolution*

To grasp the evolution of religious sites from 1966 to 1976, this study scrutinizes growth disparities between the initial phase (1966–1971) and the subsequent phase (1972–1976). Furthermore, the chapter provides comprehensive details regarding the years in which new religious sites emerged for all five major religions. Additionally, it highlights the top five provinces housing the most recent religious sites, outlining their rural and urban distribution to elucidate the geographical expansion of places of worship during this period.

Due to space constraints, an exhaustive list of over 2,500 new religious sites cannot be included here. Instead, a few spatial maps are employed to depict the locations of religious sites for each major religion in China. Finally, this study incorporates growth rates of the national population and per capita GDP as comparative benchmarks to contextualize the growth of religious sites during the Cultural Revolution. It is anticipated that these potentially contentious data and thought-provoking visual representations of religious sites from 1966 to 1976 will inspire fellow religious scholars to explore new data, methodologies, and theories in their analyses of Chinese religion and society.

13.2 Overview of Chinese religious sites during the cultural revolution

To present comprehensive data on religious sites for the five major religions, Tables 13.1 and 13.2 provide specific counts for each religion and the total number of religious sites encompassing all five religions from 1966 to 1976. Islamic mosques, exceeding five digits, stood out as the most numerous religious sites during the Cultural Revolution. Buddhist temples, in four digits, ranked as the second most prevalent religious sites within the same timeframe. Conversely, new sites affiliated with western-origin religions, encompassing both Catholic and Protestant churches, recorded the lowest numbers. This suggests that the central government and local communities may have implemented less permissive policies and measures toward these Catholic and Protestant churches.

Surprisingly, during a period often characterized as a cultural wasteland in China, the growth rate of religious sites for each major religion reached an all-time high from 1966 to 1976. Table 13.3 provides a clear illustration, showing an

Table 13.1 Number of Religious Sites for the Five Main Religions (1966–1971).

Year	1966	1967	1968	1969	1970	1971
Daoism	746	753	763	768	810	823
Protestantism	635	642	652	657	695	705
Catholicism	381	387	388	388	392	395
Islam	11,321	11,363	11,463	11,527	11,813	11,918
Buddhism	3,075	3,097	3,134	3,154	3,215	3,239
Total	16,158	16,242	16,400	16,494	16,925	17,080

Sources: Compiled from China Census Bureau, *The 2004 China's Economic Census Data with GIS Maps* (Beijing: All China Market Research Co., LTD, 2004); China Data Institute, *China Geo-Explore*, 2012, retrieved from: https://www.chinageoexplorer.com/cge/.

Table 13.2 Number of Religious Sites for the Five Main Religions (1972–1976).

Year	1972	1973	1974	1975	1976
Daoism	839	851	859	884	908
Protestantism	730	742	757	791	816
Catholicism	398	400	401	402	406
Islam	12,149	12,261	12,394	12,705	13,102
Buddhism	3,288	3,319	3,353	3,410	3,480
Total	17,404	17,573	17,764	18,192	18,712

Sources: Compiled from China Census Bureau, *The 2004 China's Economic Census Data with GIS Maps* (Beijing: All China Market Research Co., LTD, 2004); China Data Institute, *China Geo-Explore*, 2012, retrieved from: https://www.chinageoexplorer.com/cge/.

Table 13.3 Growth Rate of the Religious Sites for the Five Main Religions (1966–1976).

Sites	Number of new sites in 1966 and 1976	Total new sites	1966–1976 (%)	Rankings
Protestant Church	635 vs. 816	181	28.5	1
Daoist Abbey	746 vs. 908	162	21.72	2
Islamic Mosque	11,321 vs. 13,102	1,781	15.73	3
Buddhist Temple	3,075 vs. 3,480	405	13.17	4
Catholic Church	381 vs. 406	25	6.56	5
Total Units	16,158 vs. 18,712	2,554	15.81	

Sources: Compiled from China Census Bureau, *The 2004 China's Economic Census Data with GIS Maps* (Beijing: All China Market Research Co., LTD, 2004); China Data Institute, *China Geo-Explore*, 2012, retrieved from: https://www.chinageoexplorer.com/cge/.

increase of 28.5% for Protestant churches, 21.72% for Daoist abbyes, 15.73% for Islamic mosques, 13.17% for Buddhist temples, and 6.6% for Catholic churches during this period. In aggregate, the average growth rate for all religious sites affiliated with the five major religions surged by 15.81% from 1966 to 1976.

Figure 13.1 provides a visual representation of the gradual and consistent growth trends observed in religious sites for each religion during the Cultural Revolution. Notably, Protestant churches led in terms of growth, whereas Catholic churches exhibited their most sluggish development between 1966 and 1976.

13.3 Comparative analysis of religious sites during the cultural revolution

Before delving into the perplexing implications of these seemingly astounding growth figures, it is essential to conduct a thorough comparison of the growth rates across various time periods since 1949. This comparative analysis seeks to determine whether the proliferation of new religious sites during the Cultural Revolution outpaced or lagged behind other historical eras. The identified periods encompass the first half of Mao's China (1949–1965), the Cultural Revolution itself (1966–1976), the Deng Xiaoping era (1977–1992), and the post-Deng China (1993–2004). It is worth noting that 1949 marked the establishment of the People's

170 *Religious Sites of Five Religions during the Cultural Revolution*

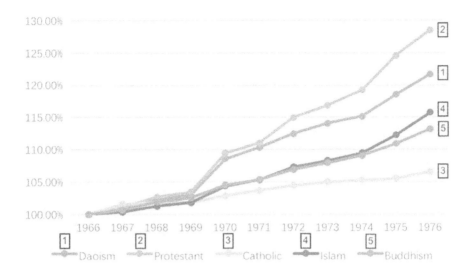

Figure 13.1 Comparison of the Religious Sites for the Five Main Religions (1966–1976).

Sources: Compiled from China Census Bureau, *The 2004 China's Economic Census Data with GIS Maps* (Beijing: All China Market Research Co., LTD, 2004); China Data Institute, *China Geo-Explore*, 2012, retrieved from: https://www.chinageoexplorer.com/cge/.

Republic of China under the leadership of Mao Zedong, while 1977 signaled the commencement of a new chapter in China's development following Mao's death, coinciding with the end of the Cultural Revolution (Zhang, 2003; Li and Lai, 2007). Deng Xiaoping's era formally commenced in 1978 after a two-year power struggle. Furthermore, following Deng's 1992 southern tour, aimed at revitalizing China's economic growth in the aftermath of the Tiananmen Square Incident, Deng's influence waned due to declining health. Meanwhile, Jiang Zemin, the emerging leader following Deng's death in 1997, wielded authority over China until 2004 (Nathan, Hong and Smith, 1999). Despite Jiang's retirement from the presidency and the position of Communist Party General Secretary in 2002, he retained leadership of the People's Liberation Army until 2004 (Tsai, 2013). Hence, the year 2004 serves as a pivotal milestone in the context of Chinese religious development.

As depicted in Table 13.4, the Cultural Revolution period from 1966 to 1976 exhibited the lowest growth rate in the context of China's religious sites across all five major religions when compared to the three subsequent significant timeframes post-1949. For instance, while the overall growth rate during the Cultural Revolution was 15.81%, the corresponding rates for the periods 1949–1965, 1977–1992, and 1993–2004 were 28.14%, 151.89%, and 46.46%, respectively. Similarly, when considering the growth rates of individual religious sites during the Cultural Revolution, there was a 13.17% increase in Buddhist temples, a 6.56% rise in Catholic churches, a 28.5% upturn in Protestant churches, a 21.72% increase in Daoist abbeys, and a 15.73% upswing in Islamic mosques.

Table 13.4 Comparison of Growth Rates of Religious Sites from 1949 to 2004.

Sites	1949–1965 (%)	1966–1976 (%)	1977–1992 (%)	1993–2004 (%)
Buddhism	28.92	13.17	151.51	77.34
Catholicism	37.55	6.56	225.18	70.23
Protestantism	71.54	28.5	582.34	128.78
Daoism	50.51	21.72	152.23	98.47
Islam	24.91	15.73	122.64	14.04
Total Sites	28.41	15.81	151.89	46.46

Sources: Compiled from China Census Bureau, *The 2004 China's Economic Census Data with GIS Maps* (Beijing: All China Market Research Co., LTD, 2004); China Data Institute, *China Geo-Explore*, 2012, retrieved from: https://www.chinageoexplorer.com/cge/.

However, it's important to acknowledge that the duration of each of the four time periods from 1949 to 2004 varies. For instance, the first period (1949–1965) spanned 17 years, the second period (1966–1976) covered 11 years, the third period (1977–1992) encompassed 16 years, and the fourth period (1993–2004) comprised 12 years. Therefore, calculating the average annual growth rate for each period is crucial to present a more accurate depiction of the increase in religious sites since 1949.

Table 13.5 provides the annual average growth rate of religious sites during the four periods from 1949 to 2004, reaffirming that the Cultural Revolution era witnessed the slowest growth. In summary, the average annual growth rate for all religious sites during the Cultural Revolution was 1.56%, while it stood at 2.51% (1949–1965), 16.45% (1977–1992), and 6.48% (1993–2004) during the other three periods, respectively. Furthermore, it is notable that the annual average growth rate for each specific religion consistently remained the lowest during the Cultural Revolution. Specifically, the number of Catholic churches experienced a mere 0.6% average annual increase from 1966 to 1976.

For a direct comparison, Figure 13.2 illustrates the highest average annual growth rate of religious sites during the 16-year post-Cultural Revolution period (1977–1992). The data reveals that Protestant churches exhibited the most significant increase, followed by Catholic churches, Daoist temples, Buddhist temples, and Islamic mosques in descending order. The collective information presented in the

Table 13.5 Annual Average Growth Rate for the Four Periods from 1949 to 2004.

Sites	1949–1965 (%)	1966–1976 (%)	1977–1992 (%)	1993–2004 (%)
Buddhism	1.70	1.20	10.10	6.45
Catholicism	2.21	0.6	15.01	5.85
Protestantism	4.21	2.59	38.82	10.73
Daoism	2.97	1.97	10.15	8.21
Islam	1.47	1.43	8.18	1.17
Total sites	2.51	1.56	16.45	6.48

Sources: Compiled from China Census Bureau, *The 2004 China's Economic Census Data with GIS Maps* (Beijing: All China Market Research Co., LTD, 2004); China Data Institute, *China Geo-Explore*, 2012, retrieved from: https://www.chinageoexplorer.com/cge/.

172 *Religious Sites of Five Religions during the Cultural Revolution*

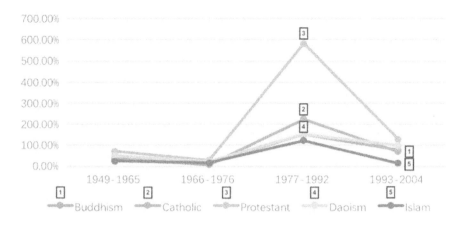

Figure 13.2 Comparative Growth Patterns of Religious Sites for the Five Major Religions (1949–2004).

Sources: Compiled from China Census Bureau, *The 2004 China's Economic Census Data with GIS Maps* (Beijing: All China Market Research Co., LTD, 2004); China Data Institute, *China Geo-Explore*, 2012, retrieved from: https://www.chinageoexplorer.com/cge/.

tables and figures unequivocally underscores that, despite some minor fluctuations, the Cultural Revolution era (1966–1976) recorded the slowest growth of religious sites across all five major religions in China, even when juxtaposed with the rest of the Maoist years characterized by stringent policies toward religion in general.

To delve deeper into the intricacies of the changes in the number of religious sites during the Cultural Revolution and provide a more comprehensive understanding of how religions fared during this pivotal decade in Chinese history, the author has opted to divide the Cultural Revolution period into two distinct phases: from 1966 to 1970 and then from 1971 to 1976.

The first phase, arguably the most destructive, was characterized by civil unrest and nationwide turmoil, resulting in the suspension of all religious activities and the persecution of religious leaders. However, efforts toward stabilization and rationalization after 1970 gradually led to the restoration of social order and economic productivity. For instance, the Ninth Party Congress held in 1969 aimed to reestablish order and stability. Additionally, the Lin Biao Incident on September 13, 1971, discouraged Mao from continuing his radical actions. During this period, Mao initiated Ping-Pong diplomacy in April 1971 and met with US President Richard Nixon in February 1972, with the hope of fostering a partial normalization of US-China relations (Hong and Sun, 2000). Notably, Mao reappointed Deng Xiaoping to oversee economic recovery and education reform in 1973, though Deng would be removed from office again three years later. Consequently, the year 1971 played a significant role in tempering the extreme agendas of the Cultural Revolution, even though it was not sufficient to bring the national upheaval to a complete halt (Gao, 1987, 2008; Clark, 2008).

Table 13.6 Growth Rate of Religious Sites for the Five Major Religions during the Two Cultural Revolution Periods (1966–1970 vs. 1971–1976).

Sites	1966–1970 (%)	1971–1976 (%)
Daoism	41.35	58.65
Protestantism	33.88	66.12
Catholicism	44	56
Islam	29.9	70.1
Buddhism	36.60	63.4
Total Average Rate	37.15	63.85

Sources: Compiled from China Census Bureau, *The 2004 China's Economic Census Data with GIS Maps* (Beijing: All China Market Research Co., LTD, 2004); China Data Institute, *China Geo-Explore*, 2012, retrieved from: https://www.chinageoexplorer.com/cge/.

Table 13.6 demonstrates that the overall average growth rate of religious sites for all five religions was 37.15% during the first phase (1966–1970) of the Cultural Revolution, while the growth rate during the second phase (1971–1976) was notably higher at 63.85%, marking a 26.7% increase. Particularly noteworthy is the stark contrast in the growth rate of mosques, with a difference of more than 40% observed between the two phases—29.9% during the first phase versus 70.1% during the second phase.

Furthermore, it holds significance to examine the top five provinces where new religious sites emerged, shedding light on the regions that played an essential role in the construction of these sites. Tables 13.7–13.10 unequivocally illustrate that Zhejiang province consistently ranked as the foremost contributor to the establishment of new Protestant churches, Buddhist temples, Catholic churches, and Daoist abbeys. This pattern aligns seamlessly with Zhejiang's geographical location on the east coast of China, which historically fostered connections with the wider world and cultivated a rich legacy of religious diversity and spiritual traditions.

Needless to say, Xinjiang was the most popular place to build the new mosques due to its historical and cultural legacy (see Table 13.11).

Finally, it is imperative to assess the growth percentages of new religious sites in urban and rural areas, respectively. Comparatively, rural areas presented a more feasible and relatively straightforward option for the construction of new sites when juxtaposed with urban areas, which bore the brunt of heavy political and religious persecutions during the Cultural Revolution. The Chinese name of a religious site often offers insight into its urban or rural location, although it must be acknowledged that some names may lack clarity or certainty in pinpointing their locale.

Hence, Table 13.12 classifies religious site locations into three distinct categories: rural, urban, and other (uncertain areas). Evidently, rural religious sites overwhelmingly constituted the majority of newly established sites during the period. In total, 93% of new religious sites were situated in rural areas, while a mere 6% were established in urban settings.

Table 13.7 Leading Provinces in the Construction of New Daoist Abbeys (1966–1976).

Province	Number of temples	Percentage of the total Daoist abbeys in the nation
Zhejiang	78	46.99
Fujian	29	17.47
Gansu	16	9.64
Hunan	10	6.02
Jiangxi	9	5.42
Total	166	85.54

Sources: Compiled from China Census Bureau, *The 2004 China's Economic Census Data with GIS Maps* (Beijing: All China Market Research Co., LTD, 2004); China Data Institute, *China Geo-Explore*, 2012, retrieved from: https://www.chinageoexplorer.com/cge/.

Table 13.8 Leading Provinces in the Construction of New Buddhist Temples (1966–1976).

Province	Number	Percentage of the total temples in the nation
Zhejiang	100	65.36
Fujian	35	22.88
Anhui	9	5.88
Heilongjiang	2	1.31
Liaoning	2	1.31
Inner Mongolia	2	1.31
Total	153	98.05

Sources: Compiled from China Census Bureau, *The 2004 China's Economic Census Data with GIS Maps* (Beijing: All China Market Research Co., LTD, 2004); China Data Institute, *China Geo-Explore*, 2012, retrieved from: https://www.chinageoexplorer.com/cge/.

Table 13.9 Leading Provinces in the Construction of New Catholic Churches (1966–1976).

Province	Number	Percentage of the Catholic Church in the nation
Zhejiang	7	28.00
Shanxi	4	16.00
Inner Mongolia	3	12.00
Shaanxi	3	12.00
Fujian	2	8.00
Hebei	2	8.00
Total	25	84

Sources: Compiled from China Census Bureau, *The 2004 China's Economic Census Data with GIS Maps* (Beijing: All China Market Research Co., LTD, 2004); China Data Institute, *China Geo-Explore*, 2012, retrieved from: https://www.chinageoexplorer.com/cge/.

Table 13.10 Leading Provinces in the Construction of New Protestant Churches (1966–1976).

Province	Number	Percentage of Protestant Churches in the nation
Zhejiang	79	43.17
Henan	22	12.02
Fujian	20	10.93
Anhui	17	9.29
Yunnan	10	5.46
Total	182	80.87

Sources: Compiled from China Census Bureau, *The 2004 China's Economic Census Data with GIS Maps* (Beijing: All China Market Research Co., LTD, 2004); China Data Institute, *China Geo-Explore*, 2012, retrieved from: https://www.chinageoexplorer.com/cge/.

Table 13.11 New Mosques in the Five Leading Provinces (1966–1976).

Province	Number	Percentage of Mosques in the nation
Xinjiang	1,390	75.58
Gansu	235	12.78
Ningxia	129	7.01
Henan	25	1.36
Yunnan	13	0.71
Total	1,839	97.44

Sources: Compiled from China Census Bureau, *The 2004 China's Economic Census Data with GIS Maps* (Beijing: All China Market Research Co., LTD, 2004); China Data Institute, *China Geo-Explore*, 2012, retrieved from: https://www.chinageoexplorer.com/cge/.

Table 13.12 Locations of New Religious Sites: Rural and Urban, 1966–1976.

Name	Rural locations (%)	Urban locations (%)	Other (%)
Catholic Church	64	36	0
Buddhist Temple	85	9	6
Daoist Temple	92	7	1
Protestant Church	76	21	3
Islamic Mosque	95	4	1
Total	93	6	1

Sources: Compiled from China Census Bureau, *The 2004 China's Economic Census Data with GIS Maps* (Beijing: All China Market Research Co., LTD, 2004); China Data Institute, *China Geo-Explore*, 2012, retrieved from: https://www.chinageoexplorer.com/cge/.

13.4 Comparative analysis of religious sites and economic indicators

In addition to examining the overall and specific growth trends of religious sites for the five major religions, this study conducts further comparisons between changes in religious sites and other economic factors, such as population growth and per capita GDP during the Cultural Revolution. Undoubtedly, religious sites and religious affairs bore a close relationship to broader social and economic developments.

During the Cultural Revolution, the total Chinese population stood at 745,420,000 in 1966 and reached 937,170,000 in 1976, reflecting an average annual growth rate of 2.34% (National Bureau of Statistics of China, 2014). As indicated in Table 13.13, the growth of religious sites for all five religions was generally slower than that of the national population, with the exception of Protestant churches. Protestant churches exhibited a 2.59% annual growth rate, surpassing the national population's growth rate by 0.25% during the Cultural Revolution.

Figure 13.3 offers a more nuanced perspective, revealing that the growth of Protestant churches did not align with the pace of national population increase until 1975. This suppression could potentially shed light on the impetus for the remarkable expansion of Protestant churches from 1977 to 1992, during which their growth soared to a remarkable 582.34%. This growth rate stands out significantly when contrasted with the development of religious sites associated with the other four major religions (refer to Table 13.4) (Tsou, 1999; Kao, 2009).

Furthermore, incorporating per capita GDP growth as an additional reference reveals further significant research findings. Notably, the 24.71% increase in per capita GDP during the Cultural Revolution surpassed the growth rate of religious sites for all five religions, as depicted in Table 13.14.

Figure 13.4 further underscores that the growth rate of GDP per capita reached a low point of −17% in 1968, a period when the Cultural Revolution pushed the country's economy to the brink of disaster. However, economic recovery gradually took hold after 1971, with GDP per capita growth outpacing the expansion of religious sites for all five major religions, except for the year 1975. During that particular year, Protestant churches accelerated their growth and exceeded the development of GDP per capita (National Bureau of Statistics of China, 2014).

Table 13.13 Comparison between Population and Growth of Religious Sites, 1966–1976.

Year	Percentage of total growth (%)	Annually average rate (%)	Rankings
Protestantism	28.50	2.59	1
Population	25.72	2.34	2
Daoism	21.72	1.97	3
Total Sites	15.79	1.44	4
Islam	15.73	1.43	5
Buddhism	13.17	1.20	6
Catholicism	6.60	0.60	7

Sources: Compiled from China Census Bureau, *The 2004 China's Economic Census Data with GIS Maps* (Beijing: All China Market Research Co., LTD, 2004); China Data Institute, *China Geo-Explore*, 2012, retrieved from: https://www.chinageoexplorer.com/cge/.

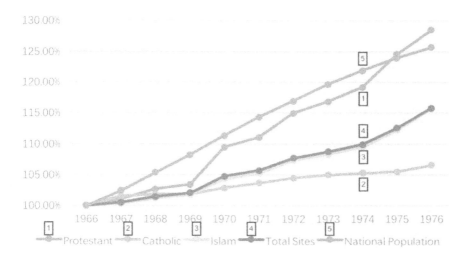

Figure 13.3 Comparative Trends in Population Changes and Growth of Religious Sites (Islamic, Catholic, and Protestant), 1966–1976.

Sources: Compiled from China Census Bureau, *The 2004 China's Economic Census Data with GIS Maps* (Beijing: All China Market Research Co., LTD, 2004); China Data Institute, *China Geo-Explore*, 2012, retrieved from: https://www.chinageoexplorer.com/cge/.

13.5 Discussion

While this chapter primarily centers on the quantitative, digital, and spatial analysis of religious sites, it is essential to offer a preliminary interpretation of why numerous new religious sites emerged during the tumultuous decade from 1966 to 1976. First, despite widespread damage to various religious sites and the suspension of religious services by the Red Guards, the growth of religious sites during

Table 13.14 Comparison between the Growth Rates of GDP Per Capita and the Religious Sites, 1966–1976.

	1966–1976 (%)	Rankings
GDP per capita	24.71	1
Protestantism	22.2	2
Daoism	21.72	3
Total sites	15.79	4
Islam	15.73	5
Buddhism	13.17	6
Catholicism	6.6	7

Sources: Compiled from China Census Bureau, *The 2004 China's Economic Census Data with GIS Maps* (Beijing: All China Market Research Co., LTD, 2004); China Data Institute, *China Geo-Explore*, 2012, retrieved from: https://www.chinageoexplorer.com/cge/.

178 *Religious Sites of Five Religions during the Cultural Revolution*

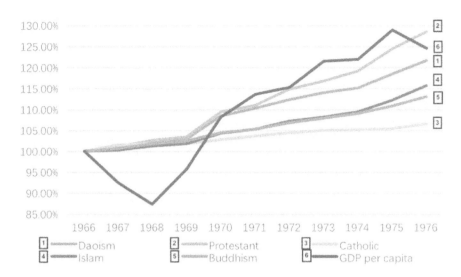

Figure 13.4 Comparative Trends in GDP Per Capita and Growth of Religious Sites, 1966–1976.

Sources: Compiled from China Census Bureau, The 2004 China's Economic Census Data with GIS Maps (Beijing: All China Market Research Co., LTD, 2014b); China Data Institute, China Geo-Explore, 2012, retrieved from: https://www.chinageoexplorer.com/cge/.

the Cultural Revolution indicates that the physical infrastructure of churches, temples, and mosques persisted. In essence, the Cultural Revolution significantly curtailed religious services and activities but did not eradicate the physical religious sites (Ahn, 1976).

Second, a considerable number of new religious sites were covert underground house churches, concealed from local governments and the general public. After the conclusion of the Cultural Revolution in 1976, these underground churches were able to organize public religious services and transform their sites into officially recognized Three-Self churches. Consequently, government records do not account for these religious sites established from 1966 to 1976, providing a partial explanation for the dramatic growth of Chinese religious sites immediately after the Cultural Revolution (Kipnis, 2001; Lai, 2005). As Kao suggests, "While the general religious revival in China became evident during the 1980s, it is very likely that Protestant growth started much earlier" (Kao, 2009: 174).

Moreover, given that new religious sites were heavily concentrated in a few provinces, further scholarly inquiry is warranted to examine the historical legacy, religious tradition, and local politics and economies of these regions. For instance, five provinces accounted for over 80% of all new religious sites during the Cultural Revolution. Notably, Xinjiang hosted 76% of new mosques, while Zhejiang became the birthplace of 65% of Buddhist temples (refer to Tables 13.7–13.11). This demonstrates that the establishment of new religious sites was not a widespread phenomenon across regions (Sun, 2013; Tsai, 2013).

Furthermore, it is plausible that local governments and religious leaders played a pivotal role in the creation of new religious sites. For example, a village leader could exercise their influence in constructing a small Buddhist temple for secret ancestor worship without incurring political repercussions, especially if the village was situated far from the central political administration. However, these temples were officially recognized after 1978 (Leung, 2005).

Additionally, a significant majority (over 65%) of new religious sites were established during the second phase of the Cultural Revolution (1971–1976), as indicated in Table 13.6. In contrast, the first phase (1966–1970) saw a growth rate of only 35%. This disparity underscores the close link between political persecution and religious suppression, as the first phase was marked by violent political upheaval and destruction. Another factor contributing to the growth of religious sites during the second phase may be overseas influence, particularly evident in the eastern coastal regions. According to Kao, the Cultural Revolution was "not only a time of disruption but also a time of formation and rebirth" for Chinese Protestantism. The interruption of religious institutions during the Cultural Revolution may have led to the reconfiguration and relocation of the religion (Kao, 2009: 174, 175).

Therefore, comprehensive interpretations of why numerous new religious sites were constructed during the chaotic decade from 1966 to 1976 necessitate additional empirical data, field research, and case studies beyond the scope of this digital and quantitative analysis. However, it is the hope that this study may inspire religious scholars to engage in interviews with leaders of these 2,500 new religious sites or local administrators to dissect this intriguing phenomenon.

Furthermore, the Chinese official data regarding the growth of religious sites during the Cultural Revolution poses challenging questions for religious scholars: Is the official data reliable and accurate? Did they systematically collect statistical data during the first half of the Cultural Revolution? What were the primary reasons for constructing over 2,500 new religious sites during the Cultural Revolution despite the prevalent anti-religious rhetoric? Who were the main contributors to this remarkable development? Does the Cultural Revolution necessitate a reassessment of its role in the growth of Chinese religious sites?

13.6 Conclusion

This study offers a unique contribution to the existing body of literature on Chinese religions by conducting a digital and spatial survey of religious sites during the Chinese Cultural Revolution. While it is acknowledged that revising the official data provided by the Chinese government with more accurate statistics from independent sources is beyond the scope of this study, it is essential to recognize its limitations. However, this research is intended to stimulate further inquiries, prompting scholars to explore new data and provide additional interpretations.

Future investigations in this field should encompass a closer examination and scrutiny of specific new religious sites established during the Cultural Revolution. This can be achieved through extensive field research, oral history interviews, and participant observation at local religious sites in China. Additionally, scholars are encouraged to employ micro-research methodologies by focusing on individual religious leaders and local government officials who may have displayed remarkable courage in safeguarding religious sites and services within their respective regions, despite the hostile religious climate prevalent during the Cultural Revolution.

Ultimately, it is imperative for all scholars to maintain an open-minded approach when reevaluating the role of the Cultural Revolution in China's religious development or regression. The value of scholarly research lies in its objectivity and impartial judgment, which can be enhanced through a combination of digital, spatial, and qualitative data analysis methods.

As I conclude this book, it seems there is still much left unsaid.

First of all, I would like to reiterate the strengths and weaknesses of this book. The most significant contribution of this work is not in the areas of religious theory, religious history, religious society, or religious economics. Instead, it introduces and applies a relatively new research method—digital and spatial studies. This conceptual design and methodological approach involves systematically selecting, verifying, integrating, and presenting data hidden in religious texts. By scientifically processing this data through geographic information systems, it can be digitalized and visualized, thus activating various information about religious sites.

At the same time, the introduction and application of this method in the book is not merely a technical show but an attempt to solve practical problems that traditional methods find difficult to address, focusing on a tough theme—the shortage of religious sites. This is an impactful research topic that directly addresses realistic and sensitive social and political issues concerning religion. A significant factor for the long-term stability of the religious market is providing and maintaining a sufficient quality and quantity of religious sites. Otherwise, demand will exceed supply, leading to overcrowding, which is detrimental to social stability, religious development, and national image. Particularly in a centralized state and society, the norm is often a shortage of religious sites rather than an excess.

Additionally, correct and advanced methods can sometimes aid in the continuous improvement of theories. Although textual evidence and empirical research are the most important research methods in the fields of religious and historical studies, quantitative research, digital studies, and spatial analysis are becoming trends, regardless of whether scholars like them or not. This is similar to online teaching, which became unstoppable after the COVID-19 pandemic, especially in the new era of AI. By using digital and spatial research methods, we can quantitatively discover the history, current situation, and future direction of religious sites. Researching the supply side of the religious market can enrich the theories and insights of religious economics and religious market studies.

Moreover, advanced research methods can effectively collect and analyze data. In fact, digital and spatial research methods are a form of evolution by combination, as advocated by complexity economics (Brian, 2018: xvii). They creatively combine existing methods of textual research, empirical research, quantitative research, historical research, induction, deduction, and abduction, presenting a comprehensive advantage (Hong, 2024:151–190). Data processed using digital and spatial methods can not only organize vast amounts of data effectively but also integrate religious data with other non-religious data, including population, urbanization, income, education, age, gender, political orientation, and prisons. Of course, it is necessary to distinguish between causality and correlation. The role of religious sites often has an indirect correlation with certain religious, social, and economic phenomena rather than a direct causal relationship, and this connection should not be overly exaggerated.

The inherent weaknesses of this book are also very evident. Due to the large number of participants and venues associated with house churches in China, which might surpass the officially registered numbers of Protestant and Catholic believers and venues (Hong, 2011, 2012a, 2012b), it is difficult, if not impossible, to accurately collect and identify this data. Therefore, the official data used in this book is very incomplete and not up-to-date. Furthermore, it is challenging to statistically account for the significant number of believers who travel from their homes to religious sites by public transportation, bicycle, or on foot, so the book only lists travel by car to attend religious services, which is also incomplete. Furthermore, because of the polytheistic nature of Buddhism and Daoism, the same believer may visit different religious sites, while Protestants and Catholics generally only go to more fixed locations, which also affects the ratio of believers to religious sites. More importantly, this study has difficulty obtaining the exact number of seats at each specific religious site, easily mixing large venues with very small ones. All of these issues await further in-depth research and more accurate data.

In addition to the strengths and weaknesses of this book, it is necessary to mention future efforts in the digital and spatial study of religion. First, data is the foundation of all scholarly research, especially digital and spatial studies. Although data does not need to be exhaustive, it must be as accurate as possible. Some official data is inherently unreliable, but private efforts to gather nationwide religious site data in China are unlikely, not only due to financial limitations but more importantly due to political constraints. In certain contexts, having enough human capital, money, and skills does not necessarily ensure success. Thus, to compensate for the incompleteness of official data, empirical research methods, including participatory observation, individual interviews, and sizable surveys, must be used. However, this approach is limited to focusing on specific regions, religions, sites, and populations, using a small-scale perspective to glimpse the general landscape of religious sites in China. Comprehensive coverage of all 31 provinces and all five major religions in China is very difficult. Therefore, it is necessary to establish more and larger data platforms, connecting existing religious data from various countries and units through big data and AI to achieve data sharing on a common platform. Additionally, since the spatial and digital platform is open to and editable by everyone, much like a wiki, it is crucial to invite scholars and practitioners living near local religious sites to contribute their insights. They can provide the most up-to-date and accurate information about these sites and their believers.

Second, choose more research themes to enhance the advantages of digital and spatial methods. For example, examining the historical evolution of the number of local churches relative to schools and prisons to determine whether adding more churches and more schools can reduce the number of prisons. Additionally, exploring the relationship between the number of religious believers and charitable activities—whether the number of believers is proportional to the number of donors and total donations. Also, examining the relationship between the number of believers and crime rates—whether there is a negative correlation between the two. Besides, by introducing reference data on urbanization, globalization, gender, consumption behavior, and investment patterns, related data can be placed on a digital and visualization platform for organic generation and comparison, promoting the integration and exchange of religious studies with other disciplines. It will promote multi-disciplinary and interdisciplinary studies, including history, economics, sociology, politics, anthropology, gender studies, urban studies, cross-cultural studies, China studies, Asian studies, digital humanities, and spatial analysis. The aim is to discover, interpret, and solve new problems from new perspectives and angles.

Third, cover more regions and periods. Although this book focuses on mainland China and introduces religious information from the US and Taiwan for comparison, such research urgently needs to expand to more regions and cover longer periods. The author believes that a new method with vitality must have broad applicability and usability. Here, two perspectives can be taken: one is a longitudinal historical perspective, focusing on different historical periods of a country for vertical comparison to identify the ups and downs and potential future directions of development. The other is a horizontal comparative perspective, not only comparing mainland China with East Asian countries and regions but also with other regions in Asia, Africa, the Americas, Europe, and Oceania. Additionally, two approaches can be adopted: focusing on countries and regions where the government tightly controls religion and comparing them with democratic countries with more relaxed religious management. The goal is to discover the different functions of the government as an intermediate variable in regulating the supply and demand management of the religious market during its development. Although such topics have already been addressed by scholars, applying digital and spatial methods might yield new findings.

In summary, the potential for digital and spatial research in religion is vast and promising, but many technical and non-technical barriers need to be overcome. The author calls for more interdisciplinary collaboration, regional exchange, and interfaith dialogue to help digital and spatial research in religion become an increasingly mature discipline.

Note

1 With the publisher's permission, segments of this chapter are excerpted from the article authored by Zhaohui Hong and co-authored by his undergraduate student, Yunbiao Zhang, "The Religious Sites during the Chinese Cultural Revolution, 1966-1976," *Journal of Advances in Social Science and Humanities*, 4 (6) (2018):1–11. Mr. Zhang has granted permission and provided written consent to exclude his name as co-author of this book. The original work has been significantly revised and updated for this book.

References

Ahn, B. J. 1976. *Chinese Politics and the Cultural Revolution: Dynamics of Policy Processes*. Seattle, WA: University of Washington Press.

Barnouin, B., and C. Yu. 1993. *Ten Years of Turbulence: The Chinese Cultural Revolution*. London and New York: Routledge.

Brian, A. 2015. *Complicity and the Economy*. New York, NY: Oxford University Press.

China Data Institute. 2012. *China Geo-Explore*. Retrieved from: https://www.chinageoexplorer.com/cge/

Clark, P. 2008. *The Chinese Cultural Revolution: A History*. Cambridge, MA: Cambridge University Press.

FitzGerald, C. P. 1967. "Religion and China's Cultural Revolution," *Pacific Affairs*, 40 (1/2):124–129.

Gao, Y. 1987. *Born Red: A Chronicle of the Cultural Revolution*. California: Stanford University Press.

Gao, M. 2008. "The Battle for China's Past: Mao and the Cultural Revolution," *The China Quarterly*, 195 (1):691–718.

Hong, Z. 2011. The Protestant House Church and its Poverty of Rights in China. In *Annual Review of the Sociology of Religion. Volume 2: Religion and Politics*, pp.160–176.

Hong, Z. 2012a. "In Search of Causes of the Poverty of Rights for Chinese Protestant House Church," *Asian Profile*, 40 (6):513–522.

Hong, Z. 2012b. "Protecting and Striving for the Rights to Religious Freedom: Case Studies on the Protestant House Churches in China," *Journal of Third World Studies*, XXIX (1):249–261.

Hong, Z. 2024. *Introduction to Propriety Economics*. Hong Kong: Chinese University of Hong Kong.

Hong, Z., and Y. Sun. 2000. "The Butterfly Effect and the Making of 'Ping-Pong Diplomacy," *Journal of Contemporary China*, 9 (25):429–448.

Kao, C. Y. 2009. "The Cultural Revolution and the Emergence of Pentecostal-Style Protestantism in China," *Journal of Contemporary Religion*, 24 (2):171–188.

Kipnis, Andrew B. 2001. "The Flourishing of Religion in Post-Mao China and the Anthropological Category of Religion," *The Australian Journal of Anthropology*, 12 (1):32–46.

Lai, H. H. 2005. "The Religious Revival in China," *The Copenhagen Journal of Asian Studies*, 18 (1):40–64.

Lee, H. Y. 1980. *The Politics of the Chinese Cultural Revolution: A Case Study (No. 17)*. California: University of California Press.

Leung, B. 2005. "China's Religious Freedom Policy: The Art of Managing Religious Activity," *The China Quarterly*, 184 (2):894–913.

Li, Y., and J. Lai. 2007. "The Implementation of Religious Policies During Mao Zedong's Era," *Journal of Political Science*, 44 (1):1–24.

Nathan, A., Z. Hong, and S. Smith, eds. 1999. *Dilemmas of Reform in Jiang Zemin's China*. Boulder, CO: Lynne Rienner Publishers.

National Bureau of Statistics of China. 2010. *Zhongguo zongjiao ditu*. (The Atlas of Religions in China). Beijing: All China Marking Research Co., Ltd. Retrieved from: https://chinadatacenter.net/Data/ServiceContent.aspx?id=1573

National Bureau of Statistics of China. 2014. *Zhongguo tongji nianjian* (China Statistical Yearbook). Retrieved from: https://www.stats.gov.cn/sj/ndsj/2014/indexeh.htm

Schoenhals, M. 2015. *China's Cultural Revolution, 1966-69: Not a Dinner Party*. Oxon: Routledge.

Shen, F. 2006. *Gang of One: Memoirs of a Red Guard*. London: University of Nebraska Press.

Sun, Y. 2013. "Popular Religion in Zhejiang: Feminization, Bifurcation, and Buddhification," *Modern China*, 40 (5):455–487.

Tsai, Y.L. 2013. "Intuitional Analysis of Chinese Communist Party's Religious Policy," *Journal of Native Taiwanese Nationality*, 3 (2):143–160.

Tsou, T. 1999. *The Cultural Revolution and Post-Mao Reforms: A Historical Perspective.* Chicago, IL: University of Chicago Press.
Walder, A.G. 2002. "Beijing Red Guard Factionalism: Social Interpretations Reconsidered," *The Journal of Asian Studies*, 61 (2):437–471.
Walder, A.G. 2004. "Tan Lifu: A 'Reactionary' Red Guard in Historical Perspective," *The China Quarterly*, 180 (1):965–988.
Welch, H. 1969. "Buddhism Since the Cultural Revolution," *The China Quarterly*, 40 (1):127–136.
Zhang, J. 2003. "Transformation and Impact of Contemporary Religious Policies in Mainland China," *New Century Religious Studies*, 2 (2):55–107.
Zuo, J. 1991. "Political Religion: The Case of the Cultural Revolution in China," *Sociology of Religion*, 52 (1):99–110.

Index

Note: – *Italicized* page references refer to figures, **bold** references refer to tables, and page references with "n" refer to endnotes.

2004 China's Economic Census 9, 83

Amity Foundation 5, 44, 57–58, 74
ArcGIS 10, 23, 69, 72, 113, 149; *see also* geographic information systems (GIS)
Atlas of Religions in China 6, 9, 22–23, 25, 32, 44, 57, 73, 84

Baidu Map 32–33, **34**
Blue Book on Chinese Religion 114
"Boya Diming" website (博雅地名网) 74, 152
Brainbridge, W. 44
Buddhism 2, 44, 100, 108; Chinese 83–84, 94; development of 86; native religions as 95; polytheistic nature of 181; principles and values of 97; regional landscape of 87; religious sites for 6
Buddhist temples 83–97, **84**, *84*, **174**; Buddhist mountain areas 84–87; in Central China **88**, **89**, *89*, *90*; in China *91*, *93*; in Chizhou City 84–87; data 83–84; in Eastern China **88**, **89**, *89*, *90*; and economic factors 92–96, **94**, **96**; and GDP per capita 94–95, *95*; growth rates of 86, 86–87, *87*, *90*, **91**, 94; in Leshan City 84–87; methodology 83–84; and other religious sites **92**, 92–96, **93**, **96**; overview 83; patterns at regional and national levels 87–92; and urbanization 96; visual representation of 87–88; in Western China **88**, **89**, *89*, *90*; in Xinzhou City 84–87; in Zhoushan City 84–87

Catholic churches 73, 92, 107, 112–117, **116**, 124–125, 127–129, 141, 169–171, 173, **174**; accessibility scores by 2SFCA 118, *119*, *120*, *121*, *122*, **123**; availability and accessibility by NAM *124*, *125*, *126*, **127**; and Daoist abbey 101, 108; density of **117**, 123; growth rates of religious sites for 108; rankings of **128**; scarcity of 113; shortage in China 112; statistical rankings of 123
Catholicism 6, 83
Catholic market 112–129; data 113–116; methodology 112–113; overview 112; results and findings 116–127
Center on Religion and the Global East at Purdue University 6
Central China 49, 51, 87; and availability of churches in 61–62, **62**; Buddhist temples in **88**, **89**, *89*, *90*; church accessibility in 76–77, **77**; church availability in 62, **62**; Daoist abbeys in **104**; density of congregations in 61, 61–62; density of Protestants (ρ) in 61, **61**; Islamic mosques in 137–141, **138**, *139*; Protestant church shortage **62**
Chengdu 48–49, 64, 66, 79; density of Protestants per church in **48**; Protestant market in 49; Protestants per church in 48–49
China: believers in 5; Catholic population in **115**, *115*; density of Catholics in **117**, *118*; historical periods (1911-2004) 4; Islamic mosques in **140**; marketization of religion 45; population data 5; religious market 2; religious sites in 5; Xinjiang mosques in **133**
China Data Institute 6
China Economic Census (2004) 23, 24, 32, 44, 57, 101, 116, 167

Index

China Geo-Explorer 14, 22–23, 25, 32, 44, 57, 73, 84, 101, 132, 148
Chinese Academy of Social Sciences (CASS) 9, 23, 44, 114
Chinese Cultural Revolution 83, 167, 179
Chinese Jerusalem 114
Chinese Muslims 137, 141, 148, 150, 152, **153**, 156
Chinese religious data 6; see also data
Christianization 32
church accessibility 9–10, 14–16, 18, 36, 69, 74–80, 112, *124*, *125*, 126, *126*, **127**, 127–129; by 2SFCA method 35, 69–70, *119*, *120*, *121*, *122*, **123**; in Central China 76–77, **77**; in Chicago 13–14, **17**; comparative analysis of 80–81; in Eastern China 74–76, **75**; in Hangzhou 13, **17**; measurement of 118; Protestant 26–28, **29**, **35**, **37**, **38**, **38**, *39*, **40**; scores and identify shortages 74; statistics 36, 123; in Western China 78–80
church availability 9–10, 26, **26**, 58, 66, 113, *124*, *125*, 125–127, *126*; in Central China 62, **62**; in Chicago *15*, **17**; in Eastern China 58–60, **60**; Fuzhou **26**, *37*, **38**, *39*, **40**; Guangzhou 37, **38**, *39*, **40**; in Hangzhou *16*, **17**, *17*, **26**, *37*, **38**, *39*, **40**; Nanjing 37, **38**, *39*; Protestant *37*, 38, **40**; Shanghai 37, **38**, *39*, **40**; Taipei 37, **38**, *39*, **40**; in Western China 63, **64**; Zhengzhou **26**
"CloudMade" website 74, 152
Communist-led Hangzhou 22
Confucianism 100
conventional economic theory 45
County and City Gazetteers 74
Cultural Revolution 4, 83, 86, 88, 100, 104, 109, 131; comparative analysis of religious sites during 169–175, 176–177; economic indicators 177–179; GDP during 176; overview 167–168; religious sites during **168**, 168–169, **169**, *170*, **171**; religious sites of five religions during 167–182

Daoism 2, 6, 44, 83, 95, 100, 108
Daoist abbeys 100–111, **102**, **106**, **174**; case studies on 101–103; and Catholic churches 101, 108; in Central China **104**; data 101; in Eastern China **104**; growth rates of **103**, **104**, **105**, *105*, *106*, **107**, **109**; growth rates of religious sites for **108**; methodology 101; overview 100; proliferation 103; regional and national landscape of 103–107; and religious sites of other faiths **107**, 107–110, **108**, **110**; and socioeconomic factors 107–110; in Western China **104**
data: Buddhist temples 83–84; Catholic market 113–116; Daoist abbeys 101; growth of registered Protestant churches 44; Islamic mosques 132, 150–156; multi-methods research design 72–74; population of China 5; religious sites 22; Taipei 31–32
Deng Xiaoping 4, 43, 83, 86, 88, 92, 100, 104–105, 107–110, 117, 131, 134, 137, 169–170, 172
density of congregations: Central China 61–62; Eastern China **58**, 58–60; Western China 63–65
density of Protestants (ρ) 31–33, **50**, 74; in Central China 61, **61**; congregations 63; per church in Chengdu **48**; per church in Chinese cities 23–25; per church in Harbin 47, **48**; per church within Hangzhou city 46, **47**; in provincial capital cities **66**; in regional provinces **52**; in Western China 64, **64**
digital humanities 1–3, 182

Eastern China 49–50, 87; Buddhist temples in **88**, **89**, *89*, *90*; church accessibility in 74–76, **75**; church availability in 58–60, **60**; church shortages in **60**; Daoist abbeys in **104**; density of congregations **58**, 58–60; Islamic mosques in 137–141, **138**, *139*; Protestant population density in *59*; Protestant population per church in 58–59
economic growth 45–46, 170

Falun Gong 100
Finke, R. 44–45
Fuk-tsang Ying's article 74
Fuzhou 31; case studies in 22–29; comparison of church availability **26**; comparison of Protestants and Protestant churches **25**; density of Protestants per church in 23–25, **24**; Protestant church availability and accessibility 25–28, *27*, **29**, **34**, 36, *37*, **38**, *39*, **40**; Protestant density rankings **34**; Protestant population in **33**; Protestant provinces in China 22

geographic information systems (GIS) 3–4, 9–10, 25–26, 32, 35, 44, 69–70, 78, 112–113, 118, 148, 150; see also ArcGIS
GIS Maps 24, 101, 167

Google Maps 26, 72, 74, 113, 150, 152
growth of registered Protestant churches 43–54; case studies 46–49; changing trends in Protestants and Protestant churches 51–52; comparison of **49**; data 44; literature review 44–46; overview 43–44; Protestant members and churches 49–51; supply and demand of Chinese Protestant market 52–54
Guangzhou 31, 59; church accessibility statistics **36**; Protestant church availability and accessibility *35, 37,* **38,** *39,* **40**; Protestant churches in **34**; Protestant density rankings **34**; Protestant population in 33, **33**
Gundlach, E. 45

Hadaway, C. K. 10, 67n2
Hangzhou 22, 31, 46–47; case studies in 22–29; church accessibility statistics **36**; comparison of church availability **26**; comparison of Protestants and Protestant churches **25**; density of Protestants per church in 23–25, **24**, **47**; Protestant church availability and accessibility 12–18, *14, 16,* **17,** *17, 18, 19,* 25–28, **29, 34,** *37,* **38,** *39,* **40**; Protestant density rankings **34**; Protestant population in **33**; Protestant provinces in China 22; shortage of Protestant churches in 9–20
Harbin 47–48; density of Protestants per church in **47**, 47–48; Protestant market in 48
Health Professional Shortage Areas (HPSA) 70, 160
Hefei: availability of Protestant churches in 25–26; case studies in 22–29; comparison of church availability **26**; comparison of Protestants and Protestant churches **25**; density of Protestants per church in 23–25, **24**; Protestant church accessibility in 26–28, **29**; Protestant provinces in China 22
Henry Luce Foundation 6, 32, 83, 148
Henry Luce project 23
Hong Kong 5, 44, 49, 74
Hua Guofeng 100
humanities 148–149; digital 1–3, 182; non-traditional research methods to 1; spatial 1–3

interdisciplinary collaboration 1, 182
Islamic mosques 131–145, **133**, *135–136,* **136**; 2SFCA 160–165; case studies in Ningxia 148–166; case studies in Xinjiang 148–166; case studies on 132–137; in Central China 137–141, **138**, *139*; in China **140**; and Chinese society **141**, 141–144; data 132, 150–156; in Eastern China 137–141, **138**, *139*; growth rates of **134**, **135**; growth rates of religious sites **141**, **142**, **143**; LAM 156–159; methodology 132, 149–150; NAM 160–165; overview 131–132, 148–149; regional and national patterns of 137–141; and social economic **143**, **144**; spatial analysis of 148–166; in Western China 137–141, **138**, *139*
Islam/Islamism 44, 83, 131

Jiang Zemin 4, 92, 100, 104–105, 107–110, 170

Kao, C. Y. 179
Klein, T. 45

Li, F. 45
Lin Biao 172
Location Analysis Method (LAM) 32, 36, 38, **40**, 149, **164**; mosque availability 156–159, *157, 158,* **159**
Luo, W. 70

Macau 49
mainland China 49; Protestant church density in 32–34; Protestant churches in **34**; Protestant density rankings **34**; Protestant population in 33, **33**; *see also* Central China; Eastern China; Western China
Mao Zedong 4, 100, 104–105, 109–110, 134, 137, 167, 172; Cultural Revolution 100, 169–170; death of 100
Marler, Penny L. 10, 67n2
McBride, M. 45–46
Meyer, C. 45
modern China 100
Mount Emei (Leshan City) 84–87
Mount Jiuhua (Chizhou City) 84–87
Mount Putuo (Zhoushan City) 84–87
Mount Wutai (Xinzhou City) 84–87
multi-methods research design 69–81; church accessibility 74–80; data 72–74; methodology 69–72; overview 69

Nanjing 31; church accessibility statistics **36**; Protestant church availability and accessibility *37,* **38,** *39*; Protestant

churches in **34**; Protestant density rankings **34**; Protestant population in 33, **33**
National Bureau of Statistics of China 5, 153
native religions 95
Network Analysis Method (NAM) 32, 36, 38, 69–70, 72–73, *73*, 75–78, 113, 123, 149–150; Catholic church availability and accessibility by *124*, *125*, *126*, **127**; church accessibility in Central China 76–77, **77**; church accessibility in Eastern China by **75**; church accessibility in Western China 78–79, **79**; church availability and accessibility by *37*, **38**, *39*; key steps 72; mosque accessibility 160–165, **164**
Ninth Party Congress 172
Nixon, Richard 172
non-market forms of sociality 45

Online Spiritual Atlas of the Global East (OSAGE) 6
Opium War 32

Paldam, M. 45
Patriotic Catholic Association 114
People's Liberation Army 170
physician availability 70
post-Deng China 131, 133–134, 136–138, 140, 142, 169
Protestant churches 49–50, **175**; availability in Hefei 25–26; availability in Zhengzhou 25–26; in Chicago 12–18, *13*, *15*, **17**; Chinese religious sites **53**; Fuzhou **25**; in Fuzhou 25–28, *27*, *29*, *34*, **36**, *37*, **38**, *39*, **40**; growth of registered 43–54; growth rates of **49**; in Hangzhou 12–18, *14*, *16*, **17**, *17*, *18*, *19*, 25–28, *29*, **34**, *37*, **38**, *39*, **40**; in Hefei 26–28, **29**; in mainland China 32–34, **34**; in Nanjing **34**, *37*, **38**, *39*; in Shanghai **34**, *37*, **38**, *39*, **40**; in Taipei *35*, *37*, **38**, *39*, **40**; in Taiwan **34**; in Zhejiang Province *12*; in Zhengzhou 26–28, **29**
Protestant church shortage 9–20, 22, 57–67; in Central China **62**; comparative perspective 12–18; national comparisons of 65–66, **67**; overview 10–11, 57–58; religious market 22; spatial studies 12–18
Protestant congregations 46
Protestant density **52**; in Chengdu **48**; rankings 34
Protestantism 2, 11, 44, 49, 51–52, **54**, 57, 81, 179
Protestant-majority Chicago 22
Protestant market: spatial measurement of 35–38; supply and demand of 46, 50, 51, 52–54
Protestant members 49–50, **50**, *53*
Purdue University 6, 32, 84, 101, 148, 167

religious economics 2, 44, 57, 69, 112, 150, 180
religious freedom 9, 31, 38, 54, 97, 100, 131
religious market 22, 43, 45; China 2; and economy 44; fundamental contribution of 45; Protestant church shortage 22; religious regulations in 45; and socialist shortage economy 22
religious market theory 44–46
religious regulations 31, 40, 43, 45–46, 110, 134
religious sites 2; for Buddhism 6; and Buddhist temples **92**, 92–96, **93**, **96**; in China 5; during Cultural Revolution **168**, 168–169, **169**, 169–175, *170*, **171**, 176–177; Daoist abbeys **107**, 107–110, **108**, **110**; data 22; growth rates for Catholic churches **108**; identified by zip codes 10; Islamic mosques **141**, **142**, **143**; Protestant churches **53**; shortage of 2
religious studies 1–2, 166; in China 20; non-traditional research methods to 1; quality of 81
Republican era 4

Shanghai 31; church accessibility statistics **36**; Protestant church availability and accessibility *37*, **38**, *39*, **40**; Protestant churches in **34**; Protestant density rankings **34**; Protestant population in 33
shortage of religious sites 2
socialist shortage economy 22
socialist system 22
spatial church accessibility *see* church accessibility
Spatial Explorer of Religion see China Geo-Explore
spatial humanities 1–3; *see also* humanities
Stark, R. 44

Taipei 31–40; church accessibility statistics **36**; methodology and data 31–32; overview 31; Protestant church availability and accessibility *35*, *37*, **38**, *39*, **40**; Protestant density rankings **34**; Protestant population for 33; spatial measurement of Protestant market 35–38

Taiwan 49; Protestant church density in 32–34; Protestant churches in **34**; Protestant density rankings **34**; Protestant population in 33, **33**
Tiananmen Square Incident 170
Tianjin 59
Two-Step Floating Catchment Area (2SFCA) 31–32, 35, *35*, 38, 69–70, *71*, 73, 74, 76, 113, 117–118, 123, 149; Catholic church accessibility scores by *119*, *120*, *121*, *122*, **123**; church accessibility in Western China 78; mosque accessibility by 160–165, **162**

University of Michigan 6, 32, 84, 101, 148, 167
US National Institute for Health (NIH) 19, 160

Wang, F. 70
Western China 49, 87; and availability of churches in 63–65; Buddhist temples in **88**, **89**, *89*, *90*; church accessibility in 78–80; church availability in 63, **64**; church shortage in **65**; Daoist abbeys in **104**; density of congregations in **63**, 63–65; density of Protestants (ρ) in 64, **64**; Islamic mosques in 137–141, **138**, *139*
Western Christianity 32
Westernization 32
Wudang Abbey 102

Xuanmiao Abbey 102

Yang, F. 2, 10, 22, 57
Ying, F.-t. 44, 58
Yuequan Abbey 102

Zeng Le 22
Zhejiang Province 4, 10–12, 46, 84, 86, 114, 173; Chinese Jerusalem in 114; new Protestant church construction in *12*; Protestant population 20
Zhengzhou: availability of Protestant churches in 25–26; case studies in 22–29; comparison of church availability **26**; comparison of Protestants and Protestant churches **25**; density of Protestants per church in 23–25, **24**; Protestant church accessibility in 26–28, **29**; Protestant provinces in China 22
zip codes 10

Milton Keynes UK
Ingram Content Group UK Ltd.
UKHW031330071224
451979UK00005B/66